CARL BECKER

ON

HISTORY AND THE AMERICAN REVOLUTION

Carl Becker
on
History and The
American Revolution

BY ROBERT E. BROWN

EAST LANSING, MICHIGAN

THE SPARTAN PRESS

1970

Other books by Robert E. Brown
*Middle-Class Democracy and the Revolution in Massachusetts,
1691–1780* (Cornell, 1955)

Charles Beard and the Constitution (Princeton, 1956)

*Reinterpretation of the Formation of the American
Constitution* (Boston, 1963)

Virginia, 1705–1786: Democracy or Aristocracy?
With B. Katherine Brown (Michigan State, 1964)

Printed in the United States of America
By The John Henry Company

PREFACE

This is the story of a man who changed his mind. Carl Lotus Becker began his professional career as a scholarly historian, then quickly abandoned scholarly detachment for commitment to the cause of social or collective democracy. Over a period of some forty years he espoused a philosophy of subjective relativism and expounded a class interpretation of the American Revolution that was to influence thousands of students and professors alike. Yet in the end, when American democracy faced the acid test posed by Communism and Fascism, Becker, largely unknown to his legion of followers, repudiated most of both his philosophy of history and his class interpretation of early American history. Too late to repair much of the damage that he had inflicted on scholarly method and interpretation, Becker, like the prodigal son, almost returned to the fold of the scholarly historian, and might well have come the full distance had he lived long enough. How this all came about and what it signifies for both the past and the present is the subject of these pages.

Given the unsettled world of today, it behooves Americans to take a second look at the American Revolution as they approach its 200th anniversary. With present-day revolutionaries using past revolutions as justification for future social change, Americans might well consider the extent to which their own Revolution embodied class conflict and internal social upheaval. The people of this country must weigh carefully the role of the past in shaping the future of democratic government, and especially the extent to which the American Revolution is exportable in today's turbulent world. And above all, Americans should be well-grounded in their own history before they choose among the alternatives that are offered on the menu for tomorrow's world. In the twilight of uncertainty that confronts us, the career of Carl Becker could well serve as a beacon light.

February 25, 1970   ROBERT E. BROWN

ACKNOWLEDGMENTS

I wish to express my special appreciation to the following persons and publishers for assistance in preparing the manuscript and for permission to quote from their letters and publications:

To the librarians at the John M. Olin Research Library at Cornell University and the Henry E. Huntington Library for their valuable aid in the use of the Carl Becker Papers and the Frederick Jackson Turner Collection.

To Professors Henry Steele Commager, Leo Gershoy, Louis Gottschalk, W. Stull Holt, and Robert R. Palmer for permission to quote from their letters to Carl Becker.

To the following publishers for permission to quote from published works. Permission for specific quotations will be noted in the footnotes.

Appleton-Century-Crofts
Cornell University Press
Harcourt, Brace & World, Inc.
Harper & Row, Publishers, Incorporated
Houghton Mifflin Company
The Macmillan Company
Princeton University Press
Random House, Inc.
Alfred A. Knopf, Inc.
United States Publishers Association, Inc.
University of Wisconsin Press
Yale University Press

In addition, I owe a great deal to my many students over the years who have served as critical sounding boards in reading courses on Becker and the progressive historians, and especially my thanks go to Anne Ousterhout for reading the manuscript. Finally, as members of the profession will well understand, of course, my wife, B. Katherine Brown has done most of the work, but, for the sake of marital harmony, has allowed me to usurp the title page.

REB

CONTENTS

CARL BECKER

ON

HISTORY AND THE AMERICAN REVOLUTION

I. THE MAKING OF A HISTORIAN, 1873-1899

> "Avoid as the very unpardonable sin any one-sidedness, any partisan, any partial treatment of history. Do not misinterpret the past for the sake of the present."
> — FREDERICK JACKSON TURNER, 1891

ANY account of Carl Becker the historian might well begin in 1899 when he published his first scholarly article, but by 1899, Becker was twenty-six years old and had undergone certain experiences which would profoundly affect his later life. A paucity of evidence renders exactness impossible, yet one can suggest some influences that went into the shaping of the distinguished career that was to follow this initial publication.

First and foremost was the fact that Carl Becker came from a family whose intellectual background or achievements enhanced Becker's chances of attending college, certainly a desirable if not a necessary factor in the training of a historian. Becker's sister Jessie claimed that their father, from whom she said Becker inherited his brilliant mind, had raised himself by his bootstraps to the extent that he passed as a college man, even though he came from poor parents and his formal education ended at the age of twelve. Migrating from New York to Iowa for cheap land, the elder Becker farmed a 240-acre tract near Waterloo for many years, then was elected county recorder and moved to Waterloo in 1884 when Carl was eleven. The mother, born of well-to-do parents, was above average in intelligence and received a good education. Not many farm and small-town boys could claim this kind of educational environment in the 1880's.[1]

[1] Jessie M. Becker to Phil Snyder, November 24, 1955, and Carl Becker to Carl Horwich, April 29, 1940, Becker Papers.

But conversely, Becker's political background was such that anyone predicting his future in 1890 would hardly have anticipated the liberalism of his later years. Sister Jessie, who undoubtedly knew nothing whatever about her brother's political views, said after his death that Carl was no real politician and she did not believe that he was either a Republican or a Democrat. If he voted at all, she declared, he voted for the man he considered most capable. On the other hand, Becker's father and the rest of the family voted the straight Republican ticket. Jessie said that her father always claimed that he supported the best man, but, she reminisced, "I remember hearing him say that the best man always seemed to be on the Republican ticket." [2]

Becker's early education indicated considerable intellectual talent but not talent directed toward the career of historian. One supposes that he attended country school until he was eleven, then he was put into a class ahead of his own, perhaps at Waterloo. His sister remembered him as a boy among boys who loved sports, became a good skater, and worked on his uncle's farm during the summer. Later he was to enjoy some reputation at Cornell as an expert at pool or billiards. Although he had an excellent record as a student, he lost interest in high school, perhaps, as Jessie said, because of inadequate teachers. But still there was no indication of any special bent toward history. [3]

It was at the University of Wisconsin that Becker found the inspiration to become a historian. After graduation from high school in Waterloo in 1892, Becker spent a year at Cornell College in Mt. Vernon, Iowa, not far from Waterloo, but after the first year, he transferred to Wisconsin. What caused the decision is not clear, but as Becker himself said, he went to Madison with no interest in history. A young lawyer friend had told him about a history professor at Wisconsin who gave his students inspiration, new ideas, a fresh light on things —

[2] Jessie Becker to Phil Snyder, November 24 and December 4, 1955, Becker Papers.
[3] Ibid.

"Old Freddie Turner" they called him. And it was "Old Freddie Turner" who inspired Becker to become a historian.[4] If Becker's memory served him right, there is no doubt that Frederick Jackson Turner the man and the historian soon made a deep impression on Becker the student. In addition to a buoyant personality, a fine voice, and a striking method of presentation (he was known for his oratorical prowess), Turner gave his students the impression that they were co-workers in a scholarly quest for new knowledge. They were all looking for something together — searching, ferreting out hidden secrets, looking into and behind the facts — some problem that concerned humanity at large. Becker said that he had "the inestimable privilege of watching an original and penetrating intelligence at work, playing freely with facts and ideas, handling with discrimination the problems of history, problems which so often turned out to be the problem of life itself." He had also, Becker continued, "the most delightful sense in the world of sitting there waiting for ideas to be born, expectantly waiting for secret meanings, convenient explanatory hypotheses to be discovered, lurking as like as not under the dullest mass of drab facts ever seen." Impressed by the man and the scholar, Becker in his junior year hitched his "tiny little wagon" to the bright Turner star.[5]

If Turner was as significant in Becker's life as Becker professed and as other historians have believed, some knowledge of Turner's ideas becomes essential. But the result is not quite what one would expect, for on occasion Becker was later to deviate in some very important respects from the teachings of his mentor. Perhaps in the long run, the negative influences of Turner were fully as important to Becker as were the positive ones.

Himself a product of the University of Wisconsin, Turner as a student early exhibited the same trend toward liberalism

[4] Jessie Becker to Phil Snyder, November 11, 1955, Becker Papers; Carl Becker, "Frederick Jackson Turner," in Howard W. Odum, ed., *American Masters of Social Science: An Approach to the Study of the Social Sciences Through a Neglected Field of Biography* (New York, 1927), pp. 273-74.

[5] *Ibid.*, pp. 273-82.

3

that would characterize Becker's social philosophy. At one point he appeared as an elitist and hereditist when he wrote the following: "The man of intellect at the top of affairs: this is the aim of all constitutions and revolutions, if they have any aim." But environmentalism soon predominated, as elitism gave way to thoughts of progress, reform, democracy, pragmatism, evolution, science, and presentism, all conceived as part of a vast program consciously designed to raise the status of the common man.[6]

The early Turner had great faith in the idea of progress, which is naturally environmentalist, a faith that Becker shared for awhile but eventually abandoned. In comparing ancient and modern civilizations, Turner favored the modern age, particularly the American, because it attempted to help the common man by improving the whole structure of society. Turner's heroes were practical men — Humbolt, Darwin, Spencer, Mill, Emerson, Morse, Fulton, Whitney, Watts — men who helped to extend liberty and light to all classes. The modern world had the noble idea of common schools and education for the masses. Plato had his Atlantis and More his Utopia, Turner wrote, but "America erected a republic based on the great progressive possibilities of a free people and on faith in democracy." [7] Present art was a "vast wave of democratic utilitarianism," and the improved political status of men set in motion a "wave of democracy that is now sweeping the world." [8]

To Turner the student, even war held an honorable place in the march of progress and democracy to raise the common man, a view that Becker would later reject only to accept again in due time. Turner praised the French Revolution as a destroyer of aristocracy and monarchy, those twin enemies of democracy. Modern poetry, he declared, was expressed by the grand meter of armies marching to rescue shackled slaves,

[6] Turner Collection, Vol. III, Commonplace Book 1, 1881, Huntington Library. Hereafter the Collection is cited as TU.
[7] *Ibid.*, 1882.
[8] *Ibid.*, 1882-83.

while the grandest lyric of all was the Emancipation Proclamation.[9] Later, Turner expressed the belief that the North was right in the Civil War, although centuries would pass before the world grasped the significance of the cause — the fight for peace not only for America but for the world and the "liberty of labor." [10]

Like the later Becker, Turner by 1884 had begun to question whether unregulated capitalism was capable of achieving progress for the common man as he desired. Turner saw the wealthy paving the way for their own demise by spending money for luxuries rather than jobs for common men. The people would be little disposed to demand justice for the rich if the capitalist overlooked the poor, for civilization must not advance the few at the expense of the many. Wealth is often a matter of accident, not merit, Turner declared, for capital is social, not individual, and results from the work of many men.[11] Becker would eventually be an ardent advocate of collective democracy, something hinted at by Turner at this early date.

In addition to thoughts on a liberal social philosophy, the young Turner expressed ideas on philosophy of history that have some relationship with the future Becker. At one point Turner wondered whether too much concern for the writing and thinking of the masters might not unfit one for original thinking and writing.[12] On quoting Franklin that honesty is the best policy, and honesty is perhaps the most important attribute of the scholar, Turner had this comment: "Honesty — for it is the law of God's universe and beautiful in itself — policy or not." Then Turner made the following entry which was particularly applicable to Becker later: "He who neglects what is, in order to follow what *ought to be*, will sooner learn how to ruin than how to preserve himself." [13]

There were also ideas about early American society and the American Revolution expressed by the youthful Turner that

[9] *Ibid.*, 1882.
[10] *Ibid.*, Book 2, 1885.
[11] *Ibid.*, 1884.

[12] *Ibid.*, Book 1, 1881.
[13] *Ibid.*, Book 3, 1886.

would find their way into Becker's writing. Turner became famous for his frontier thesis that political and social democracy in America came as a result of economic democracy on the frontier, a democracy made possible by the availability of cheap land. But Turner, as did Becker later, seemed to assume that the frontier which produced democracy after the American Revolution was not equally effective toward the same end before the Revolution. Turner saw violations of democracy in colonial Virginia because of the long assembly, restrictions on the franchise, and poll taxes which fell heaviest on the "laboring classes." [14] But unlike Becker in his later doctoral dissertation, Turner did not interpret the American Revolution as a social movement. He pointed out that the new state constitutions which emerged from the Revolution had an "aristocratic basis" — property requirements for voters, additional qualifications for officeholders, and checks and balances to limit democracy.[15]

At the age of thirty, Turner in 1891 had arrived at a mature philosophy of history which apparently did not change materially in succeeding years. In a paper, "The Significance of History," he again expressed a belief in progress, but now it was not a progress that continued upward without abatement. He said that primitive people sometimes brought retrogression when they supplanted civilized people. Turner also placed great emphasis on economic causation in history. He characterized as extremely important Thorold Rogers' *Economic Interpretation of History* (1889) which, he said, truly asserted that the real cause of great political and social events was often economic. Yet Turner was not an economic determinist, for he insisted that there was still much truth in the concepts of history as past literature, past politics, past religion, and past economics.[16]

[14] TU, XIV, No. 2 (1887-88), pp. 27, 28, 83.
[15] *Ibid.,* XV, No. 1 (1887-88), p. 119.
[16] Frederick Jackson Turner, "The Significance of History," *Wisconsin Journal of Education,* October and November, 1891, reprinted in *Early Writings of Frederick Jackson Turner* (Madison, 1938). See pp. 44-47, 51-52, 55-57.

More important for any consideration of Becker was Turner's philosophy of history as a link between the past and the future. As the self-consciousness of society, Turner said, history promotes mental growth, enables us "to behold our own time and place as a part of the stupendous progress of the age," and helps us to realize the richness of our inheritance, the possibility of our lives, and the grandeur of the present. As training for good citizens, history lets the community see itself in the light of the past and suggests reforms for a still better future.[17] Becker would later have little confidence in the "richness of our inheritance" or "the grandeur of the present," but he was to accept fully the idea that history allowed humanity to see itself in the light of the past and that it suggested reforms for the future.

There was something in Turner of the cult of the common man that James Harvey Robinson and the "New Historians" would foster later and that would appear in Becker's "Everyman His Own Historian." "The focal point of modern interest," Turner declared, "is the great mass of the people." History recorded the annals of the few but it also revealed the tragedy of the tillers of the soil, the slaves of Greece, and the serfs of Rome. More often than is known, he continued, underlying facts affecting the breadwinners of a nation have determined the nation's rise or fall. Compared with this, much that has passed as history "is the merest frippery." [18]

Turner then tackled the problem that would eventually concern Becker — whether truth or literary style takes priority in historical writing. He said that some writers strove "to give to history the coloring and dramatic action of fiction" and did not hesitate "to paint a character blacker or whiter than he really was." In contrast, the historian, Freeman, declared that the best possible style would be wasted if it were used to prove that "any two sides of a triangle are not always greater than the third." Turner hit on a compromise: "But after all these criticisms we may gladly admit that in itself an interesting

17 *Ibid.,* p. 58.
18 *Ibid.,* pp. 47-48.

style, even a picturesque manner of presentation, is not to be condemned, *provided the truthfulness of substance rather than the vivacity of style be the end sought."* [19] In short, Turner believed that the historian must tell the truth but tell it as well as possible. What Becker believed will appear in good time.

Although the phrase "truthfulness of substance" suggests some absolute truth in history, there was also a hint of the subjective relativism in Turner's thinking that would play such an overriding role in Becker's career. On one hand, Turner referred to "real facts" and to historians who attempted "to reconstruct the truth." But at the same time, said Turner, "each age tries to form its own conception of the past. *Each age writes the history of the past anew with reference to conditions uppermost in its own time."* There is objective history or the events themselves, and subjective history or man's conceptions of the events. The way of looking at things altered with each age, Turner said, but the real events of any given age did not change — only our comprehension of the facts changes.[20] This idea that each age rewrites history with reference to its own milieu would become one of Becker's strongest convictions.

Turner's solution for the problem of the nature of historical knowledge is perhaps no more satisfactory than most answers to this perplexing question. According to Turner, what happened in the past is the absolute truth and cannot be changed. Yet the reconstruction of this absolute truth depends on the historian's conception which changes with each age. In reality, Turner seemed to be saying that historians cannot examine the same body of evidence and arrive at the same conclusions. Neither history nor the writing of history would ever be final. History will be a continuous process as long as man is on earth, and since the function of the historian is to explain the present by revealing its origins from the past, each new present, being different, will require the writing of history anew.

[19] *Ibid.*, pp. 43-44. Italics added.   [20] *Ibid.*, pp. 50-52.

Perhaps the element in Turner's philosophy from which Becker would later deviate so completely was Turner's insistence that the historian should never distort the past for partisan causes. Turner condemned those historians who used their writings as "an arena whereon are to be fought our present partisan debates" with the choice of sides by the historian "victorious at whatever cost to the truth." [21] "Of one thing beware," he wrote. "Avoid as the very unpardonable sin any one-sidedness, any partisan, any partial treatment of history. Do not misinterpret the past for the sake of the present." History's sanctuary must not be fouled by "carelessness of truth about the dead that can no longer speak." [22] The historian must not "judge the past by the canons of the present, nor read into it the ideas of the present. Above all, the historian must have a passion for truth above that of any party or idea." [23] How far Becker departed from this scholars' code will be apparent in due time.

Shortly before Becker became known to Turner, there occurred one other event of great significance for an understanding of the later Becker. In 1893, Turner delivered a paper at the meeting of the American Historical Association entitled "The Significance of the Frontier in American History." In it, he made two major points. First, he contended that the American West, rather than the East or Europe, was the proper point from which to view American history. And secondly, he declared that American institutions and ideas were shaped by repeated contacts with the raw frontier, and that American democracy in particular had resulted from the fact that economic opportunity on the frontier promoted political democracy both in this country and in Europe. [24]

But again, as he had done earlier, Turner did not visualize the frontier as a great democratizing force until after 1789. He had previously noted the aristocratic nature of Revolutionary constitutions because of property requirements for voting

[21] *Ibid.,* p. 48.   [22] *Ibid.,* p. 67.   [23] *Ibid.,* p. 55.
[24] Frederick Jackson Turner, *The Frontier in American History* (New York, 1920), pp. 1-4, 29-32.

9

and even higher requirements for holding office. But the frontier states that entered the Union during the first quarter of a century after the adoption of the Constitution "came in with democratic suffrage provisions." Since these democratic states attracted people from the older aristocratic states, "an extension of the franchise became essential" in the old states. In Turner's opinion, western New York forced a liberalization of the suffrage for all New Yorkers in 1821; western Virginia compelled the "tidewater aristocracy" to extend the suffrage and grant more equitable representation to the frontier in 1830. Hence, said Turner, "the rise of democracy as an effective force in the nation came in with western preponderance under Jackson and William Henry Harrison, and it meant the triumph of the frontier."[25]

There are two points to note in Turner's "Frontier" article as they related to Becker's later writing. One is the extent to which Turner missed the democratizing influence of the frontier before the American Revolution and the degree to which Becker perpetuated Turner's error. The second is Turner's emphasis on the voting franchise and representation as the main ingredients in democracy. The latter idea will assume increasing importance after Becker's death when his work is subjected to a critical evaluation.

It was at this stage of Turner's career that the paths of the Wisconsin historian and the boy from Iowa, who had no interest in history, met. The boy had the advantage. He had already heard about "Old Freddie Turner," and it was doubtless this knowledge that directed him into Turner's classes. Considerable time would elapse, however, before the man became much impressed by the boy.

If Becker's memory served him correctly, Turner was the fountainhead of many ideas about history that would come to agitate Becker. In a highly eulogistic article on Turner, Becker later praised his former mentor for his techniques in training graduate students. Turner raised the question, he said, of what historical facts are, a question that Becker would later

[25] *Ibid.,* pp. 30-31.

consider at length in a paper delivered at a meeting of the American Historical Association. Turner also asked whether there was a difference between facts and inferences, or facts and interpretations of facts, whether inferences could be proved (and thus rested on other "facts"), and whether historians can be satisfied with inferences. Although Turner seldom answered his own questions to Becker's satisfaction, Becker would find answers in due time. Becker also claimed that Turner pursued his scholarly efforts with detachment. As practiced by Turner, however, detachment was not synonymous with complete indifference, as Becker had once believed, for Turner, he said, was not indifferent.[26] But again Becker did not always follow in Turner's footsteps. Having acquired the concepts of detachment and objectivity under Turner, Becker subsequently came to believe that objectivity was impossible and that a detached mind was a dead mind.

Evidence that Becker himself could be detached or objective in his research and thinking at this early stage of his career can be seen in two term papers on nominating conventions preserved in the Turner Collection. Both papers appear to be as objective as anything Turner could have expected from a graduate student, for Becker analyzed evidence carefully and arrived at interpretations which followed logically from this evidence. In criticizing the work of another historian, he wrote, "Let us now see if the evidence which he offers will bear out this statement." Then followed a close analysis of the other man's evidence which showed that it did not support his interpretation or conclusion.[27] The implication was that interpretation and fact must go together and that there was a logic in the evidence, some absolute quality, from which the historian would depart at his own peril.

During the years that Becker was a student under Turner, Turner published articles which were to give Becker the mistaken notion of eighteenth-century America that he would later incorporate into his own dissertation. In spite of his

---

[26] Odum, *American Masters of Social Science*, pp. 283-87, 291-92.
[27] TU Miscellaneous, Students' Papers.

emphasis on the democratizing influence of the frontier, Turner interpreted colonial society as essentially aristocratic rather than democratic, with its focus directed toward Europe. He believed that aristocracy continued after the Revolution, for the property-holding minority of the tidewater apportioned state legislatures so that they could outvote the more populous backcountry. In the West, however, free land provided economic equality which led to political equality, individual liberty, and the "exaltation of the common man." New frontier states, "with democratic provisions for the suffrage," captured the government and rallied to their aid the coastal "laboring classes." [28] Again Turner implied that the frontier was not an effective democratizing agency before the Revolution, an interpretation that Becker would later follow.

One final item must be included as part of the Wisconsin heritage for Becker. In October, 1899, the *American Historical Review* published Becker's first article, "The Unit Rule in Nominating Conventions," the subject on which Becker had written his two term papers and which appeared at this time to be his intended doctoral dissertation under Turner. Here Becker argued persuasively from the evidence that the two-thirds rule for nominating presidential candidates and the unit rule whereby convention delegates voted as a state unit rather than as individuals were devices used by the Democratic Party, not the Republican, to bolster slavery and states' rights. Again Becker demonstrated his ability to uncover relevant evidence and to draw logical conclusions. He was also able to show that another writer on the same subject was "wide of the mark" in his interpretation.

Thus it was that when Becker left Wisconsin in 1898 to continue graduate work at Columbia, he had the potential for developing in any one of several directions. He could continue as a scholarly historian, for he had learned from Turner that there was something called "truth" in history which must not be prostituted either to good literary form or to partisan desires. He had himself written some good

---

[28] Turner, *The Frontier in American History*, pp. 205-07, 212, 214, 216.

history which in effect condemned the party of democracy for developing a political device in the interests of slavery and states' rights. But Becker could also follow Turner in other directions. He could write on early American history with an interpretation based on Turner's faulty assessment of the impact of the frontier, and he could walk through the door of subjective relativism which Turner had left ajar. Turner had introduced the notions that each generation must rewrite history in the light of its own milieu, that there was the objective fact and the subjective historian, that dull facts could be used to solve fascinating human problems, that the historian must create a past that is the product of all the present, and that progress for the common man was a desirable philosophy of history. Time and circumstances would determine which path or paths Becker would follow.

II. THE BECKER "DUAL REVOLUTION" THESIS

> "I am immensely confirmed in my idea that the Revolution was only incidentally a matter of home rule, and primarily a matter of democratization of politics and society."
>
> — CARL BECKER, 1909

THE second major stage in Becker's intellectual development came with the evolution of the "Becker thesis" between 1898 and 1907. Turner believed that Becker should have training at another major graduate school besides Wisconsin. He could not get a fellowship for Becker at Harvard, but was successful at Columbia where Becker spent a year working, among others, under Herbert Levi Osgood in early American history and James Harvey Robinson in the French Revolution and European intellectual history. The supposition, apparently, was that Becker would spend a year at Columbia, obtain a position in a college or university, and return to Wisconsin in 1900 to take his degree, presumably with nominating conventions as his dissertation.[1]

Becker, however, did not follow the expected plan. After considerable difficulty in securing a position in 1899, he went to Pennsylvania State College for two years, then to Dartmouth for a year, and, in 1902, to the University of Kansas. It was not until 1907 that he returned to Wisconsin to take his final degree, and when he did, his thesis was quite different from the one he had started under Turner. In the meantime, Becker shocked his family somewhat in 1901 by marrying, not the "gracious and talented" Waterloo girl

---

[1] Turner to A. B. Hart, March 5, 1897; to Seth Low, February 23, 1898; to Becker, November 7, 1898, TU Box 2, Correspondence, 1895-99.

whom he knew during the Wisconsin years, but a widow with a seven-year-old daughter whom he had met at Columbia.[2]

A preview of what the Becker thesis would eventually be came when the *American Historical Review* published two articles by Becker in 1901. The first was entitled "Nominations in Colonial New York," an indication that he was still interested in the problem of selection of candidates for political office, even though the time had changed from the early national period of Turner to the colonial period of Osgood. The second, "The Growth of Revolutionary Parties and Methods in New York Province, 1765–1774," was further evidence that Becker was shifting away from Turner and toward Osgood.[3]

The general thesis of the two articles was both an affirmation and a denial of the Turner thesis. On the one hand, the concept that colonial society was aristocratic, first expressed in Turner's student notebooks and later in his articles on the frontier, provided the basic framework for Becker's articles. The departure from Turner appears, however, when Becker depicted an emergence of democracy in the eighteenth century, while Turner did not see American democracy until it was fostered by frontier conditions in the nineteenth century. In addition, Becker found the impetus for democracy much more among the disfranchised urban workers than among the enfranchised settlers on the frontier.

In the first article, Becker, as did Turner, saw the society which produced the American Revolution as fundamentally aristocratic. There was a governor, council, and assembly, he said, but the really vital political fact in New York was not these formal governing bodies. Of much greater importance was "the existence of a few rich and influential families," whose power rested on ability, social position, and close organization secured by prudential marriages. Land was largely in

---

[2] Jessie Becker to Phil Snyder, November 24, 1955, Becker Papers. On Becker's difficulties in securing a position, see Turner to Becker, April 19, June 25, July 14, August 5, and September 10, 1899.

[3] *American Historical Review*, January, 1901, pp. 260-75, and October, 1901, pp. 56-76.

the hands of the few, thus presumably restricting the impact of the frontier; representatives of the great families helped to carry out a more or less concerted plan of action; manor lords and important city families were tied together by interest and blood relationship; the aristocracy was coherent and well-organized.[4]

In addition, Becker continued, the political system was structured in such a way that this aristocracy could dominate politically as well as economically and socially. A sharply-limited electorate because of suffrage requirements, infrequent and irregular elections, and the manner of voting all militated against democracy. Becker placed great emphasis on the franchise which was "limited to freeholders, and the freemen of the corporations," New York and Albany, with the result that "the whole voting population, on account of the limitations of the suffrage, was small." Furthermore, elections were held "sometimes at such short notice that the total voting population, such as it was, could not be got to the polls." As for the political power of tenants, Becker, without benefit of evidence, said this: "That tenant voters would be largely influenced by the lords of the manors is perhaps sufficiently obvious." The aristocracy was able to cow even the few who could vote, for voice voting meant that "every man voted in full knowledge of the candidates and of the powerful leaders. . . . Every voter was watched, we may be sure, and his record was known." As a result, according to Becker, "New York was controlled by an aristocracy of wealth and ability."[5]

The nominating convention, then, became an instrument that would help to break the power of this dominant aristocracy. Under the old system, nominations "were made practically by the controlling members of the aristocracy," for the essence of aristocracy is "that men are governed by personality rather than by principle." The issues were men, not measures. But as the century wore on, there was a "growing democratic spirit, a coming consciousness of equality," and the nominating convention played a significant role in this development.

[4] *Ibid.,* January, 1901, pp. 260-75. [5] *Ibid.*

In fact, said Becker, "the nominating convention is an incident in the effort of the masses to pull down authority from the top and place it on the ground — an instrument by which they try to get vital control of the business of governing." This weakened the influence of the great families, who now had to win the support of the voters.[6]

Instead of perpetuating aristocracy, as Turner had assumed, the American Revolution became part and parcel of the democratizing process. It gave a powerful impetus to the new method of making nominations, "it destroyed the old by breaking up and driving out the old aristocracy," and it taught the lessons of formal organization, mass meetings, committees, and resolutions — lessons that remained after the Revolution.[7]

Becker's second article carried his thesis of the Revolution several degrees beyond the first. He included the thesis of the previous article that the new method of nominating candidates was an important development in the evolution of democracy. This method, he said, had its origins in the growth of the democratic spirit; a consciousness of equality cut into old factions and recognized parties on a basis of principle. The Revolution gave a great impetus to this movement by hastening and to some extent completing the change by teaching a minority the necessity of organization and the uses of political machinery. Becker then repeated a former statement that the Revolution in New York was a culmination in theory, and to a considerable degree in fact, of the effort of the "masses" to pull down authority from the top and place it on the ground.[8]

But the Revolution did much more than merely give impetus to the institution of nominating conventions. The Stamp Act, Becker maintained, brought virtually unanimous opposition in New York to British measures, but after the Stamp Act, resistance took on "a more radical character." Especially in New York City, "where the Revolutionary movement centered from first to last," this resistance was increasingly dominated by the lowest class, "the unfranchised

[6] *Ibid.*   [7] *Ibid.*   [8] *Ibid.*, October, 1901, pp. 56-76

mechanics and artisans." As a result, the propertied and commercial classes began to draw back and to assume a more conservative attitude. The organization which represented this unfranchised class and assumed the leadership of the more radical phase of the movement was called the Sons of Liberty. While the exact origins of the Sons of Liberty remain clouded, Becker declared, "what is true is that the Sons of Liberty represented the lowest of the four classes, the artisan and laboring classes of the city, and that they directed the conflict in so far as popular agitation and mob violence formed a part of it." [9]

The injection of radicalism into the controversy by lower classes who cried liberty and destroyed property very quickly sharpened class divisions. As Becker put it: "But opposition of this sort was not to the liking of the propertied classes, however much they may have disapproved of the levy and collection of the stamp tax. A little rioting was admirable, it is true, so long as it remained entirely under their own control and was directed to the one end of bringing the English government to terms. But when destruction of property began to be relished for its own sake by the classes which were propertyless, and when the cry of liberty came loudest from those who were most conspicuous for their lack of political privileges, it seemed well to draw back; these men might not cease their shouting when purely British restrictions were at an end. The ruling class in New York saw clearly that 'liberty' and 'no taxation' were arguments that might be used with as great potency against the home government — arguments which indeed the unfranchised classes were already making use of." [10]

In actuality, however, Becker indicated that the break between upper and lower classes was only partial as a result of the Stamp Act violence. While this episode detached the landed classes from the more radical Sons of Liberty, there was as yet no sharp separation of the merchants from the mechanics and artisans who filled the ranks of the Sons of

[9] *Ibid.*   [10] *Ibid.*

Liberty. But the merchants were becoming conscious of mob violence and resented the interference by unfranchised classes. And thus it was that when nonimportation was used as a weapon against the Townsend Acts, nonimportation resulted in a split between merchants and Sons of Liberty. Of the merchants, Becker said that they were "actuated rather by jealousy of the growing political influence of the unfranchised classes, and by the fear of their undisciplined methods of resistance, than by difference of opinion as to the nature of British policy." [11] This thesis would later be developed more fully by Arthur M. Schlesinger, Sr., in his own doctoral dissertation, *The Colonial Merchants and the American Revolution.*

The near approach of the Revolution merely widened the gap between classes in New York. When "radicals" dumped tea in New York, said Becker, once more "the Sons of Liberty, the representatives of the unfranchised classes, had scored a victory over the propertied enfranchised classes." Extreme conservatives dropped out of the opposition to become Tories as the question sharpened in New York over whether policy was to be guided by the "radical unfranchised classes" or by "moderate men of property" who were accustomed to exercise political privilege.[12]

Although Becker stopped his account short of the Revolution and therefore did not carry this class conflict for democracy between a disfranchised lower class and an enfranchised propertied class to its logical conclusion, the implication from both articles was that the Revolution brought great gains for democracy and the lower class. Class conflict, to Becker, thus became inextricably interwoven with the controversy between Britain and her colonies, with democracy the ultimate prize.

One might well wonder what Turner's reaction to this new thesis on the origins of American democracy might be, especially since it seemed to contradict in some respects his own thesis that the frontier brought democracy. Becker had shifted the center of revolution from the farm to the city and from

[11] *Ibid.*   [12] *Ibid.*

19

the "embattled farmer" to the "masses" of propertyless and unfranchised artisans and mechanics. But if Turner saw the emerging Becker thesis as a threat to his own, he never gave any indication of an adverse reaction. Turner's only comment was that he enjoyed Becker's articles on New York in the *Review*.[13]

More than five years would elapse before the completed Becker thesis would see the light of day, but at least when it was finished, it came as no surprise to Turner. Meanwhile, Becker, now at the University of Kansas, began to use book reviews as the vehicle for making known both his social philosophy and his ideas on history.

Turner's concern for progress and the welfare of the common man, while implicit in Becker's two articles on New York, now became much more obvious. In reviewing Simon N. Patten's *Heredity and Social Progress,* Becker "heartily approved" of Patten's analysis that prosperity creates and adversity lessens energy, but that progress is blocked unless the strong protect the weak. Patten declared that "the initial step in progress is protection and a flow of income from the strong to the weak," a philosophy which Becker echoed by saying that "the more freely we give to the weak, the more is gained by the strong." [14]

On the question of scholarly method in history, Becker continued to uphold high standards for historical research and writing which he had ostensibly gained from Turner. He upbraided conservative Henry Cabot Lodge for his approach in *The Story of the Revolution.* To those who believed that "good history consists in explaining past events in the light of truth rather than in the light of 'patriotism'," Becker declared, and to the "serious historian with careful methods and rigid standards," Lodge's book was "worth less than nothing and was not history at all." [15] The implication here was that there was an entity called "truth" which the serious historian, using careful methods and rigid standards, could uncover.

[13] Turner to Becker, November 9, 1901, TU Box 3.
[14] *The Nation,* June 11, 1903.   [15] *Ibid.,* November 5, 1903.

20

On another occasion, Becker also had the opportunity of demonstrating that he understood perfectly the stuff of which good historical writing was made. In a summary of the meeting of the American Historical Association in New Orleans in 1903, Becker said that President Lea urged historians not to use history for illustrating ethical principles or teaching conventional moral doctrines. The duty of the historian, he declared, was to reconstruct the past in as close approximation to reality as possible. He must explain how an institution came to be what it was at any given time and how it was transformed in response to the needs of a new environment. Great figures in history must be understood from their own point of view and that of their age to show that they were the product of their age. Becker concluded that Lea had clearly set forth all that is vital in the historic conception, all that makes valuable the serious study of history.[16]

Then in 1904, nearly three years before he submitted his dissertation at Wisconsin, Becker used a book review to announce his famous "dual-revolution thesis," previously hinted at in his articles on New York. Historians had viewed the American Revolution "too exclusively as a movement for independence of England," he declared, when the real keynote was to be found "in the conflict between the extreme radicals and the moderate conservatives." [17] On the one hand, there was a war between Britain and her colonies involving American independence, but at the same time there was an internal class war of great importance in progress.

Judging by the emphasis in the review, Becker seemed to feel that the internal class conflict, involving the evolution of democracy in this country, took priority in importance over the war with Britain. Said Becker: "There were bound up in the Revolution, in fact, two great questions, not necessarily connected with each other — the questions of the relation of the colonies to England, and the question of the extension of political privileges to the unfranchised in the colonies. In the colonial period the assemblies were in the hands of the

[16] *Ibid.,* February 4, 1904.   [17] *Ibid.,* August 18, 1904.

property classes, but, in resisting the royal governors, they were forced to justify themselves by an appeal to natural rights and popular welfare. They seemed to stand for democratic principles in government, and their constant insistence upon the rights of the colonists as against the governors fostered the democratic spirit and led the unfranchised classes to hope for political equality." [18]

To Becker, then, the American Revolution became an important social movement for improving the status of the lower classes. It "opened the door for the unfranchised" who were working fully as much for political equality with the propertied classes as they were for home rule against Britain. The propertied classes, which had steadily resisted colonial governors, became conscious of their inherent conservatism and from 1765 on they opposed the growing influence of those who had previously possessed no share in political action. We cannot completely understand the Revolution if we regard it exclusively from the standpoint of home rule, Becker concluded, for home rule was complicated by the question of equality or political privilege.[19]

In a 1905 review of Edward Channing's *History of the United States,* Becker again appeared to accept Turner's concept of the great historian as one who sought the "truth" yet did not minimize breadth or literary style. Earlier he had condemned those historians whose "interest in the minutiae of documentation so often obscures the breadth of view essential to great historical writing." [20] In Channing, however, Becker found the ideal. Instead of a specialist who wrote monographs about a limited area of history, Channing ventured "to write the whole history of his country in extended form with the ideals of a man of letters and the conscience of a scholar." Becker praised Channing's scholarship and style, a style which permitted one "to tell the exact truth." [21] Again there was the suggestion that there is an "exact truth" in history which the historian could uncover through the use of proper scholarly methods.

[18] *Ibid.*   [19] *Ibid.*   [20] *Ibid.*, November 20, 1902.   [21] *Ibid.*, July 3, 1905.

There was one discordant note in the review, however, with reference to Turner's view of history and Becker's own philosophy later. Turner had emphasized that while the present is the product of the past, the past is also a product of the present, and the proper perspective from which to view history is the present. The historian, therefore, works from results back to causes. But Becker praised Channing precisely because he *did not* study history from the vantage point of the present. He said that Americans had endeavored to explain events by their results rather than their causes, but that Channing, who viewed American history as part of British history, wrote of the growth of the United States from the standpoint of that which preceded rather than that which followed.[22] Eventually, however, Becker would revert to the presentism of Turner.

Becker finally completed his dissertation in 1907, but the details of the process, which assume some importance later, are not completely clear. In November, 1906, Turner asked to see portions of the work so that he could make suggestions, but at that point the title had not been settled.[23] Whether Turner saw any of the dissertation before it was completed we cannot tell, but in April, 1907, he instructed Becker to send the manuscript to Washington where he was doing research.[24] Then on May 25, Turner wrote that he would begin to work on the dissertation on the 26th, and on June 8 came his only comment: "I like your thesis exceedingly." [25]

Thus was born the "Becker thesis." Becker received his doctor's degree at the age of thirty-four, and in 1909 the University of Wisconsin published the dissertation under the title, *The History of Political Parties in the Province of New York, 1760–1776*.

In final form, the Becker thesis was what might have been predicted from his two articles on colonial New York and his Patten review in 1904. "The American Revolution was the

[22] *Ibid.,* July 13, 1905.
[23] Turner to Becker, November 28, 1906, TU Box 7.
[24] Turner to Becker, April 13, 1907, TU Box 9.
[25] Turner to Becker, May 25 and June 8, 1907, TU Box 9.

result of two general movements; the contest for home-rule and independence, and the democratization of American politics and society," Becker wrote. There was no doubt in his mind, however, as to which of these two aspects he considered the more significant: "Of these movements, the latter was fundamental; it began before the contest for home-rule, and was not completed until after the achievement of independence." He then closed his first chapter with this oft-quoted statement: "The first was the question of home rule; the second was the question, if we may so put it, of who should rule at home." [26]

Lest there should be any question of the extent to which he rejected imperialism and sectional controversy in favor of internal class conflict as causes of the Revolution, Becker explained his interpretative emphasis in a letter to Turner in 1909. He contended that in New York there was neither sectional conflict between seacoast and interior nor any significant imperial issue. Said he: "I am immensely confirmed in my idea that the Revolution was only incidentally a matter of home rule, and primarily a matter of democratization of politics and society." [27]

Becker must also have realized that the Becker and Turner theses on the origins of American democracy were drifting poles apart, for this letter to Turner appears as an effort to reconcile the two and especially to involve Turner in the Becker thesis. After denying that there was a sectional conflict between the aristocratic seacoast and the democratic frontier in New York, Becker went on in this vein to emphasize his own version of democratization: "The history of revolutionary parties must be rewritten on that line, I think, and your paper points the way unmistakably for that as for other ventures." [28] Becker was referring to Turner's article, "The Old West," which Becker had just read but which, in fact, stressed sectionalism.

[26] Carl L. Becker, *The History of Political Parties in the Province of New York*, 1760-1776 (Madison, 1909), pp. 5, 22.
[27] Becker to Turner, March 19, 1909, TU Box 12.　　　　[28] *Ibid.*

Thus did Becker the student appear to part company with the frontier thesis of Turner the master, yet in a way that kept the personal relations between the two intact. Both were interested in the evolution of American democracy, it is true, but their interpretations of the process by which democracy was to be achieved were vastly different. Having rejected sectionalism and imperialism, Becker placed the American Revolution in the city rather than on the frontier with class conflict between disfranchised lower classes and propertied upper classes the major issue.

III. A CRITIQUE OF THE BECKER THESIS

> "The number of freemen was small; so late as 1790 there were only forty-five in Albany and ninety-three in New York. . . ."
>
> — CARL BECKER, 1909

THE Becker thesis was to become one of the most famous and influential in American history, and since it had such a profound impact on other historians and since it provides the foundation for all of Becker's other writings on American history, it must undergo the kind of critical analysis to which all major works should be subjected.

So we ask of Becker the same questions that any scholar must apply to his own and other works in his field of competence. Did Becker examine a sufficient amount of the available primary sources to give his conclusions a firm foundation? Are his conclusions or generalizations based on evidence and are they justified by the logic of the evidence which he presented? Are there conflicts or contradictions in his evidence or conclusions that would cast doubt on the validity of his thesis? In short, would the Becker thesis stand up under the most critical cross-examination that it could receive in the highest court of the land where accepted rules of evidence were mandatory?

Becker uses his first chapter both to state the dual revolution thesis and to present much of the foundation on which the important half of the thesis, the democratization of an aristocratic American society, rests. In a sense, the thesis can be said to stand or fall on the strength of the evidence which Becker presents in this chapter.

Fundamental to Becker's interpretation was the domination by a ruling aristocracy of New York colonial society. Through grants of land and special privileges, he said, early governors had in fact established the "peculiar social conditions that characterized New York in the eighteenth century," for by the close of Cornbury's administration, "a very large part of the most valuable land in the province was in the hands of a few families." Wealthy merchant families in New York City were closely associated with the great landowners, and in particular, intermarriage among these families helped to solidify the position of the aristocracy.[1]

In addition to wealth and family ties, the ruling upper class had other methods for maintaining its position of dominance. One was through the landlord-tenant relationship both on the manors and on other landed estates. The manorial estates, "homes of a numerous tenantry," operated under "quasi-feudal" lease tenures advantageous to the "manor lords." In politics, said Becker, "it was taken as a matter of course that tenant voters would follow their landlords." Non-manorial proprietors, although without "some of the distinctive privileges of lords of the manors," nevertheless had great influence because of their wealth and the relations they sustained with their tenants.[2]

Becker declared that it was through a rigged political system, however, that the aristocracy was best able to sustain its dominance. Below the aristocracy was a "mass" of freeman and freeholder electors. Freemen were voters who had purchased the privilege of engaging in certain occupations in New York City and Albany. Freeholders were voters if they "possessed, free of encumbrance, an estate in fee, for life, or by courtesy, of the value of £40." But the number of these nonaristocratic electors was strictly limited. "The number of freemen was small," Becker declared, for as "late as 1790 there were only forty- five in Albany and ninety-three in New York." At that time, 1790, the proportion of electors to the total population was only twelve per cent, he continued, but this was not

[1] Becker, *History of Political Parties*, pp. 8-10, 12-13.
[2] *Ibid.*, pp. 10, 14.

27

a true reflection of voters among the people, for many of the twelve per cent were members of the aristocracy.[3]

Of greatest significance to Becker in explaining aristocratic domination, however, was the large number of disfranchised men who were excluded from all political activity. This constituted Becker's third class in the population — freeholders with estates too small to qualify their owners, leasehold tenants, and those who worked for others, such as clerks, journeymen, and day laborers, often called inhabitants or mechanics. The size of this group is best expressed by Becker's statement that "it is perhaps safe to say that over half of the male population above the age of twenty-one years was without political privilege of any sort." Hardly a factor in politics earlier, this "very absence of privilege became a matter of tremendous significance" during the revolutionary period, for it was this class that would gain most by the internal democractic revolution.[4]

Representation was also rigged in favor of the upper class, according to Becker. Since political privilege rested on property, it was only natural that the assembly should represent the interests of those property holders who could elect assemblymen. As Becker phrased it: "Technically the assembly did not represent the people; it represented a privileged class whose interests were in reality threatened by the spread of democratic notions."[5]

Over all hung a pall, a smog, of privilege and deference which threatened to smother any democratic aspirations. Until the middle of the eighteenth century, and even later in rural areas, "the democratic ideal was without significance. The aristocratic flavor which everywhere permeated society prevented the common man from taking the initiative, and even from expressing independence of judgment on political questions. To look up to one's superiors and follow their lead

---

[3] *Ibid.,* pp.10-11.

[4] *Ibid.,* p. 11. What Becker meant by leasehold tenants who were disfranchised is not clear, for previously he stated that tenants on the manors with "lease tenures" had voted with the lords of the manors.

[5] *Ibid.,* p. 16.

was quite the proper thing." The absence of a secret ballot meant that a voter was always subjected to the scrutiny of his superiors, while a common man who presumed to run for office was doomed to both failure and censure. At every election, "aristocratic methods of political management were in striking evidence." New York before the American Revolution was certainly not the "age of the common man." [6]

Yet the winds of change were beginning to stir after mid-century. "The rise of democratic ideals" tended to lessen upper-class influence and "to give weight to the common man." Frontier conditions contributed to the levelling process, the absence of a law of entail resulted in the breakup of great estates, there was a democratic flavor to the aristocracy which was based on wealth rather than birth, and "equality of opportunity" helped to break down artificial social and political barriers.[7]

It was at this point, said Becker, that the British-American controversy became paramount in the democratization process. In resisting the governor and Great Britain, the assembly had to justify its position with arguments based on natural rights and the general welfare. "A local and an aristocratic assembly could not consistently oppose monarchical and external authority by pleading the natural rights of a class or the general welfare of the few." The net outcome of the conflict between governor and assembly was "to foster the theory of political equality" and the notion that governments should derive their authority from the consent of the governed.[8]

The result of these new ideas was the gradual transformation of politics. Men who learned that "they might have opinions of their own" began to think in terms of political rights, governmental policy, or social change. The great families, particularly in New York City, found it necessary to alter their political practices by winning over support through reason rather than through personality. Public nominations for office replaced private "arrangements," and candidates began to appeal for public support on the basis of "principles."

[6] *Ibid.*, pp. 14-16.   [7] *Ibid.*, p. 16.   [8] *Ibid.*, pp. 16-17.

Later, when the "unfranchised" began to demand rights, the upper classes drew back, but until they saw the light, they encouraged "the very spirit which threatened their peculiar privileges." [9]

Eventually the contest for "home rule" between governor and assembly would broaden to include Parliament and the colonies, a development which gave impetus to the question of "who should rule at home." Extralegal committees and congresses replaced the official assembly, and "this extra-legal machinery was the open door through which the common freeholder and the unfranchised mechanic and artisan pushed their way into the political arena." Thus according to Becker did the American Revolution become primarily a social revolution for democracy in the interests of the common man.[10]

How, then, does this social-revolution interpretation stand up under scrutiny? If American democracy today is what it is because of the way it developed out of the past, it is of great significance to our understanding of ourselves to know what that past was. In the light of today's discussion among historians about the relative importance of conflict or concensus as forces in our development, it behooves us to know the extent to which the beginnings of American democracy resulted from class conflict.

Contrary to his thesis, Becker made it clear that before 1765 the central fact in New York political history, the contest between governor and assembly, was imperial rather than class. The two sides represented different interests and opposing principles. In the matter of interests, the assembly was concerned with local rather than imperial problems, and used its position to exact "tremendous concessions" from Britain in matters of local government. As for principles, the governor held to monarchical traditions of the past, while the assembly, even though it was not based on manhood suffrage, in fact "guarded the general interests with an over-scrupulous care." [11]

Three governors, Hunter, Clark, and Clinton, presented another clue to the imperial conflict as represented by the

[9] *Ibid.*, p. 17.   [10] *Ibid.*, pp. 21-22.   [11] *Ibid.*, pp. 5-6.

contest between governor and assembly, Becker continued. They suggested that the dominance of the assembly had become so great that the entire process of government would be taken over by the assembly unless the king took the colony in hand. Implied is actual if not nominal independence, suggesting the possibility that British action after 1760 was designed more to enable the king to take the colony in hand than to govern an expanded empire.[12]

The names of the two parties involved in the governor-assembly controversy give additional insight into the nature of the struggle. The men who attached themselves to the governor's interest were called the "court party" while those who made use of the assembly to thwart the governor's interest were known as the "popular party." [13] One suggests an absence of democracy, but the word popular, then as now, had the connotation of something based on wide support by the people — something approaching the idea of democracy.

Becker's account of this governor-assembly conflict raises some troublesome questions. If the imperial contest was predominant before 1765, how much more important would it have been after 1765 when efforts to enforce imperial restrictions increasingly encroached on the assembly's sphere of power? Does the action of the assembly in guarding general colonial interests "with an even over-scrupulous care" imply internal conflict or concensus? If the assembly party was known as the "popular party," is it not possible that the power of the assembly had a much broader basis of enfranchisement among the common people than Becker implied? And could it be that democracy before 1765, as represented by the assembly, threatened to take over all power in the colony and thus led the king to attempt a restoration of monarchical authority?

Another major question relates to the solidarity of the upper or aristocratic class. After saying that the aristocracy was able in large measure to control provincial politics because of economic and social conditions, and that the leaders

---

[12] *Ibid.*, pp. 6-7.   [13] *Ibid.*, pp. 8, 11-12.

of the aristocracy stood between governor and assembly, using either as occasion demanded, Becker offered considerable evidence that the aristocracy was, in fact, widely split. The Philipse family "remained loyal to the governors" and De-Lancey was "best known as the leader of the court party," but Robert Livingston, on entering the assembly, almost at once found himself at odds with the governor, and his descendants became "the most distinguished leaders of the popular party." [14]

Attesting to the lack of solidarity among the aristocracy was the fact that even members of the same family appear on opposing sides. Becker quoted a contemporary observer on the point that R. R. Livingston failed of election in Dutchess County in 1769 "owing to all the tenants of Beekman and R. G. Livingston voting against him." [15] If one Livingston opposed another for election, and a Beekman, who was related to the Livingstons by marriage, also was in the opposition, what happens to the class solidarity on which Becker built his aristocracy?

An election in 1769 further clouds the issue of aristocratic control. The contest, according to Becker, was between the Livingston and DeLancey factions, again indicating class fragmentation. But in addition, the "Livingston or popular party" was backed by the lawyers and dissenters (Protestants who did not subscribe to the Church of England) while the DeLancey or court party was backed by the Church of England and the mercantile interest.[16] This alignment suggests issues far different than those put forward by Becker.

Becker's account of tenant voting against Livingston poses the question of the number of freeholders and tenants who were voters. He said that there were both freeholders and tenants on the manors, and while we do not know how the freeholders voted, in this one particular election "all the tenants" of Beekman and R. G. Livingston voted. If *all* of these tenants voted, the possibility is that most tenants throughout the colony could also vote. In addition, Becker

[14] *Ibid.*, pp. 11-12.   [15] *Ibid.*, p. 14n.   [16] *Ibid.*, pp. 18-19.

said that the freeholders on the manors of Livingston and Rensselaerwick were numerous enough to control the elections of Albany county, and that the freeholders of Livingston Manor were as numerous as those in Kings and Richmond counties, having a militia of more than 650 men.[17] Thus to find out how large the disfranchised element was, Becker needed to ascertain with some degree of accuracy how many freeholders and tenants actually possessed the franchise.

A recent detailed study of a New York manor shows that most of our notions about manors and their proprietors are erroneous. There were no "lords of the manor" as proprietors early lost their powers of government. By pre-Revolutionary times, the manors had been so divided by sale and inheritance that they really ceased to resemble manors. There were numerous proprietors with tenants, as the defeat of Livingston indicates, but there were also many freeholders who owned land outright. There were no quasi-feudal relationships, for obligations had been commuted to rents and governmental functions were exercised by county and colonial officials.[18]

Most important of all, however, was Becker's use of evidence on the question of the number of freemen who could vote in New York City. Since Becker saw the Revolution as centering in New York rather than in the rural areas, and since he emphasized the conflict between disfranchised and enfranchised, the number of enfranchised freemen in the city becomes crucial to the Becker thesis.

In the first place, Becker uses figures that were completely irrelevant to his thesis even if they were true, which they were not. He said that the number of freemen was small, and that even as late as 1790 there were only ninety-three in New York City.[19] But the number of freemen in 1790 has no relevance for a thesis that is concerned with the dates 1760–1776 unless Becker can demonstrate the relevance. If the Revolution was primarily concerned with disfranchised nonfreemen, we must

[17] *Ibid.*, pp. 14n., 11 and note 39.
[18] Sung Bok Kim, "The Manor of Cortlandt," unpublished Ph.D. dissertation, Michigan State University, 1966.
[19] Becker, *History of Political Parties,* p. 10.

know how many adult men in New York City from 1760 to 1776 were unfranchised and how many were not. The source of the information for Becker's erroneous 1790 figures will be discussed later.

Fortunately for the historian, the exact figures on all New York freemen are available, but unfortunately for the Becker thesis, they prove quite the opposite of what Becker implied. Stranger yet, Becker cited the source for the freemen in both his article and in Chapter I of his dissertation,[20] yet he made no use whatever of the information to be found there. The source is a volume of the *New York Historical Society Collections* for 1885 which contains the requirements for freemanship as well as the names and most of the occupations of all men admitted as freemen after 1684.

What, then, could Becker have discovered about the freemen of New York if he had used this document as historians customarily use documents?

Instead of being exclusive, as Becker implied, freemanship was in fact a *requirement* for anyone carrying on a gainful occupation in the city. Every man engaged in productive work of any sort, whether manual or professional, was required to become a freeman. He purchased a freemanship if he was able, but if he was too poor, it was given to him gratis. If he served an apprenticeship to a trade in the city, his master had to purchase his freemanship for him so that he could engage in his trade. Instead of being a privilege for the few, it was a requirement for everyone including Jews, and even a few women were granted freemanships. Officials were concerned, not with restricting the number of freemen to the select few, but in forcing men to become freemen when they apparently preferred the status of nonfreemen to paying the fee for a freemanship.[21]

Then if quantification was important, as it must be in a problem involving the unenfranchised and as he indicated

[20] *Ibid.,* p. 10n.
[21] *New York Historical Society Collections,* 1885, pp. 47-49, 58-71, 169, and *passim.*

that it was by giving the figure of ninety-three, Becker could have found out exactly how many men became freemen from 1760 to 1776 and what most of their occupations were. Obviously, many men who became freemen before 1760 were still freemen after that date, so in Table I, I have compiled figures on male freemen for both 1740 to 1759 and 1760 to 1776.

The number and occupations of these freemen give quite a different impression of the New York City electorate than that given by Becker. There is a considerable discrepancy between ninety-three and 2,493, and the number of bakers, blacksmiths, bricklayers, carpenters, coopers, cordwainers, laborers, and shipwrights, not to mention a hundred other occupations represented, does not add up to an aristocratic society.

The extent to which freemanship was nonexclusive can be seen from the number of men admitted on single days during these years. On January 31, 1769, a total of 171 men became freemen, but there were also 164 admitted on October 1, 1765, and 128 on September 11, 1770.

Figures on freemen *admitted* from 1740 to 1776 do not, of course, tell us how many freemen were actually in New York from 1760 to 1776, the years of the Becker thesis. To the total must be added all men who were admitted as freemen before 1740 and who were still alive after 1760. But at the same time, the number of men who died or who left New York must be subtracted from the total. It would probably be impossible to arrive at an exact figure of freemen who were actually in the city during this period. But the deeds, wills, tax lists, church records, records of vital statistics, and the newspapers would contribute much information.

If they had been relevant to his thesis, which they were not, Becker could also have found the names and occupations of all men who were admitted freemen between 1784, when the British evacuated New York, and 1790, the date he cited. These freemen, however, were not relevant to the Becker thesis, which presumably ended in 1776, but they are relevant to a critique of the Becker thesis in a way that will be clarified in due time. The number and occupations of freemen in this later period are included in Table II.

TABLE I

NUMBER AND OCCUPATION OF MEN ADMITTED AS FREEMEN
IN NEW YORK CITY, 1740–1759 and 1760–1776.[22]

Occupation	1740–1759	1760–1776	Occupation	1740–1759	1760–1776
1. Attorney	3	0	39. Cutler	2	1
2. Armourer	0	4	40. Dancing		
3. Baker	36	52	master	1	0
4. Barber	2	1	41. Distiller	6	2
5. Blacksmith	32	41	42. Druggist	1	3
6. Blockmaker	8	11	43. Dyer	2	0
7. Boatman	3	2	44. Farrier	2	0
8. Bolter	9	1	45. Feltmaker	15	5
9. Bookbinder	2	2	46. Founder	0	1
10. Bookseller	0	1	47. Fuller	0	1
11. Brassfounder-			48. Gardener	1	5
brazier	4	10	49. Gauger	0	1
12. Breechesmaker	1	6	50. Gentlemen	24	97
13. Brewer	0	1	51. Glazier	1	1
14. Bricklayer	23	14	52. Glover	1	0
15. Brickmaker	2	0	53. Goldsmith	7	8
16. Butcher	18	21	54. Grocer	1	1
17. Buttonmaker	0	1	55. Gunsmith	15	6
18. Cabinetmaker	1	7	56. Hatter	5	17
19. Carpenter	50	81	57. Heelmaker	0	2
20. Carman-			58. Hosier	0	2
cartman	16	11	59. Innkeeper	16	25
21. Carver	1	0	60. Instrument		
22. Chairmaker	1	5	maker	1	1
23. Chandler	4	0	61. Jeweller	2	2
24. Chimney-			62. Joiner	29	17
sweeper	0	1	63. Laborer	362	43
25. Chocolatemaker	2	1	64. Lastmaker	0	1
26. Clerk	0	1	65. Leatherdresser	4	6
27. Clockmaker	0	1	66. Limner	1	1
28. Clothworker	0	1	67. Malster	1	0
29. Coachmaker	0	2	68. Mariner	91	49
30. Collarmaker	0	1	69. Mason	9	6
31. Compass maker	0	1	70. Mastmaker	1	1
32. Confectioner	1	0	71. Measurer	0	1
33. Cooper	55	40	72. Merchant	79	62
34. Coppersmith	0	1	73. Miller	0	1
35. Copper refiner	0	1	74. No occupation	16	3
36. Cordwainer-			75. Organist	0	1
shoemaker	86	95	76. Painter	6	14
37. Corkcutter	1	0	77. Perukemaker-		
38. Currier	4	5	wigmaker	31	24

[22] *Ibid., passim.*

TABLE I (Continued)

Occupation	1740–1759	1760–1776	Occupation	1740–1759	1760–1776
78. Peddler	1	0	103. Soapboiler-tallowchandler	1	4
79. Pewterer	2	5	104. Stationer	1	0
80. Physician	5	0	105. Staymaker	3	6
81. Plasterer	0	1	106. Stocking weaver	3	2
82. Potter	0	3	107. Stone cutter	1	4
83. Practitioner Dr. of Physick	1	2	108. Sugar refiner-baker	2	5
84. Printer	3	1	109. Surgeon	7	7
85. Razor grinder	1	0	110. Surveyor	0	1
86. Retailer	0	2	111. Tailor	45	46
87. Rigger	3	0	112. Tallow chandler	6	3
88. Ropemaker	5	8	113. Tanner	1	5
89. Ropemerchant	1	0	114. Tinman-tinplater	4	2
90. Saddler	8	11	115. Tobacconist	3	5
91. Sailmaker	6	7	116. Trader	0	1
92. Saltmeasurer	0	1	117. Turner	9	6
93. Sawyer	2	0	118. Upholsterer	0	4
94. Schoolmaster	10	5	119. Vendue master	0	1
95. Scrivener	2	11	120. Victualler	5	0
96. Shagreen casemaker	0	1	121. Watchmaker	3	3
97. Ship chandler	0	2	122. Weaver	24	6
98. Shipwright-joiner	73	17	123. Wheelwright	2	8
99. Shopkeeper	30	48	124. Whitesmith	0	1
100. Silversmith	2	8	125. Yeoman-farmer	16	15
101. Skinner	0	1	Totals	1390	1103
102. Snuffmaker	1	1			

Although the 2,493 freemen before 1776 were all qualified voters, these 565 freemen admitted after 1784 were not voters unless they also possessed a certain amount of property. The New York constitution of 1777 abolished freemanship in New York and Albany as a qualification for the franchise and imposed a property qualification in its place, hardly a democratizing trend. But the constitution of 1777 also said that while new freemen in the two towns did not become voters unless they had property, all freemen who had been freemen in 1775 still qualified as voters simply by virtue of their freemanship. The constitution was not retroactive: it did not deprive freeman of the vote if they had once possessed the vote. Since Becker cited figures for 1790, he ought to have

TABLE II
NUMBER AND OCCUPATION OF MEN ADMITTED AS FREEMEN
IN NEW YORK CITY, 1784–1790[23]

Occupation	Number	Occupation	Number
1. Baker	3	26. Innholder	4
2. Barber	1	27. Ironmonger	2
3. Blacksmith	13	28. Laborer	68
4. Blockmaker	1	29. Last & heelmaker	1
5. Boatman	2	30. Mariner	3
6. Brassfounder	1	31. Measurer	1
7. Brewer	1	32. Merchant	3
8. Bricklayer	2	33. Public cryer	1
9. Butcher	3	34. No occupation	16
10. Cabinetmaker	3	35. Ropemaker	2
11. Carpenter	17	36. Saddler	1
12. Cartman	322	37. Shipwright	4
13. Chairmaker	1	38. Shopkeeper	2
14. Chocolatemaker	1	39. Silversmith	3
15. City marshall	1	40. Stonecutter	2
16. Coachmaker	1	41. Surgeon	1
17. Cooper	9	42. Tailor	7
18. Coppersmith	1	43. Tallow chandler	1
19. Cordwainer-shoemaker	17	44. Tanner	5
20. Distiller	1	45. Tinman	1
21. Farmer	3	46. Tobacconist	2
22. Gentleman*	10	47. Upholsterer	1
23. Grocer	10	48. Watchmaker	2
24. Hatter	4	49. Weaver	2
25. Heelmaker	1	50. Whitesmith	1
		Total	565

*Included Washington, LaFayette, Von Steuben, Gates, L'Enfant, and Clinton.

consulted the constitution of 1777 to see who could vote in 1790.[24]

The constitution of 1777 explains where Becker got his figure of ninety-three freemen in New York in 1790 and the extent to which he misused the document containing these figures. The document, "A Census of the Electors and Inhabitants of the State of New York, 1790," indicated that 1,209 men in New York City possessed £100 freeholds, 1,221

[23] Ibid.

[24] Francis Newton Thorpe, ed., The Federal and State Constitutions, Colonial Charters, and Other Organic Laws . . . 7 vols. (Washington, 1909), V, 2630-31.

had £20 freeholds, and 2,661 rented 40 shilling estates. The constitution of 1777 provided that men with £100 freeholds could vote for senators while those who possessed £20 freeholds or rented tenements with a rental of forty shillings a year could vote for representatives. Since a man *had to be a freeman* to work in New York, most of the freeholders and renters either had to be freemen or they were violating the law. But in addition to these property-holding voters, there were ninety-three men who qualified as voters simply because they had been freemen in 1775.

Naturally a question arises as to Becker's use of this evidence so vital to his thesis: did he make an honest mistake or was this a deliberate falsification of the record? One would like to believe that it was an honest mistake, but the evidence says otherwise. The evidence was absolutely fundamental to his thesis and he cited both documents as support for his statements. His background had demonstrated that he could analyze evidence with great skill, although all that was necessary was a little grade-school arithmetic. It seems doubtful that any trained scholar, who was dedicated to "the love of truth and the disinterested search for it," could make such an error. Over many years, literally hundreds of graduate students in seminars and reading courses have been exposed to Becker's use of evidence as part of their training, and their reaction has invariably been one of shock and disbelief. The verdict must be that Becker had to have an undemocratic New York society or he had no thesis, and that he created the impression of having used original documentation when, in fact, that documentation annihilated his thesis.

A corollary to the first question is this: why did Frederick Jackson Turner allow Becker to prostitute scholarship in this way? As his dissertation director, it was up to Turner to check on Becker's work. Here the circumstances noted earlier might have been a factor. Turner was doing research in Washington when Becker submitted his dissertation and had little time before Becker was to take his final examination. More plausible, however, is the fact that Turner had long assumed that colonial society was undemocratic and therefore did not question Becker's use of evidence. If Becker was saying what Turner already believed, and Turner told Becker that he liked the dissertation very much, one could easily imagine that Turner did not bother to do any checking.

The Becker thesis, predicated on a mass of disfranchised men who were seeking political rights, appears, then, to have no validity. If there were many freeholders, both on and off the manors, who could control elections, and if all the tenants were voters, this leaves only the city "proletariat." But they were also freemen and voters. This, in turn, would make the assembly a democratically elected body, not an aristocratic one, and would explain why this assembly "guarded the general interests with even an over-scrupulous care," as Becker said it did. The assembly did not represent "a privileged class whose interests were in reality threatened by the spread of democratic notions," but was, in fact, as it was called, the center of the "popular party."

The fact that the people of New York elected Livingstons and DeLanceys to represent them does not in any way invalidate a contention that, except for British authority, New York society was a democratic society. With everyone now having the vote, New Yorkers still elect Harrimans, Rockefellers, and Kennedys, and they do it in the belief that these men will represent their principles and interests. By the same token, there is no reason to suppose that the men who were elected to the assembly before 1776 did not also reflect the wishes of a majority of their constituents. The defeat of Robert R. Livingston in 1769 by the tenants is not-so-mute evidence of what could happen to a so-called "aristocrat" who did not please a sufficient number of the voters. Thomas Hutchinson in Massachusetts and Landon Carter in Virginia, also labeled "aristocrats," met similar fates when they displeased their constituents.

The positing of a democratic society in turn helps to explain other contradictions in Becker. Becker noted, but did not develop, the ideas that the leveling influences of the frontier, the absence of entail, and equality of opportunity tended to raise the status of the common man. Instead of fostering the theory of political equality, therefore, the contests between governor and assembly might well have involved rights which the people already had and which they intended to keep. And if leaders had to win popular support for election, as Becker said, this fact itself reveals a democratic society at a time when it should have been aristocratic. Becker indicated that this process began as early as 1739, not after 1763, and that it involved "a great number of freeholders and freemen" in New York City.[25]

Some of the fallacies of Becker's class-conflict thesis are apparent in his own account of the election of 1769. Not only was Robert R. Livingston defeated by the tenants of Beekman and R. G. Livingston, but in New York City the issues were obviously something other than class. The election, said Becker, was a conflict between the Livingston or popular party, supported by lawyers and Dissenters, and the DeLancey or court party, backed by the Church of England and the merchants. The major issue, according to Becker, was opposition by the merchants to the election of a lawyer, John Morin Scott, and the appeal of the merchants was to the "respectable tradesmen and other electors." The two other issues which Becker suggests were important, "the religious quarrel, and the supplying of British troops," hardly got mentioned by Becker. Needless to say, it is difficult to find any controversy here between enfranchised and disfranchised even though the other issues appear to have been important to those concerned.[26]

Throughout the remaining ten chapters of his dissertation, Becker attempted to impose an internal class conflict on a controversy which his evidence adequately demonstrates to have been a sharp difference between Great Britain and her American colonies over the status of Americans in the British Empire. The key thread, according to Becker, was the process

[25] Becker, *History of Political Parties*, p. 18.
[26] *Ibid.*, pp. 14 and n. 58, 18-20.

by which the disfranchised lower classes used what Becker considered to be a minor controversy to force their way into the political arena against the desires of the enfranchised upper classes. As Becker put it, "the entrance of the unfranchised classes into the political arena" and the measures proposed by their leaders, "created the first broad distinction between radicals and conservatives." [27]

Unfortunately, the source cited by Becker as proof for the entrance of the unfranchised classes into politics makes no mention whatever of the unfranchised. This source is a letter by Silas Deane in 1781, although Becker has it 1785, which indicates that Deane disapproved of what was happening in the country as a result of the Revolution. Deane saw "noisy and designing men who had risen from the lowest order, and displaced the best and most respectable members of society," but there is nothing in the letter to indicate that this "lowest order" was ever disfranchised.[28] One would have to check carefully to see what Deane meant by the lowest order, for his statement is somewhat reminiscent of those of Thomas Hutchinson, governor of Massachusetts before the Revolution, who always referred to the opposition as the lower orders when often they were among the wealthiest and best-educated people in the colony.[29]

One can go even further and say that, throughout the entire book, none of Becker's sources which are used to document the disfranchised classes and their entry into politics in any way prove the presence of a large disfranchised class of artisans, mechanics, and laborers. The reason is quite obvious, for if all workers in New York had to be freemen, as the law required, and all freemen had the vote, the only people who were disfranchised were those who successfully avoided payment of their freemen's dues.

The title of Becker's second chapter, "The Stamp Act.

[27] *Ibid.*, p. 28.
[28] Becker's citation, p. 28n., was Deane to Root, May 20, 1785 [1781], *Deane Papers*, IV, 349-50.
[29] See Robert E. Brown, *Middle-Class Democracy and the Revolution in Massachusetts, 1691-1780* (Ithaca, 1955).

Radicals and Conservatives," gives a good indication of his class-conflict approach. On the one hand, there is the "home rule" issue, of which the Stamp Act controversy of 1765 is an integral part. But on the other hand, the terms "radical" and "conservative" have social class overtones which raise the question of "who shall rule at home," the second and most important part of the Becker thesis. These are the terms, as we shall see, that James Harvey Robinson, under whom Becker had received part of his graduate training, was using at Columbia University.[30] And these are also the terms that Becker used repeatedly to indicate class conflict in New York.

In fact, throughout the entire book, Becker describes a British-American conflict, then imposes a class-conflict interpretation which is either unsupported by any citations of sources whatever, or is supported by citations which do not prove his interpretation. The following example is typical of Becker's technique. After a long discussion of the Stamp Act and colonial reaction, in which he pictured colonial opposition as virtually universal,[31] Becker injected this undocumented interpretation into his narrative: "This sort of thing brought men of property to a realization of the consequences of stirring up the mob. A little rioting was well enough, so long as it was directed to the one end of bringing the English government to terms. But when the destruction of property began to be relished for its own sake by those who had no property, and the cry of liberty came loudest from those who were without political privilege, it was time to call a halt. These men might not cease their shouting when purely British restrictions were removed. The ruling classes were in fact beginning to see that 'liberty and no taxation' was an argument that might be used against themselves as well as against the home government. The doctrine of self-government, which for so many years they had used to justify resistance to the colonial governors, was a two-edged sword that cut into the foundations of class privilege within the colony as well as into the foundations of royal authority

[30] Becker, *History of Political Parties,* p. 23.   [31] *Ibid.,* pp. 23-30.

without. Dimly at first, but with growing clearness, the privileged classes were beginning to perceive the most difficult problem which the Revolution was to present to them: the problem of maintaining their privileges against royal encroachment from above without losing them by popular encroachments from below. It was this dilemma that gave life and character to the conservative faction." [32]

But there is absolutely nothing in Becker's evidence to substantiate this interpretation. Everything points to the Stamp Act as the only issue, and when the people were assured that the stamps would not be distributed, the "mobs" and the riots ceased. Becker's "radicals" turn out to be those who opposed the British most violently, while his "conservatives" preferred more moderate methods. In fact, as one contemporary observer said, it was the "gentlemen" who had "all along made the principal opposition to the Stamp Act." [33] There is no mention of the "disfranchised" in the sources, and the differences over method of opposition were the kind that could have existed in any democratic society where there are always liberals and conservatives who differ on both means and ends.

Becker continued to inject the "unfranchised" into his account even though it is obvious that differences were simply over methods of opposing Britain. This appears in the controversy over whether the colony should stop all business in protest against the Stamp Act or resist the act by conducting business as usual without stamps. Becker said that the conservative men of property and political influence opposed all illegal opposition and believed that matters should be settled by legal voters, not by the unfranchised. Said Becker: "The entrance of the unfranchised into the political arena was as distasteful to them as the early November riots had been, for their political supremacy was threatened by the one as their property was threatened by the other." There is no citation

---

[32] *Ibid.*, pp. 31-32.

[33] *Ibid.*, p. 37. In footnote 55, Becker injects the words "the radicals" in brackets, but the source itself merely shows people who were strongly opposed to Britain.

for this conclusion, however, and no evidence whatever to support it.[34]

Having attempted without evidence to identify the radicals with the unfranchised, Becker next joined radicals and Sons of Liberty — again without evidence. Nowhere do the sources use the terms radical or unfranchised to describe the Sons of Liberty whose followers, according to Becker, "were recruited from the poorer classes." Quite the contrary, in fact, for at a meeting held at Mr. Howard's, "a great number of gentlemen, Sons of Liberty, assembled," and pledged their lives and fortunes to prevent enforcement of the Stamp Act. And in their resolutions, the Sons spoke of "the preservation of our rights and privileges" from the threat of British encroachment, not the acquisition of rights and liberties by the disfranchised from a dominant upper class. Their "extreme radicalism" consisted merely in desiring to carry on business without stamps and had nothing to do with a modification of the social structure within the colony.[35]

Still in the same vein, Becker pointed out that the repeal of the Stamp Act resulted in a dissolution of the Sons of Liberty, yet he continued to insist that the Sons and the unfranchised radicals were virtually one and the same. He referred to "the increasing activity of the unfranchised classes" and to "radical leaders" who "depended more and more upon the unfranchised classes whose poverty made them radical." The Sons of Liberty, he said, represented "in fact, the protest of the unfranchised classes, guided by leaders partly sincere and partly interested, against the determination of the privileged classes to retain an exclusive control of political affairs." Becker used the terms radical and conservative to imply social conflict, but the issues always turn out to be British-American, and again there is never any mention in the *sources* of the unfranchised.[36]

Although Becker continued in his attempt to develop internal social conflict during the controversies of 1767–1770, he was no more successful than he was in handling the Stamp

[34] *Ibid.*, p. 38.   [35] *Ibid.*, pp. 41-44.   [36] *Ibid.*, pp. 48, 50-52.

Act crisis. The title of Chapter III, "The Economic Crisis of 1768–1770: The More Complete Differentiation of Radicals and Conservatives," promises but does not deliver class conflict. The issues all revolved around British policy, and the victory of the court party over the popular party in 1768 did not appreciably change the opposition of the assembly to British measures.[37]

After leading the reader to expect social conflict, Becker spent twenty pages showing why the Americans had perfectly good reasons for fearing British measures, even to the fear of a military government, and then proceeded to demolish his class interpretation. In the election of 1768, the radical Sons of Liberty, presumably composed mainly of the disfranchised, helped to elect the conservative DeLancey "court" party to the assembly. This assembly, however, passed resolutions against British measures that were considered seditious, and the assembly was dissolved. A new election, said Becker, "registered the popular approval of the conduct of the assembly, for the old members were returned almost to a man." Then came this strange admission of concensus from Becker: "Both the merchants and the *Sons of Liberty* voted the DeLancey ticket," yet he had emphatically contended earlier that the Sons of Liberty were the disfranchised lower classes.[38]

At this juncture in his story, Becker injected an account of previous activities in marked contrast with his earlier interpretation. The issue was nonimportation in 1770. In the Stamp Act crisis, he said, some leading merchants had opposed the violence of the Sons of Liberty, but "as a class they were, however, largely identified with the radicals, and neither the elections of 1768 and 1769, nor the formation of the nonimportation association, had revealed any hostility between fair trader and smuggler, or between merchant and mechanic." Previous to 1769, celebration of the repeal of the Stamp Act had resulted in "a cordial cooperation of all classes in this event; merchant, mechanic, lawyer, and landowner had as-

[37] *Ibid.*, pp. 53-60.
[38] *Ibid.*, pp. 60, 74-75.

sumed for the day the title of *Sons of Liberty*." Concensus now replaced class conflict, yet all along Becker had insisted that social class differences were paramount.[39]

The real break between radicals and conservatives would come over the question of continued nonimportation in 1770, Becker assured the reader, but again the promise failed of fulfillment. Repeal of the Townshend taxes except the tax on tea raised the issue of whether or not the colony should resume importation of untaxed articles, especially since there were rumors that other colonial ports were violating nonimportation. A subscription or popular referendum was circulated among the people, Becker said, "apparently not limited to the legal voters, but in spite of that fact the conservatives had a majority." Cadwallader Colden said that 1,180 persons favored importation, about 300 "were neutral or refused to declare their sentiments, and few of any distinction declared in opposition to it." [40] So once again concensus rather than radical-conservative conflict seems to have been the order of the day.

The Tea Act of 1773 provided Becker with the additional opportunity of imposing class conflict on an episode that was purely imperial. He pointed out that repeal of the Townshend duties in 1770 left New York "exceptionally quiet and peaceful," an indication that the issues were external rather than internal. Becker's statement that "neither the city elections nor the celebrations of the repeal of the stamp act occasioned any factional conflicts; the lower classes were prosperous and contented; the *Sons of Liberty* were no longer heard of" indicates that agitation occurred only when British measures engendered it. But when Britain passed the Tea Act in 1773, opposition was virtually universal again, both because the act posed a threat of monopoly and a threat to "liberty," the latter a suggestion that Americans already had liberties. The association against the Tea Act was signed by "a great number of the principal gentlemen of the city, merchants, lawyers, and other inhabitants of all ranks." Practically everyone

[39] *Ibid.*, pp. 83, 86.   [40] *Ibid.*, pp. 85, 90-93.

favored use of force to prevent the landing of the tea, and after the New York Tea Party, which destroyed only tea and not other property in general, "the great part of the town was perfectly quiet," as Colden wrote. The issues were imperial, and again the result was concensus against British measures rather than internal class conflict.[41]

Yet on the tea episode, which demonstrated a remarkable degree of concensus, Becker imposed a radical-conservative dichotomy involving the "unprivileged" and the "unfranchised" classes. Even though action against the tea was practically unanimous, he said, "nevertheless, the event aroused the old conservative fear of mob-violence, and the old opposition of the intrusion of the unprivileged classes in political affairs." As evidence, Becker cited one writer in *Rivington's Gazetteer,* a notorious Tory newspaper, but this writer really said that the "cobblers and tailors" were running the town, not that there were any "unfranchised classes." [42]

Again Becker's evidence does not support his interpretation. He said that the tea episode momentarily united radicals and conservatives but ultimately brought out more sharply than ever essential differences between them. The coercive acts resulting from destruction of the tea led to extralegal organizations, he said, and raised the question "of whether the unfranchised" should share in elections. Conservatives realized that they must influence the Sons of Liberty, "now controlled by the radicals." Then after saying that the Sons enjoyed "wide popular support," Becker cited this statement of Colden, which says nothing whatever about unprivileged or disfranchised classes: "After the destruction of Captain Chamber's tea and some other violent proceedings of the pretended patriots, the principal inhabitants began to be apprehensive and resolved to attend the meetings of the inhabitants when called together by hand bills. The consequence is that Scott, MacDougall, Sears, and Lamb are all in disgrace, and the people are now directed by more moderate men." [43]

[41] *Ibid.*, pp. 95, 96, 106, 108-10. [42] *Ibid.*, p. 110.
[43] *Ibid.*, pp. 110-11 and note 81.

In the struggle in New York over selection of delegates to the First Continental Congress in 1774, Becker again imposes the issue of enfranchisement on a controversy which patently revolved around colonial countermeasures against the coercive acts. Nowhere does the evidence point to "unfranchised classes" or to proposals by the "radicals" to achieve enfranchisement of the lower-class masses. The issue was purely that of strong, moderate, or conciliatory measures to be adopted against the British to preserve "the liberties of America." Becker even attempted without success to impose conservatism on the colony outside New York City — the "conscious conservatism of the great landowners" and "the instinctive conservatism of the small farmers" — but then Becker was puzzled when the rural areas demanded complete nonintercourse just as New York City "radicals" had done.[44]

Withal, there is only one piece of evidence that lends any credibility to the Becker thesis, and even that has nothing about the unfranchised classes which he emphasized so much. Becker quoted John Adams to the effect that Philip Livingston seemed "to dread New England, the levelling spirit," and then went on as follows: "Mr. MacDougall gave a caution to avoid every expression here which looked like an allusion to the last appeal. He says there is a powerful party here who are intimidated by fear of a civil war . . . another party, he says, are intimidated lest the levelling spirit of New England should propagate itself into New York. Another party are prompted by Episcopalian prejudice against New England. Another party are merchants largely concerned in navigation, and therefore afraid of nonimportation . . . agreements. Another party are those who are looking up to government for favors."[45]

One might make something of the ideas of civil war and leveling spirit, but the civil war was between colonies, not classes, and it would seem that New York was divided vertically into interest groups rather than horizontally into classes of radicals and conservatives. Furthermore, the unfranchised

[44] *Ibid.*, ch. V, especially pp. 112-13, 117, 119-21, 123, 136.
[45] *Ibid.*, p. 117n.

never entered the picture, and John Adams' description of the "radicals" makes them anything but poor.[46]

Actions by the First Continental Congress in adopting the rebellious "Suffolk Resolves" and nonintercourse in the form of a Continental Association merely emphasized the fallacies in the Becker thesis. Throughout Chapter VI, Becker's theme was that conservatives favored conciliatory measures toward Great Britain while radicals and "ultra-radicals" looked on violations of the decrees of Congress "as a treasonable desertion of the American cause." Yet Becker could not resist the inclusion of his thesis. On one hand, "the old conservative faction" in New York "had hitherto embraced the great majority of the inhabitants," even though he had previously said that more than half of these inhabitants were disfranchised. Then after showing that the issue, beyond doubt, was loyalism rather than internal class conflict, Becker, without evidence, had conservatives desiring control "by men of property with political privileges to lose rather than by men of no property who had at best only political privileges to gain." [47]

In his discussion of the rise of loyalism and the election of delegates to the Second Continental Congress, Becker continued to use the terms radical and conservative, implying internal social conflict, but again his evidence all points to British-American difficulties. The "extreme conservatives" now became loyalists, but their writers were "mainly Episcopalian clergymen." [48] Then in the election to decide on an extralegal provincial congress, Becker declared that the fight, where there was a fight, was "between those who were going the way of revolution and those who were going the way of loyalism." This was, in fact, the real issue, and did not involve "radicals" versus "conservatives" in internal class warfare.[49]

In showing the loyalist-patriot controversy, Becker, in viola-

[46] John Adams, *The Works of John Adams,* Charles Francis Adams, ed., 10 vols. (Boston, 1850-56), II, 345-51.

[47] Becker, *History of Political Parties,* ch. VI, especially pp. 142-43, 148, 153-57.

[48] *Ibid.,* pp. 158-59.   [49] *Ibid.,* p. 187.

tion of his thesis, also presented much evidence on democracy in New York. In an approaching election, he said, one side expected to get the votes of "part of the trade, part of the church, all of the non-Episcopals, and all of the liberty boys." [50] This was anything but a class alignment; and in addition, if the "liberty boys" were voting, they obviously had the right to vote, a fact that Becker had continually denied. Earlier, Becker had characterized "voice voting" as a device by which conservative aristocrats could control the voters, but in 1774, with the election limited to legal freemen and freeholders, "the decisive method of election by ballot was to be replaced," indicating that elections had been by ballot rather than voice voting, and now it was the radicals, not the conservatives, who were using this device. Becker interpreted the switch to mean that "the suffrage ceased to be a matter of importance," but since all men by law had to be freemen and voters, the suffrage had never been "a matter of importance." [51]

Two elections cited by Becker, both prime examples of a misuse of evidence and logic, actually refute the Becker thesis. In one, two committees, presumably representing radicals and conservatives, had agreed on a ticket for a new committee of sixty with the choice to be submitted to the voters. Becker called the result "a victory for the radicals" even though the ticket was actually elected "without a dissenting voice" and, as he said, "all shades of opinion were represented in it." Rather than a victory for radicals, this election would appear as a verification for concensus, especially as only thirty or forty voters took the trouble to vote. [52] But as an indication of how many potential voters there were, and how one-sided the result was, in an election for delegates to an extralegal provincial congress, 825 freemen and freeholders voted for the ticket while 163 voted against. In a footnote, Becker said that the total vote, 988, "was about two-thirds of the voting population which, at that time, was over 1500." [53] If Becker knew

[50] *Ibid.*, p. 164n.
[51] *Ibid.*, p. 166.

[52] *Ibid.*, p. 167 and note 33.
[53] *Ibid.*, p. 186 and note 39.

that there were more than 1500 qualified voters in the city in 1774, why did he imply ninety-three in 1790 instead of using this figure of over 1500, which more nearly conforms with the number on the freemen's list?

Becker ended his chapter on election of delegates to the Second Continental Congress by demonstrating again that the real issue was British-American rather than class. Said he: "The conservative program was rapidly breaking down; and of the old members of the conservative faction, one part was becoming indistinguishable from the revolutionists, while the other was in part already identified with the loyalists." [54] In other words, as Britain and her colonies approached a showdown, men who hoped for some sort of reconciliation were gradually forced to take sides.

Contrary to Becker's interpretation, his description of events of 1775 surrounding the election and activities of a revolutionary provincial congress to replace the assembly again indicates no internal revolution. A new Committee of One Hundred was elected by a vote "limited to freemen and freeholders," and the vote was by ballot as usual. Opposition to the list of candidates for the committee was not based on their social views, but on the fact that the list was too long and contained names of men "whose loyalty to America was doubtful." The successful "radical" policy was "directed by men of conservative temper." And again in October, 1775, a second election was to be held with the "suffrage being limited to the electors of representatives in the assembly," but this was modified to allow the vote to tenants holding property worth £80, a move to enlist their support against Britain. There is nothing in the chapter signifying internal class conflict, but much indicating a protest against imperialism. [55]

The closer New York got to independence, the less the conflict appears as one to democratize American society and the

[54] *Ibid.*, p. 192.

[55] *Ibid.*, pp. 180, 194-96, 222 and note 227. Since we know that all the tenants of Beekman and Livingston voted, the meaning of this £80 provision is difficult to determine.

more it appears as a problem of imperialism if one looks at Becker's evidence. On one occasion, seven persons were denied the right to vote because they were not freeholders, but their vote made no difference in the outcome of the election, and the fact that they were excluded certainly does not indicate increased democracy. An election on November 7, 1775, was based on the usual suffrage requirements while opposition or support for candidates depended on their loyalist views.[56] A poll on the same day in Queens County registered 1,009 voters, which does not seem overly restricted, the "multitude" were anti-British, and in an election of the fourth provincial congress in 1776, voters were freemen, freeholders, and persons possessed of property worth £40.[57] In short, the move toward independence did not result in any substantial change in voting requirements.

After what has already been said, the reader should not be surprised when Becker ended his final chapter without achieving the social revolution to democratize American society which he considered the important half of his thesis. "Radicals" become merely "revolutionists" for Becker characterized both John Adams and Gouverneur Morris as radicals although both were undoubtedly social conservatives.[58] Instead of a social revolution in New York, the city election in 1776 resulted in a conservative victory as "the entire conservative ticket was elected." In the counties "elections were in most cases uncontested" and probably "the rural counties registered a conservative victory." The contest, as Becker said, was "between loyalists and revolutionists" — but this was what it had been from the beginning. There were differences of opinion over when independence should be declared, whether or not the provincial congress should write a constitution, and who should elect delegates to the Continental Congress, the provincial congress or the people. But there is no evidence whatever that "the people" were demanding to be included in politics, and the fourth provincial congress in June, 1776, was

---

[56] *Ibid.*, pp. 230-32.   [57] *Ibid.*, pp. 237, 242, 252 and note 157.
[58] *Ibid.*, pp. 253, 256, 267.

elected under the same suffrage requirements that prevailed in the previous election.[59]

Since the nature of a revolution can be determined only by a comparison of the society which produced the revolution and the society which emerged from the revolution, Becker's sudden termination of his account with the Declaration of Independence is particularly frustrating. That the social revolution never came off is abundantly clear. Said Becker: "The fear of British oppression was transformed into the fear of oppression by the national government, while the demand of the unfranchised classes for recognition . . . was to find its ultimate answer only in the achievements of Jefferson and Jackson. . . . Of the rivalry between conservative and radical, which the question of the new government gave rise to, we hear but little." Becker admitted, without producing evidence, that the new constitution in New York was "measurably aristocratic," but he said that the history of revolutionary parties must end with the Declaration of Independence, for the later conservative-radical controversy properly belonged to the history of the Federalist and Anti-Federalist parties under the Confederation.[60]

But the historian of social revolution cannot stop here. He must turn at least one more page in the record to ask this question: how revolutionary, in fact, was the first constitution in New York, and why was it what it was? If there is only one law in history, that is, that history demonstrates both continuity and change in human affairs, we need to know the extent of continuity and the extent of change resulting from the Revolution. This, in turn, will cast some light on the issue of concensus and conflict in interpretations of this period of American history.

It is well for the Becker thesis that Becker did not examine his thesis in the light of the New York constitution of 1777. In the first place, the fourth provincial congress, which wrote the constitution, recited the background which was, as Becker's own *evidence* proves, clearly a matter of British imperial

[59] *Ibid.*, pp. 258, 259, 262, 266, 268, 273-74.   [60] *Ibid.*, pp. 275-76.

encroachments rather than radical-conservative class conflict. Then the constitution itself was not what one would label ultra-liberal. There was a check and balance legislature composed of an assembly and a senate, but there was also a council, composed of the governor, the chief justice, and at least two judges of the supreme court, who had veto power over laws and whose veto could be overridden only by a two-thirds vote of both assembly and senate.[61]

When we turn to the voting franchise, the heart of the Becker thesis, we find requirements both more liberal and more conservative than had previously prevailed. On the liberal side, free adult men could vote for assemblymen if they paid taxes and possessed a freehold of twenty pounds or rented a tenement worth forty-shillings rent a year. This was definitely more liberal than the forty-pound freehold requirement before the Revolution. On the conservative side, men who were freemen in Albany and New York before October, 1775, retained the right to vote on the basis of their freemanship only, but new freemen would henceforth have to meet the property requirement. Even more conservative, however, were the qualifications for electors of governors, lieutenant governors, and senators. Instead of a forty-pound freehold, these voters must now possess a freehold of one hundred pounds clear of all debts.[62]

Unlike some states, however, New York did not impose conservative property requirements for holding office. The governor was to be "a wise and discreet freeholder," senators were to be freeholders, but not necessarily wise or discreet, and there was no specification whatever for the lieutenant governor who might eventually become governor.[63] Since a freehold could be as minimal as a lot in town or half an acre in the country, the freehold stipulation was virtually without meaning. Presumably the constitution makers were satisfied that anyone who acquired enough prestige to gain high office

[61] Thorpe, *Constitutions and Charters*, V, 2623-29.
[62] *Ibid.*, pp. 2630-34.   [63] *Ibid.*, pp. 2631-34.

would have accumulated property or that voters with property would not elect propertyless officials.

Other election provisions in the constitution were also a mixture of liberalism and conservatism, but were certainly not evidence of internal social revolution. The secret ballot, instead of a combination of ballot and voice voting, was to be tried but could be eliminated if the legislature considered it unsatisfactory. Governor and lieutenant governor were to serve for three years rather than one year, as one might have expected if democracy were the aim of the Revolution. Conservatism prevailed in the election of senators who were to serve four years, with one fourth being elected each year. Supreme court justices were appointed by the governor, not elected, and held office during good behavior, while a whole host of other officials — sheriff, coroner, county judge, court clerk, register, and marshall — were all appointed rather than elected.[64]

Further evidence of an absence of internal revolution is to be found in the fact that the state retained British as well as colonial laws that were in effect before the Revolution. The constitution declared that "such parts of the common law of England, and of the statute law of England and Great Britain, and of the acts of the legislature of the colony of New York, as together did form the law of the said colony on the 19th day of April, in the year of our Lord, one thousand seven hundred and seventy-five, shall be and continue the law of this State" until altered by the legislature. The exceptions were the repeal of all laws establishing any church, certainly a liberal provision, as well as all laws relating to allegiance to the king. Land grants and charters made before October 14, 1775, were also validated. The constitution guaranteed complete religious toleration, but this merely confirmed an established practice, for Jews as well as Christians had long enjoyed toleration in the colony.[65]

On balance, the New York constitution of 1777 does not appear as a very "revolutionary" document. If it was more

[64] *Ibid.*   [65] *Ibid.*, pp. 2635-37.

democratic than the old system on voting for assemblymen, it was not particularly democratic in the election of other officials or in their terms in office. Whether in actual practice the constitution made much difference one way or the other is difficult to say, but in theory, at least, the city artisans and workers should have felt the £100 restriction more than did the rural population. Yet it was in the city that Becker concentrated his discontent and presumably this was the area which should have benefited most by the internal revolution.

One final item should be noted about the thesis. Becker's dissertation was on New York alone, but his dual revolution thesis embraced the entire Revolution in all the colonies. Becker opened Chapter I with the statement that "the American Revolution was the result of two general movements," not that this was characteristic of the Revolution in New York.[66] Unfortunately his projected generalized view has been widely accepted by later writers as valid for all the colonies.

In short, the Becker thesis does not stand up under critical analysis. It literally bristles with the words radicals, conservatives, privileged classes, underprivileged classes, franchised, and unfranchised, all designed to impress the reader with the importance of the internal revolution. But Becker's *evidence* points to a middle-class, democratic society living under an imperial system which the people opposed when the British attempted to make it effective. The question of home rule was fundamental; that of who should rule at home involved only the usual conflict between liberalism and conservatism that exists in any democratic society. Elimination of British imperialism was obviously a great gain for American democracy, but as the constitution of 1777 demonstrates, New York fought to preserve the kind of democracy it enjoyed, not to achieve a new brand of lower-class democracy. In later years, Becker himself would confirm this analysis.

[66] Becker, *History of Political Parties,* p. 5.

IV. PROGRESSIVISM AND SUBJECTIVE RELATIVISM, 1909-1918

> "There is profound truth in the biting remark of Voltaire, that, after all, history is only a pack of tricks we play on the dead. If useful social ends are served, it does not harm the dead, who had in any case tricks of their own."
>
> — CARL BECKER, 1910

BECKER'S "dual revolution" thesis signaled a fundamental transformation in philosophy of history from the objectivism implied in his early work on nominating conventions, and since this new philosophy dominated his thinking on history for the ensuing thirty years, some knowledge of its background and its salient features is imperative.

No doubt many influences were at work, perhaps influences that even Becker would have had difficulty in tracing. But some factors are apparent from the evidence at hand. "Certain inspiring teachers," as he acknowledged in the preface of his dissertation, left their mark on him. These included Frederick Jackson Turner, Charles H. Haskins, Victor Coffin, Herbert Levi Osgood, John W. Burgess, and James Harvey Robinson. The impact of two men was particularly significant — Turner who continued to influence Becker, and Robinson whose ideas began to affect Becker at Columbia. Then there was the "climate of opinion" or the general intellectual milieu of the historian's own day which Becker himself would stress at great length and which, judging from his own writings, did much to shape his philosophy of history.

In his earlier years and despite his emphasis on democracy, Becker's "inspiring" teacher, Frederick Jackson Turner, was not what one would call ultra-liberal or anticapitalistic in his social philosophy. Although Turner in 1893 had emphasized the impact of the frontier on the development of democracy, he also insisted that frontier democracy had certain undesirable features — selfishness, individualism, intolerance, anti-intellectualism, and the pressing of individual liberty "beyond its proper bounds." In particular, the colonial and Revolutionary frontier brought forth the "worst forms of an evil currency" and lax financial integrity similar to recent Populist agitation. Turner said that a primitive society can hardly be expected to show intelligent appreciation of the complexity of business interests in a developed society. So in 1893, Turner does not appear to have been anticapital in his outlook.[1]

After 1900, however, when the climate of opinion included an element of anticapitalism engendered by progressivism, Turner's attitude toward capitalism appears to have changed. For example, a colleague at Northwestern, in hiring a man to teach international law, felt the need to justify his actions to Turner as follows: "I wanted you to know that this was in no sense a selling out to the capitalists." [2] In the spring of 1906, the Turners had entertained the Socialist or Marxist historian Algie M. Simons and his wife in Madison. Simons, editor of *The Chicago Daily Socialist* and also *The Appeal to Reason,* a new Socialist magazine, asked Turner to excuse the faults of the first issue as parts of it were "written intentionally for propaganda." Simons then denied that he had "ever consciously distorted facts," but his articles on American history were written for a working-class audience and were "intended to off set the traditional prejudices of the conventional school history." Simon's letter leaves the impression that Turner was not unsympathetic with Simon's social philosophy.[3]

There is also evidence that Turner was feeling the increasing pressure of the relativism and subjectivism which were looming larger after 1900 as part of the intellectual climate. In a paper, "Social Forces in American History," he insisted

[1] Frederick Jackson Turner, *The Early Writings of Frederick Jackson Turner*, compiled by Everett E. Edwards with an introduction by Fulmer Mood (Madison, 1938), pp. 219-22.

[2] James Alton James to Turner, May 1, 1906, TU, Box 7.

[3] Algie Martin Simons to Turner, December 3, 1906, TU, Box 7.

in 1907 that the historian must find "the essential, the really typical and vital" in his material, but under no circumstance must he enforce a creed, a philosophy, a political dogma, or a pet theory which historical material can provide, "ready for the artful combination and presentation." Having made this plea for objectivity, however, Turner immediately denied that his canons of historical scholarship were possible. No historian had completely succeeded, Turner continued, for he was a man, "played upon by prepossessions, affected by his own experience and his own ideals, dominated — try however he may to resist them — by the influence of his nationality, by the class in which his lot is cast, by the age in which he lives."[4] Becker would later write a similar paper, but he would eliminate any pretense at objectivity.

Turner left Wisconsin for Harvard in 1910, and among the many letters of appreciation by former Turner students is a magnificent one from Becker attesting to Turner's influence. Among the items mentioned were the following: Turner had said that it was impossible not to have some kind of philosophy of history, the vital point being only whether one's philosophy amounted to anything. Becker interpreted Turner's statement that history is the self-consciousness of humanity to mean what he himself had recently stated — "we must have a past that is the product of all the present." But even more important for an understanding of Becker was his assertion that nothing could be duller than historical facts and nothing more interesting than the service they could be made to render in the effort to solve the everlasting riddle of human existence. It was from Turner more than anyone else, he said, that he had "learned to distinguish historical facts from their uses."[5] The importance of this statement will appear in due time.

An analysis of Turner's work by Professor Merle Curti indicates some of the influences which Turner had on Becker,

---

[4] "Social Forces in American History," address before the Phi Beta Kappa Society at the University of Nebraska, June 1907, TU, 55.

[5] Becker to Turner, May 15, 1910, Becker Papers, and TU, Vol. I, Red Book.

especially on his ideas of subjectivism and relativism. Curti said that Turner "denied the objective and permanently truthful and adequate character of even the best historical scholarship," for each age must rewrite history in the light of conditions uppermost in its own time. Turner anticipated the emphasis that Carl Becker, Charles Beard, and others later placed on the relativity of historical knowledge — on the frame of reference concept. In many ways, Curti concluded, Turner was a forerunner of James Harvey Robinson and his philosophy of "the New History." [6]

The Turner-Becker relationship was by no means a one-way proposition, however, for within a short time after Becker received his degree, elements of his thesis began to appear in Turner's writing and teaching. When he wrote "The Significance of the Frontier in American History," Turner's emphasis was on sectional controversy rather than class conflict, with democratic west pitted against aristocratic east. But in "The Old West" (1908) and "The First Official Frontier of the Massachusetts Bay" (1914), class conflict becomes more in evidence. Capitalist land speculators, conservatives of the older sections, absentee landlords, eastern men of property, poverty-stricken frontiersmen, class conflicts in the towns, traditional class control, property-holding class of the coast and the debtor class of the interior, and other expressions indicate class as well as sectional interpretation. Turner, who cited Becker, also took over the "dual revolution" concept as the following quotation demonstrates: "Indeed, there were two revolutions in Pennsylvania, which went side by side: one a revolt against the coastal property-holding classes, the dominant Quaker party, and the other a revolt against Great Britain, which was in this colony made possible only by the triumph of the interior." [7]

There is also evidence that Turner at this time was empha-

[6] Merle Curti, "Frederick Jackson Turner," in *Wisconsin Witness to Frederick Jackson Turner: A Collection of Essays on the Historian and the Thesis,* compiled by O. Lawrence Burnette, Jr. (Madison, 1961), pp. 184-203.

[7] Turner, *Frontier in American History,* pp. 56, 60, 62, 63, 65, 70, 75, 78, 79, 81, 94, 110, 111, 113.

sizing conflict rather than concensus in his classes in American history, especially internal class conflict in the early period. One student in his lecture notes pointed out that Turner explained the "whyfore" of many modern movements, such as "insurgency." As for the early period, he recorded, Bacon's Rebellion was a conflict between democrats and aristocratic Cavaliers; the frontier was settled mainly by freed indentured servants who were democratic; leading planters controlled the government; there was unequal suffrage because of tax qualifications; petty lords in New York controlled the legislature and escaped payment of their taxes; democracy existed on the frontier with the Scotch-Irish, inequitable representation favored aristocratic seaboard over democratic backcountry; the frontier compelled much democracy in the state constitutions and resisted adoption of the federal Constitution; a minority on the coast *"ruled the whole country;"* in 1776 the backcountry under Jefferson's leadership threw off the dominance of the coast; the Revolution ushered in the philosophy of equality and the new constitutions provided equality for the west; the east had to submit to taxes ("horrible thought") to improve the west; the "Rev. destroyed, at least temporarily, the aristocracy of landowners and raised democracy;" seaboard and backcountry were antagonistic; in all the colonies there was a conflict between the western frontier radical elements and the conservatives of the coast; Virginia was the "Prussia" of the United States until 1830; and anticipating Charles A. Beard, those who favored the Constitution were the wealthy, commercial creditors of the coast, while those who opposed were the unsettled, debtor rural areas.[8]

Thus it is not too difficult to understand why Turner accepted Becker's thesis apparently without any critical evaluation of Becker's evidence. Even though Becker's dissertation was not grounded in the frontier and sectional controversy, Becker was probably saying the kind of thing that Turner approved of in 1907. Most of what Turner had to say about early American history would not meet the test of evidence;

---

[8] E. Emerson, Notes on History 17, TU, Vol. XXIII, 1910.

he, himself, on occasion had stated that the new revolutionary constitutions were not really very democratic, and some of the papers of his students proved with credible evidence that Turner's aristocratic coast versus democratic backcountry was largely myth.[9]

A second man of major importance to Becker was James Harvey Robinson of Columbia University. Born in 1863 of a well-to-do family in Illinois, Robinson studied at Harvard, then took a doctorate in history at the University of Freiburg, presenting as his dissertation a study on the American Constitution. In the beginning of his career, Robinson was a meticulous, objective research historian who placed great emphasis on original evidence from the sources and interpreted these sources strictly in the setting of their own time. He also sent his students to the sources for firsthand evidence and refused to tolerate any careless references to secondary accounts.[10] Among the Becker Papers is a letter from Robinson, written in 1899, the year Becker published his first article, praising Becker's work in general and especially his good grasp of historical method.[11]

In the course of time, however, Robinson abandoned both his dissertation field of the American Constitution as an area for further study and his objective scholarly approach to history. Modern Europe, especially the French Revolution and intellectual history, replaced his interest in American history. And instead of the objective research scholar, Robinson became a generalizer and popularizer with a commitment. Harry Elmer Barnes, who knew Robinson well as student and colleague, said that Robinson's very popular intellectual history course departed from the sources, becoming "more uni-

[9] See especially the student paper by Arthur Boggess, "The Struggle Between the Coast and the Interior in Virginia," TU, Student Papers.

[10] For sympathetic accounts of Robinson see Harry Elmer Barnes, "James Harvey Robinson" in Odum, *American Masters of Social Science,* and Harvey Wish's introduction to James Harvey Robinson, *The New History* (First Free Press Paperback Edition, New York, 1965). Barnes was closely associated with Robinson as student, colleague, and chief exponent of Robinson's philosophy of history.

[11] Robinson to Becker, September 3, 1899, Becker Papers.

versal in its scope and more interpretative in character as Robinson utilized historical knowledge in the interests of human betterment and social reform." As the course became "more popular and more propagandist, in the best sense of that term," Barnes declared, "it became more useful as a weapon for clarification of thought and for the promotion of social reform." What had once been an objective historian now became to Robinson merely a historian without an objective.[12]

Robinson's objectives soon became those of the Progressives of the period — liberal reform to promote progress, especially liberal reform in the interests of the common man. Under the influence of William James, John Dewey, Thorstein Veblen, James T. Shotwell, Charles Beard, Richard Henry Tawney, and Voltaire, Robinson developed an interest in pluralism and pragmatism in philosophy, a psychological and genetic approach to history, an anticapitalism, anti-business, pro-common man social philosophy, and a preference for pagan rather than Christian cultures. Unhappy with the conservatism of Columbia under Nicholas Murray Butler, Robinson resigned in 1919 to launch the ultra-liberal New School for Social Research where liberals would be unhampered in their research and teaching.[13]

Robinson's most famous and influential book, *The New History,* published in 1912 at the height of the liberal Progressive Movement, was a clarion call for historians to use history in the interests of progress and liberal reform. Although the book was composed of various papers and speeches that Robinson had written over a span of many years, these papers and speeches, as Robinson said in his preface, all illustrated in one way or another his conception of the "new history" and the uses to which it could be put.[14] Barnes has rightfully declared that *The New History* will remain the

---

[12] Barnes, "Robinson," in Odum, *American Masters of Social Science,* pp. 321-37, 375-76.

[13] *Ibid.,* pp. 353, 356, 370, 395.

[14] James Harvey Robinson, *The New History* (New York, 1912), preface.

chief criterion for judging Robinson's place in the history of historiography and marks his shift from research history "to that of social betterment and intellectual reform." [15]

In the first chapter, entitled "The New History," Robinson called for the kind of history that would aid society in its "tremendous and unprecedented effort to better itself." This New History would concern itself with the typical and the significant, not the spectacular or the unusual; with the way things in the present had developed, not simply with how things were in the past. It would help us to solve our present problems, not by providing precedents from the past, but by giving us a perfect understanding of the present on which to base current decisions. It must show, as historians had not done in the past, "what lies behind our great contemporaneous task of human betterment," and especially it must expose the "anachronisms in conservative economic and legal reasoning." The part played by each individual would depend on his understanding of the historical development of the present out of the past — on historical mindedness — and this, in turn, would "promote rational progress as nothing else can do." Said Robinson: "The present has hitherto been the willing victim of the past; the time has now come when it should turn on the past and exploit it in the interests of advance." [16]

The history of history itself demonstrated progress, Robinson continued, but this was not apparent until history became a genetic social science rather than a branch of literature. Karl Marx had contributed greatly to the historian's development, and while Robinson did not accept Marx's economic determinism in toto, he did believe that Marx's doctrines "explain far more of the phenomena of the past than any other single explanation ever offered." Because of man's nature, history, though more science than art, could never become an exact science. Yet there was one scientific law of history, the law of continuity, "based on the observed fact that every human institution, every generally accepted idea, every

---

[15] Barnes in Odum, *American Masters of Social Science*, p. 391.
[16] Robinson, *New History*, pp. 21, 23, 24.

important invention, is but the summation of long lines of progress." Not until the eighteenth century "did the possibility of indefinite human progress become the exhilarating doctrine of reformers, a class which had previously attacked existing abuses in the name of the 'good old times.' No discovery could be more momentous and fundamental," Robinson continued, "than that reform should seek its sanction in the future, not in the past; in advance, not in reaction." [17]

Succeeding chapters of *The New History* also dealt with the relationship of history to various aspects of progress and reform. The historian must make use of the new social and natural sciences which, by applying evolutionary theory, had "progressed marvelously" in revealing man to himself and without whose assistance history could not hope to progress. Intellectual history would reveal "the manner in which our convictions on large questions have arisen, developed, and changed," and thus enable us to cast off authority and anachronisms which obstruct progress. Democracy has brought an appreciation of and respect for the common man, while the industrial revolution has made possible material progress for the common man. Knowledge of evolution has altered our ideas of morals, politics, and religion — has taught us that truth is not merely relative but that this relativity is conditioned by our constant increase in knowledge. A "new history" for the common man would not only enable him to understand his role in industrial production but would also suggest ways in which he could better his lot through social progress. The fall of Rome demonstrates continuity which is the essence of progress. And the French Revolution, with its liberty, fraternity, and equality, should be looked upon as one of the great social movements in all history. Robinson would have welcomed a study on "The French Revolution Considered as a Social Movement" such as J. Franklin Jameson wrote on the American Revolution.[18]

Robinson saved his big progressive and reformist guns, however, for his last chapter. Entitled "The Spirit of Con-

---

[17] *Ibid.*, pp. 51, 63, 64. [18] *Ibid.*, chs. III-VII.

servatism in the Light of History" and pitting "radicals" against "conservatives" in the battle for liberal progress and reform, Robinson contended that history, by showing progress, is the natural weapon of the radical, and, said he, "it is the chief end of this essay to indicate how it can be used with the most decisive effect on the conservative." [19]

The idea of progress, though a relatively recent discovery, was in Robinson's eyes "the greatest single idea in the whole history of mankind in the vista of possibilities which it opens before us." The ancients did not comprehend progress and the Christians were more concerned with the afterlife than with improving conditions on earth for mankind. It was experimental science that made progress possible: it was Lord Bacon who popularized the possibilities of science. Only by turning to the study of real things in the world was it possible to improve man's estate, and only in an obviously dynamic social environment and with the growth of historic perspective could the idea of conscious progress develop. [20]

Of extreme importance in Robinson's mind was the need to challenge authority if progress was to continue. Lord Bacon led the way, for it was Bacon who undermined "reverence for the past by pointing out that it rests on a gross misapprehension." Instead of accepting the traditional approach that mere age gave sanction to an institution or a belief, Bacon and Bruno weakened "the strength of authority and tradition." Conservatives turned to the hoary past for support, yet, said Robinson, "the process of weakening authority has been very rapid, considering its novelty and its fundamental character." A liberal Italian priest, Beccaria, reminded conservatives "that the past was after all only an immense sea of errors from which there emerged here and there an obscure truth." [21]

Thus, in effect, one of the most important functions of the study of history for Robinson was the destruction of traditional authority which held its sanction from the past. If it was true that every idea and institution was the result of

[19] *Ibid.*, ch. VIII, esp. p. 252.   [20] *Ibid.*, p. 247.   [21] *Ibid.*, pp. 246, 249.

progress, then any idea or institution would be less desirable at any stage of its development in the past than it was at present or would be in the future. History must show that there was no "golden age" to which men could look in the past. The most golden age which mankind had experienced had to be the present, and if man were to look for a more golden age, he must of necessity, because of the idea of progress, look to the future.[22]

Progress fed on progress, with history as the catalyst. Evolution, by showing the development from animal to man, demonstrated that man himself, as well as his external institutions, had progressed. Science opened infinite possibilities for the future, pointing up the fact that man could learn indefinitely more than his predecessors had known and could "better his estate indefinitely by the use of this knowledge and the desertion of ancient prejudices and habits." Early progress was unconscious, but it eventually awakened mankind so that it is only recently that he *"came to wish progress, and still more recently that he came to see that he can voluntarily progress, and that he has progressed."* This, according to Robinson, was "the most impressive message that history has to give to us, and the most vital in the light that it casts on the conduct of life."[23]

Once men realize that progress is possible, Robinson continued, the supreme value of history lies "in the suggestions that it may give us of what may be called the technique of progress." If social betterment is "the chief interest in this game of life," then those phases of the past which bear on this essential point should engross our attention. Heretofore, conservatives have invoked history to prevent progress, but except for the Marxian socialist, who "uses his version of the past in support of his plan of social amelioration," radicals have generally neglected history as a weapon. The radical as yet has not perceived the tremendous value to him of an understanding of the past, that the past is his weapon by right, and that he should wrest it from the hand of the conservative.[24]

[22] *Ibid.*, pp. 249-52.   [23] *Ibid.*, pp. 251, 252.   [24] *Ibid.*, p. 252 and note.

According to Robinson, the chief responsibility for the radical's failure to use history in the cause of radicalism rests on his misunderstanding of the essence of human nature. Most of what is generally called human nature is, in fact, human nurture or the result of education in the broad sense, he said. The conservative opposes reform because it involves change in human nature, but he constantly mistakes acquired and thus nontransmissible aspects with those that are hereditary and transmissible. Thus, said Robinson, *"Those things that the radical would alter and the conservative defend are therefore not traits of human nature but artificial achievements of human nurture."* [25]

The historian and the radical can therefore rule out the fundamental conservative appeal to human nature which blocks progress, Robinson contended. Conservatives were inevitable products of the period before men woke up to the possibility of conscious betterment. Now they justify existing conditions by standards of the past rather than those of the present or future without realizing how things have changed in the past or how much they could be improved in the future. If the conservative agrees that there has been some improvement, he also assigns to himself the task of brakeman to prevent progress from running headlong into disaster. But there is no need for such a brake, Robinson declared, for there are already too many obstacles without conscious conservative opposition. Yet despite these obstacles, many seemingly hopeless or preposterous dreams of the past have come true without conservative assistance.[26]

Now is the time, warned Robinson, for the radical to nullify the obstructive influence of the conservative on social progress. Conservatives have been victimized by a misunderstood past, and radicals, who have appealed to an untried future, can now rest their case on past achievement and current success. The radical can now see what has been done in the past, what is being done in the present, what remains to be done in the future, and, as never before, how to get it done. The great

[25] *Ibid.,* p. 254.   [26] *Ibid.,* pp. 258-66.

reforms — abolition of poverty, disease, and war, and the pro-motion of happy and rational lives — would be hopeless with-out recent advance and more advance in the future. Thus it is clear that "the conscious reformer who appeals to the future is the final product of a progressive order of things." Thus it may be that the long-disputed sin against the Holy Ghost is the refusal to cooperate with the vital principle of betterment, for history seems to condemn conservatism as a hopeless and wicked anachronism.[27]

The real remedy for the radical, Robinson concluded, rested in a change in the educational system. In the past there had been no consistent effort to cultivate a progressive spirit in school children. Their histories reveal none of the real lessons of the past; they are reared with too much respect for the past and too little for the future. Education in reality becomes a barrier to progress rather than a guidepost to betterment. Teachers should emphasize to their students the relative character of the instruction they offer and urge students to transcend this instruction as fast as a progressive world permits.[28]

Thus did Robinson develop a philosophy which would make history a weapon to be used by the radical against the conservative in the interests of the future progressive society. Based on evolution, science, the industrial revolution, com-mon men, common things, and democracy, this philosophy accepted the doctrine that progress in human affairs meant that the past could not be as good as the present or the future. The radical, therefore, had history on his side, for he could point out to the conservative that progress had taken place in spite of conservative efforts to prevent it. Radicals need no longer rely on an appeal to an untried better order in the future in their efforts to improve social conditions for the common man.

Some of the extent to which Becker accepted the philosophy of *The New History* is to be found in Becker's friendly and lengthy review of Robinson's book. Becker began with the

[27] *Ibid.,* p. 264.   [28] *Ibid.,* pp. 265-66.

implication that relativism and subjectivism precluded the possibility of definitive history and that "new history" had to be written continually because of new points of view and novel methods of treatment. He then emphasized Robinson's statement that the time had come for the present to turn on the past and use it in the interest of advance. In fact, the eighteenth-century philosophers announced a new history, "a history which was to tell the average man, not what actually happened, but what he ought to think about what happened, and especially about what might happen; and this new history did indeed exploit the past most effectively in the interest of advance, or what was supposed to be advance." This idea would later be the thesis of a Becker book, *The Heavenly City of the Eighteenth Century Philosophers*. Becker then went on to show that historical writing in the past was shaped by the pressure of social needs and served certain useful purposes. Von Ranke, for example, wrote the kind of history that would counteract the radicalism that came out of the French Revolution. Convinced by sharp experience that conscious attempts at radical social reconstruction were dangerous, conservatives of the nineteenth century wished to exploit the past to disprove the doctrine of natural rights and to condemn the methods of the French Revolution. The business of history, Becker declared, is to arouse an intelligent discontent and to foster a fruitful radicalism. If conscious effort toward social regeneration is to result in anything more than temporary expedients, the distinction between what is natural and permanent in human society (heredity) and what is artificial and temporary (environment) must be drawn clearly.[29]

It is this background of Turner, Robinson, and the Progressive climate of opinion or frame of reference which goes far in explaining the Becker thesis and the Becker philosophy. This is not to say that specific elements in Becker's thinking can be traced exactly to their source in Turner and Robinson, for it is quite possible that all three men were drinking

[29] *The Dial,* July 1, 1912.

at the same intellectual fountain. But since Becker acknowledged and continued to acknowledge the impact of Turner and Robinson, it is at least not unreasonable to suppose that Becker consciously appropriated as much of Turner and Robinson as suited his purposes.

Published in 1910, an article by Becker entitled "Detachment and the Writing of History," which provided the first clue to this new philosophy, developed the thesis that scholarly, objective history was neither possible nor desirable. The relativism of knowledge and the subjectivism of the historian made detachment impossible. Detachment was not desirable because the historian should possess a deep philosophy of life, a social commitment, for which he should write history.[30]

Becker began his article with a debunking of historians and the kind of history they wrote. He spoke of "the witty remark of Dumas, that Lamartine had raised history to the dignity of romance," of scientists who reproached history with being entertaining but useless, and of others who lamented the futility of present historical methods. At a time when all other departments of knowledge made great and useful advances, "historians alone were industriously engaged in aimless endeavor." Becker chided orthodox historians for amassing facts without meaning, facts which they put into books because they knew not what else to do with them.[31]

One of the chief reasons for the historian's futility, according to Becker, was his failure to realize that truth was relative, not absolute. Evolution had contributed the "law of change and adaptation," implying that everything changes, yet historians seemed to exempt truth itself from this law. But pragmatists were asking whether truth and reality, instead of

[30] Carl Becker, "Detachment and the Writing of History," *The Atlantic Monthly,* October, 1910. The editors, who were "struck by the brilliant common sense" of the article, still made the usual request that he cut out a thousands words or so. Editors to Becker, November 16, 1909, Becker Papers. Quotations are reprinted from Carl L. Becker: *Detachment and the Writing of History: Essays and Letters of Carl Becker.* Edited by Phil L. Snyder. © 1958 by Cornell University. Used by permission of Cornell University Press.

[31] *Ibid.*

being absolute, were not also subject to the law of change and adaptation. Becker said that historians had not yet been disturbed by the idea that truth itself is not absolute but relative to a changing milieu. As a result, historians, "not sufficiently aware of the disastrous influence of the milieu," had "unconsciously read the objective facts of the past in the light of their own purposes or the preconceptions of their own age." [32]

The statement that historians are swayed by their own purposes and the preconceptions of their own age suggests that the relativism of truth and subjectivism of the historian are so inextricably interwoven that they are difficult to distinguish separately. On the one hand, historical facts were not something substantial, material, cold, and hard, but, said Becker, "in truth the historical fact is a thing wonderfully elusive after all, very difficult to fix, almost impossible to distinguish from 'theory,' to which it is commonly supposed to be so completely antithetical." But on the other hand, fact and historian are inseparably locked together, for "the 'facts' of history do not exist for any historian until he creates them, and into every fact that he creates some part of his individual experience must enter." [33]

It was the historian's experience which gave meaning to the facts, not the facts which conveyed meaning to the historian. The historian's experiences not only helped to shape the image, according to Becker, but they were also "the final court of appeals in evaluating the sources themselves." We must have a past that is the product of all the present, that is, a past that conforms with our experiences, and if the sources say otherwise, we will not only not accept the sources but will make them say what we want them to say. As Becker phrased it, "Even the will to be purely objective is in itself a purpose, becoming not infrequently a passion, creating the facts in its own image." [34]

This, in turn, raises the question of which comes first, the fact or the concept, and Becker's answer is not difficult to

[32] *Ibid.*   [33] *Ibid.*   [34] *Ibid.*

surmise. Facts were useless until synthesized around a meaningful concept, but the very selection of some facts and rejection of others introduces the idea of importance which is subjective. Why does the historian accept some facts and reject others — "do the facts come first and determine the concept or does the concept come first and determine the facts?" [35]

In answering this conundrum, Becker again expressed his low opinion of the historian and his history by equating his thought processes with that of a child. The child, he said, lives in a dream world far removed from the world of adults. Reality is whatever relates to his interests, and if left to himself, he will select the facts that are important for his concepts, thus constructing a synthesis quite true and valuable for his purposes. The method of the trained historian was not essentially different from that of the child, for while his concepts are different, he will, like the child, select the facts that are important for him. Thus, said Becker, it is the concept which determines the facts, not the facts the concept. Rather than the historian sticking to the facts, it is the facts which stick to the historian, and his history will be valuable only if his ideas are many, vivid, and fruitful.[36]

Instead of detachment, which was neither possible nor desirable, Becker made a plea for commitment, which was both. "Complete detachment would produce few historians and none worth while," he declared, "for the really detached mind is a dead mind." The detached historian would not be able to take sides or decide what was good or true or useful. But in the world as it was, it was difficult not to take sides. Historical synthesis was only "true relatively to the age which fashioned it," and this fact, plus the doctrine of evolution, made it difficult to see how detachment could long remain the fashion among historians. The detached mind was not the kind "to care greatly what happened," but whatever value the notion of detachment might have in the present, the time might come, as it had in the past, when caring greatly what happened was more important than being detached.[37]

[35] *Ibid.* [36] *Ibid.* [37] *Ibid.*

In the end, Becker, through the combination of relativity and subjectivity, virtually reduced history to the status of propaganda to be used by the committed historian on behalf of the issues for which he cared greatly. "There is profound truth in the biting remark of Voltaire, that, after all, history is only a pack of tricks we play on the dead," he declared, then added, "if useful social ends are served, it does not harm the dead, who had in any case tricks of their own." [38]

History playing tricks on the dead to serve useful social purposes — this, I think, is the key to Carl Becker during the ensuing thirty years of his career. With facts elusive and almost indistinguishable from theory, and with the historian creating the facts in his own image, there was no objective basis for judging historical writing. "History is what the historian says it is," a participant on a recent panel discussion told me, which is about the position to which Becker had reduced history as a scholarly discipline.

In 1910, also, Becker gave expression to the useful social purposes — the progressive or liberal society — for which history should be written. In a chapter entitled "Kansas," part of a *Festschrift* to Turner on his departure from Wisconsin to Harvard, Becker insisted that most great men were progressives. They were men of faith — faith in themselves and in the rightness of things at the center of the universe. Idealists who attempted to mold the world in their own image, they believed in the perfectibility of mankind, and in an equality leveled up to their own high vantage.[39]

Becker then proceeded to combine the frontier of Turner with the progress of Robinson. Kansas was an exemplification of the spirit of progress, he said, as Kansans lived more for the better day of the future than for the present. Their idealism was colored by the humanitarian liberalism of the early nineteenth century, by an unquestioning faith in indefinite progress toward perfectibility. The people had a loyal devo-

[38] *Ibid.,* p. 27.
[39] *Essays in American History: Dedicated to Frederick Jackson Turner* [New York, 1910], reprinted by Peter Smith (New York, 1951), pp. 88-105.

tion to such words as liberty, democracy, equality, and education, and while they disliked the word "socialism," they nevertheless applauded governmental control of corporate wealth. Thus anyone interested in getting Kansas or America to accept the essential features of socialism should use the term equality, not socialism. Kansas, which legislated to equalize, believed that the welfare of society was always superior to that of the individual, yet no Kansan doubted that perfect liberty was the birthright of every man. Becker ended his essay with the plea of the liberal environmentalist that society is responsible for creating the kind of just environment that will allow all men to reach a high level.[40]

If "Kansas" did not indeed reflect the virtues of Kansas, and there is a chance that it did not, there is little doubt that it did reflect the social philosophy of Carl Becker. The implication was that great men are progressives and that progress involves the collective effort of all men, call it equality rather than socialism, to create the proper environment for the fullest development of man's potentialities. In addition, the article undoubtedly had great appeal to men of similar social ideals.

If "Kansas" was far more philosophical than historical, more the expression of the social ideals of one man than the collective philosophy of a state, there can be no doubt that the essay served the very practical purpose of calling Becker to the attention of the historical profession. Reviews of the *Festschrift* singled out Becker's essay for the highest praise. One reviewer spoke of the "penetrating, brilliant, and altogether delightful analysis of the temper and ideals of Kansas by Professor Carl Becker of the University of Kansas." Another reviewer praised Becker's literary ability — his facility for telling good and apt stories and for turning sentences with a pleasant wit.[41]

[40] *Ibid.*
[41] *The Nation,* April 20, 1911; Becker Papers, March, 1911; letter of Henry Adams to John Franklin Jameson, in letter of Harold Dean Carter to Becker, September 4, 1944, Becker Papers.

The end result was two position opportunities which reveal another important deviation by Becker from the Turner influence. As a result of the "Kansas" essay, Claude H. Van Tyne at Michigan, who was considering Becker for a position in modern European history, said that he had changed his mind about Becker whom he had considered unprepossessing, curt, indifferent, and wanting in the social amenities.[42] Illinois was also looking for a man to replace Guy Stanton Ford, who was going to Minnesota. But strangely, both positions were in European, not American history. At Illinois, Evarts B. Greene was confronted by the fact that while Becker was probably a good man with much literary skill, he had "never made any contributions in the field of European history" which would enable Illinois to judge his future potential.[43]

Neither position materialized, but here was Becker, a Turner Ph.D. who had published articles on colonial and early national America, a dissertation on colonial and revolutionary New York, and an essay on Kansas, yet was being considered for positions at major universities in the field of modern European history. Since it is quite common for men to continue their professional work in the general area of their doctoral dissertations, this switch by Becker from American to European history takes on added significance, especially given the amount of time that Becker had spent under the tutelage of Turner.

Shortly after the publication of "Detachment," Becker reinforced his philosophy of subjective relativism in two book reviews. One author was John Fiske, whom Becker praised as a writer of excellent English and a philosopher concerned with the "large general ideas" so unfashionable among scientific historians. With tongue in cheek, Becker said, "One suspects that Fiske was often guilty of the terrible crime of getting an idea first and then finding the facts to support it." But his work would be read when the works of others had

---

[42] Van Tyne to Turner, February 1, 1911, TU, Box 16.
[43] Greene to Turner, April 29, 1913, TU, Box 19.

been forgotten, and after all, it was not easy "to point out the value of histories that nobody reads." [44]

The second author was Houston Stewart Chamberlain, a subjectivist whose book, *The Foundations of the Nineteenth Century*, Becker considered one of the most significant books written in the nineteenth century. To understand Chamberlain, said Becker, one must forget that there is such a thing as objectivity. Chamberlain was the committed historian who believed that there were prizes to be won, ideals to be fought for, possessions of the heart to be cherished. If there is nothing worth fighting for in the present, the past has no human value; if there was something worth fighting for, the historian should be in the thick of the conflict. But this approach demanded that the historian have a "real standard of value" with which to judge history. Chamberlain's standard was culture, by which man raised himself above nature and the mechanically ordered universe, and becomes the arbiter of his own destiny. Becker approved of Chamberlain, even though Chamberlain came perilously close to saying that there were some absolute truths in the world worth fighting for.[45]

Then in a third book review in 1911, Becker gave some additional hints of the social purposes for which the historian played tricks on the dead — social purposes that he considered worth fighting for. At the time of Cavour, he said, liberalism was looked upon as a halfway house, or perhaps only the first stage, on the road from absolutism to democracy. The highly respectable and conventional bourgeoisie found liberalism exactly to their liking. There must be liberty, but not too much, and only for the right people. This meant political liberty for those who had enough money to appreciate its advantages, industrial liberty for those who wished to increase profits but not for those who desired to raise wages, and intellectual and religious liberty for all except the indecently eccentric or the uncomfortably original — nothing too much. But this brand of liberalism was not enough for Becker. He called for freedom in government, industry,

[44] *The Nation,* November 2, 1910.   [45] *The Dial,* May 16, 1911.

78

thought, and religion to the end that every man could develop the best that was in him, for only thus could justice prevail, ignorance, superstition, and intolerance disappear, poverty and war be banished, and peace, prosperity, and happiness be universally diffused.[46]

By 1912, Becker was spelling out more precisely the social purposes for which he was to use history. In a paper delivered before a meeting of sociologists, entitled "Some Aspects of the Influence of Social Problems and Ideas Upon the Study and Writing of History," he not only reemphasized the influence of the milieu upon the historian, but he also stated unequivocally the social philosophy which would color his own thinking for many years.[47]

First Becker found "scientific" proof for his view that the historian was swayed by the intellectual and social conditions of his own age and thus wrote "an interpretation of the past in terms of present social interests." What was this "scientific" proof? Said Becker: "The latest fashion among psychologists and philosophers seems to be to regard the individual intelligence, not as an instrument suited to furnish an absolute test of objective truth, but as a tool pragmatically useful in enabling the individual to find his way about in a disordered objective world." Whether or not scientists would accept "the latest fashion among psychologists and philosophers" as scientific proof, this kind of "scientific" verification seemed to satisfy Becker.[48]

Having laid a "scientific" foundation for subjectivism in history, Becker then proceeded to show how this subjectivism had functioned in practice. The general intellectual activity of any period had its origins in practical interests, he said, and derived its validity from the service it rendered in solving community problems. Historical thinking, part of the general

[46] Review of William Roscoe Thayer, *The Life and Times of Cavour,* in *The Dial,* November 16, 1911.

[47] Apparently the sociologists approved of this sociological article by a historian, for they published it twice in *Publications of the American Sociological Society,* VII (1912), pp. 73-112, and *American Journal of Sociology,* XVIII (March, 1913), pp. 641-75.   [48] *Ibid.*

intellectual milieu, was also "a social instrument, helpful in getting the world's work more effectively done." Historians had attempted without success to be scientific, but in fact their writing had "been determined by the pressure of social problems and ideas." Practical conditions probably had more to do with enriching the historian's conception of the content of history than had speculative thought.[49]

Most important of the practical factors in shaping the historian's thinking were the pressing social problems which the old liberalism had failed to solve. Becker declared that classical economists and liberal statesmen earlier hoped that if the state guaranteed individual freedom, "there must follow a greater welfare for all, but especially for the least favored classes." Such expectations for liberalism had not been realized, however, for instead of increased freedom, the result had been exploitation of the lower classes. These economic facts of life had forced historians to recognize the importance of economic influences in history.[50]

It was this disillusionment with the old liberalism, then, that goes far in explaining the Becker thesis. Becker added this significant statement that in the previous twenty years, active study of the economic basis of the American colonial system had "radically changed the interpretation of Colonial and Revolutionary history popularized by Bancroft." Bancroft had depicted a democratic society in which there was much concensus in American opposition to British mercantilism and imperialism. In contrast, Becker's colonial society was class-ridden and undemocratic, with internal conflict between classes rather than concensus against the British the significant factor.[51]

A new day was dawning, however, for the outmoded idea of scientific history was giving way to a new faith in progress. At one time it was thought that the historian, like the objective and detached natural scientist, must "avoid the warping effects of religious or party bias, the insidious influence of temperamental prepossessions, the alluring temptation to read

---

[49] *Ibid.*   [50] *Ibid.*   [51] *Ibid.*

into the facts any meaning suggested by a preconceived theory." But during the past two decades, Becker declared, a revival of faith in the possibility of social regeneration, a profound belief in progress, had emerged from the wreck of old creeds. Born of science and democracy, and about the only vital conviction left to us, this belief in progress held that society, by taking thought, could modify conditions of life and thus greatly improve the happiness and welfare of all men.[52]

As a result, said Becker, pragmatists were making the imperative demand that knowledge should serve useful purposes and learning should be applied to the solution of human problems. Results were already in evidence. Jurisprudence was coming to be considered as a science of rights, not just a knowledge of law; economics was becoming a science of human welfare, not merely a science of wealth. Men were asking what light the past could throw on problems of the present and the future, and philosophy had provided a "conception of history which liberates the present from slavish dependence on the past." Becker believed that the study of history was bound to be influenced "by this new faith in progress and the possibility of social regeneration." And as evidence that this was in fact happening, Becker cited the statement by James Harvey Robinson that the time had come for the present to turn on the past and exploit it in the interest of advance.[53]

But if men are to use history in the interest of progress, if they are to control events and not be controlled by them, Becker continued, they must know what constitutes "advance." This means that the importance of facts can no longer be measured by the facts themselves; they must be judged by some standard of value derived from a conception of what it is that constitutes social progress, some conception of moral quality or present practical purpose.[54]

If history is to guide our actions in the present in order to bring progress for the future, Becker declared, historians must subordinate the past to the present. Robinson and Charles

[52] *Ibid.*   [53] *Ibid.*   [54] *Ibid.*

Beard were so doing, and while this did not mean distortion of the facts, it did mean that the present is the standard for judging history and that we study history for the sake of the present. The historian may legitimately emphasize the facts of history according to their importance for *our* time instead of *their* time; that is, he may interpret the past in terms of the present. Becker also gave the example of Turner who emphasized the present as a basis for studying the past, and who insisted that statesmanlike treatment of present problems demanded that they be seen in their historical relations in order that history might hold the lamp for conservative reform.[55]

Another method for estimating the importance of historical facts, Becker continued, is to bring them to the test of some conception of moral quality. The historian explains actions of the past by the standards of their own age, but he judges these actions by the standards of his, the historian's age. This implies a standard of value not furnished by the facts themselves, and therefore the historian needs "a brave philosophy of life" before he interprets the past, for it is his subjective judgment that gives ultimate meaning to the past.[56]

Once again Becker called for a deep commitment on the part of the historian if he would make history serve its proper function in forwarding progress. He cited with approval the declaration that the historian cannot stand aloof but must be sympathetic with men who lived the good life. The historian must condemn those who act only from selfish interest and praise those who act from principle. His heroes must be sincere and righteous, not iniquitous; beneficent, and not malignant; loving and lovable, not hating and hateful; promoters of light and not darkness, and men who choose right over wrong. The historian cannot state the facts and then sit aloof, impartial between good and evil, success and failure, progress and retrogression. He must love and hate, and at his peril love aright and hate what is truly hateful. This was "clearly a new note," Becker concluded, and while the new

[55] *Ibid.*   [56] *Ibid.*

methods of historians differed, "they seem all inspired by a common desire, namely, to appropriate out of the past something which may serve that ideal of social progress which is the sum and substance of our modern faith." Knowledge of history is useless, he said, unless we can transmute it into motives for effective social service.[57]

Not all members of the panel where Becker gave this paper were willing to accept subjective relativism as a valid philosophy of history, even though Becker's views later became widely accepted among historians. A. J. Todd of the University of Illinois declared that Lamprecht, whom Becker cited and who was searching for some underlying explanation of history, had left the objective world of science and had plunged into subjectivism. If the historian assumes some reality beyond his facts, he cannot convey reality, said Todd, for such a process gives us a delusive philosophy of history which is neither sound philosophy nor truthworthy history. The historian must collect and interpret a wide range of facts, but the interpretation, if it is to yield good history, must, like the facts, be objective in reference and expression. If the historian insists on the subjectivist attitude, Todd contended, he must reject historical method and adopt poetry or the delphic incoherencies of swoon and dream as his medium.[58]

As for the Becker thesis itself, Becker had two major opportunities to publicize his ideas beyond the published dissertation. One was in *The Nation* where he reviewed the third volume of Edward Channing's *History of the United States,* the volume in which Channing covered the period of the American Revolution. Since *The Nation* had long been a magazine for liberals, this review was certain to reach many people who would be sympathetic with Becker's views. The second exposure came in Becker's *The Beginnings of the American People* (1915) in which he would interpret American history to the Confederation period in terms of class conflict.

In the Channing review, 1912, Becker modified his thesis somewhat, but he also used most of the review to expound his

---

[57] *Ibid.*　　　[58] *Ibid.*

own ideas rather than to evaluate Channing's. Previously, Becker had praised Channing highly for his objective scholarship and impressive literary style. Now he admitted that Channing was fairer than other historians in presenting both the British and the American sides of the Revolution and that Channing well understood the desires of Americans for home rule. But there was another aspect of the Revolution, Becker declared, though perhaps not as significant as the contest for home rule, which Channing either did not understand or ignored. This, said Becker, "may be called the class conflict within the colonies themselves." Becker, who had once believed that class conflict explained the Revolution entirely, was now conceding that the conflict with Britain was more important than internal revolution.[59]

Much of the review of Channing was simply a summary of the Becker thesis. In every colony, Becker declared, there were little aristocracies resting on wealth and family ties and aping the British gentry in manners and clothing. These families, associated with the governor, were entrenched in the Council, dominated the Assembly much as the English aristocracy did the House of Commons, and controlled colonial politics and society. Opposed to this aristocracy was another class with different interests and ideals — backcountry farmers, unenfranchised city artisans and laborers, debtors, ambitious young lawyers, and dissenting clergymen. By 1760 the conflict between these classes had begun, a conflict between east and west, franchised and unfranchised, rich and poor, privileged and underprivileged which, in one form or another, has characterized American society ever since.[60]

The Revolution, Becker continued, was in part a class war for increased democracy. Conservative classes feared the rising democratic spirit in the colonies almost as much as they feared British encroachments. They sought to control the movement for home rule and to maintain privileges against British interference without extending them to their own lower classes. Their difficulty lay in claiming rights of man

[59] *The Nation*, November 12, 1912.   [60] *Ibid.*

from the British and explaining rights of property to their inferiors at home. This conservative dilemma opened the door for the "radicals" or all those who had little to lose and much to gain. Desiring more than home rule for the rich and wellborn, the radicals used the home-rule issue to break the power of the colonial aristocracy.[61]

In this review Becker also expressed the belief that class conflict continued as the very substance of American history after the Revolution. Channing, said Becker, neglected class-conflict aspects of American history after the American Revolution, for from 1760 to 1830 the persistent issue was the conflict of democratic and aristocratic interests and ideals. Perhaps, he said, this was the primary issue of the Revolution; it certainly was in 1789 and 1828. The radicals, according to Becker, won much in the Revolution (his thesis had not demonstrated this but the implication was there), lost a great deal in 1789 with the conservative counterrevolution under the Constitution (a forerunner of the Beard thesis in 1913), and then won something again under Jeffersonian democracy in 1800. But when Andrew Jackson, the backwoodsman of Scotch-Irish descent who could fight better than he could spell, broke the power of the Virginia Dynasty and destroyed the United States Bank, frontier democracy for the first time came into its own.[62] Thus was presented the familiar outline of early American history which would captivate the support of so many academicians later.

The second vehicle for publicizing the Becker thesis was the publication in 1915 of his book *The Beginnings of the American People*. The title page and introduction tell us a great deal of what Becker had accepted and rejected of Turner and Robinson. Becker was designated as "Professor of European History," again indicating that he had chosen the field of Robinson rather than Turner. The editor, William E. Dodd, said that Becker approached early American history "from the standpoint of the student of modern European history. The infant colonies are to him merely offshoots of ancient

[61] *Ibid.*   [62] *Ibid.*

Europe" — which was certainly not the Turner approach. The presentism of both Turner and Robinson was apparent, for, said Dodd, "the object has been to portray only those things which seem to have counted in the final makeup of the Confederacy of 1783, and of the United States of today." Turner and Robinson, but especially Robinson, were visible in the stated purpose of emphasis on the common people — their amusements, manners, religion, and everyday occupations instead of mere accounts of government and arguments of jurists.[63]

As he had done in his thesis on New York, Becker painted colonial society as class-ridden. Side by side with the landowners, but sharply differentiated, was "a servile laboring class which formed a large part of the total population." Indentured servants, "unfortunate and dispossessed," were "driven and whipped like the Negro slave." Small farmers were pitted against large landowners, with the lower classes "excluded from the tidewater by the engrossers of great estates, or oppressed by its restricted social conditions." Colonial society was definitely deferential, for the colonists had transferred their class system to America and accepted their position within this class structure. Becker cited the statement of one Devereaux Jarrett to indicate the extent of deference accorded the upper by the lower classes. In all, an aristocratic tidewater was opposed to a democratic frontier where "primitive radicalism" held sway.[64]

Unfortunately for his thesis, however, Becker also depicted colonial society as one in which economic opportunity abounded and social mobility was plainly evident. He said that easily-obtained rich land "assured an easy living and the prospect of accumulating a competence" so that Virginians described America as "God's country, abounding in every good thing." "Initiative and industry, rather than the dead hand of custom, marked a man for distinction and prefer-

---

[63] Carl L. Becker, *The Beginnings of the American People* (Houghton Mifflin Company, New York, 1915). Quotations are used by permission of Houghton Mifflin Company.   [64] *Ibid.*, pp. 71-74, 174-77, 182.

ment." America was a "land of opportunity where the servant could become the farmer, [and] the farmer a planter." There were classes but no castes, for "not birth or title, but individual enterprise determined rank and influence." The possession of a great estate was not a social grievance but evidence of success, the measure of personal prowess, and the test of civic virtue. If Devereaux Jarrett emphasized deference, he himself rose to considerable eminence. The careers of John Adams, Franklin, and many others indicated that America was a place where law and custom were most in accord with the philosophers' ideal society; where, in contrast with the oppression, tyranny, inequality, superstitions, and worn out institutions of Europe, America was a "new land of promise where the citizen was a free man, where the necessities of life were the sure reward of industry, where manners were simple, where vice was less prevalent than virtue and native incapacity the only effective barrier to ambition!" [65] Obviously all of this does not add up to a class-ridden society, but Becker seemed not to recognize his own contradictions.

The same lack of consistency that appears in Becker's analysis of colonial economic and social life is also to be found in his account of political affairs. His general thesis was that, politically, colonial America was a class-ridden society. The great planters of the South dominated by controlling elections, furthering their own interests, and forming a ruling oligarchy. Massachusetts was an undemocratic society where the people showed deference to the magistrates. With property tests restricting the number of voters and no secret ballot to protect even those few who could vote, the result was "effective control" in the hands of the eminent few. It was presumptuous for the common man to dispute the opinion of his betters or contest their right to leadership. Becker said that William Byrd II of Virginia left his son 179,000 acres of land "and the right to represent his county in the assembly" — a suggestion that political office was hereditary — and that

[65] *Ibid.*, pp. 69-70, 79, 172, 174, 181, 196-200.

Byrd and Thomas Hutchinson were "the genuine colonial aristocrat[s]." [66]

But then Becker contradicted these unsupported statements about an aristocratic political structure just as he had done about an aristocratic economic and social structure. He quoted the English official Randolph as saying that colonial representatives were "mostly an inferior sort of planters," not aristocrats. Although Becker had declared that Massachusetts was undemocratic, he also stated that the fall of the Puritan theocracy (c. 1690) was followed a half-century later by the rise of Puritan democracy. If men such as Patrick Henry, John Adams, and Benjamin Franklin, all of obscure origin, could rise to positions of prominence, America, as Becker said, must have been a "new land of promise where the citizen was a free man." If colonial assemblies were aristocratic, they were strange aristocracies indeed, for they passed paper money bills whereby "debtors profited at the expense of creditors." Becker went even further by showing that the "upper classes" opposed British restrictions on paper money. And if Thomas Hutchinson was an aristocrat living in an aristocratic society, he must have been completely unaware of this fact, for Becker quoted Hutchinson as saying that men of the "best character and estate . . . decline attending Town Meetings where they are sure to be outvoted by men of the lowest orders." [67] Becker did not seem to question the nature of an "aristocracy" where the "lowest orders" outvoted men of the "best character and estate."

In his account of the American Revolution as a class conflict as well as a war for independence, Becker again contradicted himself. The upper classes, he said, could "defend liberty against the encroachments of their equals in England, without sharing it with their inferiors in the colonies." These same upper classes also realized that mobs and popular mass meetings undermined "security of property rights and their own long-established supremacy in colonial politics." They

[66] *Ibid.*, pp. 75-77, 99, 165, 167, 170.
[67] *Ibid.*, pp. 121, 194, 196-200, 209, 218, 245.

desired to protect their privileges from British encroachments "without sharing them with the unfranchised populace." "Not for home rule alone was the Revolution fought, but for the democratization of American society as well," Becker declared, for the greatest opposition to Britain came from those who felt themselves inadequately represented in colonial assemblies. Half of the denunciation of corruption in England was inspired by jealous dislike of high-placed American families whose ostentatious lives and condescending manners were offensive to the laboring poor and to ambitious men of talent. The quarrel with England was a heaven-sent opportunity for all who resented the favorites of fortune who vainly called themselves the better sort and monopolized privilege in nearly every colony. Loyalists who had once opposed British policy looked with increased apprehension upon the growing influence of obscure leaders who proclaimed the rights of the people. The presence of mobs, the entrance of the unfranchised populace, and the leveling principles all led conservatives to consider whether their interests were not more threatened by insurgent radicalism in America than by alleged British oppression.[68]

At the same time, however, Becker actually demonstrated that the Revolution involved fundamental principles rather than class interests and that concensus was more important than conflict. American contact with British claims of superiority during the French and Indian War, he declared, brought unity within and helped cause the final separation. British measures were looked upon generally as a malignant design to destroy British liberties in America; the Stamp Act raised the "issue of fundamental rights;" American opposition was based on principle rather than on interest alone; and the British-colonial conflict involved principles and freedom, for the common people supported the American cause with a religious fervor of men doing battle for the welfare of the human race. Becker shows that it was the legally-elected representatives who carried Virginia into the Revolution, not the disfranchised mob, that John Adams refused to be bought

[68] *Ibid.*, pp. 172, 227, 240-41, 244-45.

off by Thomas Hutchinson, and that it was the imperial coalition of the Hutchinson party and Britain which caused a perpetual struggle threatening the liberties of the colonies. Becker also praised the fundamental principles of the Declaration of Independence that governments derive authority from the consent of the governed and that civil society is grounded upon the inherent and inalienable rights of man. Of outstanding importance in western culture, its glittering generalities, he declared, formulated truths which no criticism can seriously impair and to which minds of men must always turn as long as faith in democracy endures.[69]

The results of the American Revolution, the real test of any revolution, also do not substantiate the Becker thesis. On the one hand, Becker said, the "radical party" in Virginia, led by Henry, Jefferson, and the Lees, destroyed the domination of a little coterie of great planters by abolishing entail, disestablishing the Anglican church, and proclaiming a state constitution founded, "in theory if not altogether in fact, upon the principles of liberty and equality and the rights of man." The new state constitutions, which should have reflected the internal revolution most, gave Becker considerable trouble. If, as he said, these new constitutions gave formal expression to the philosophy of the Revolution, they also limited popular sovereignty by basing the suffrage upon property and often half defeated it through checks and balances. In one place Becker declared that the constitutions marked a safe and conservative advance toward "establishment of a more equal liberty;" in another, he said that "detailed arrangements followed closely the practices and traditions inherited from the colonial period." [70] If the United States at the end of the war was the exhausted and half-ruined champion of those principles of liberty and equality which would soon transform Europe, it was, by Becker's own statement, a land of great opportunity and freedom, a new land of promise before the Revolution.

And finally, Becker did an about face on the conservative

[69] *Ibid.,* pp. 192, 217, 219, 221, 239.   [70] *Ibid.,* pp. 241, 263, 272.

upper classes who became loyalists. After seemingly condemning this group as aristocratic monopolizers of privilege and adamant foes of democracy and the common man, Becker declared that independence was won only by the sacrifice of much that was best in colonial society. "Something fine and amiable in manners, something charming in customs, much that was most excellent in the traditions of politics and public morality disappeared with the ruin of those who thought themselves, and who often were in fact, 'the better sort.' " [71]

A friend and former colleague at Kansas, Wallace Notestein, gave what seems to be a fair appraisal of *The Beginnings of the American People.* Then at Minnesota where Becker would soon follow, Notestein said that Becker's chapters on the Puritans interested him but that some of Becker's generalizations seemed "a little more suggestive than true." [72] The same could be said in fact for the entire book — it was a little more suggestive than true.

That Becker looked upon the American Revolution as an integral part of the progressive movement appeared in a review in 1916. As in an earlier review, he had some second thoughts about the dual revolution, for again he said that the war was "primarily" a movement for independence. But having said this, Becker proceeded to use most of the review to expound the class-conflict aspects of the Revolution. The war with England was accompanied, and greatly complicated and intensified, by a conservative-democratic conflict in nearly every colony, with conservatives endeavoring to maintain old privileges and democrats attempting to acquire new ones. Colonial aristocrats wished to achieve separation without disturbing existing class relationships while "progressives" sought to establish a government of equal rights, a democratic state. It was difficult, however, to demand rights from the king while denying them to the people. Radicals were partially successful from 1776 to 1779, but a conservative reaction then set in, resulting in the Federal Constitution and rule by the Federalists (the Beard thesis in part). Nevertheless, the Revolution

[71] *Ibid.*, p. 272.   [72] Notestein to Becker, ? 1915, Becker Papers.

was the beginning of the democratization of American politics and society, a movement inseparably associated with the names of Jefferson, Jackson, and Lincoln, and Becker added, shall we say Bryan, Roosevelt, and Wilson.[73]

The Becker thesis also underwent modification, but it still remained as part of the progressive movement toward a more democratic society. Starting with the belief that the internal class aspects of the Revolution were virtually everything and that the struggle for independence was of little importance, Becker had come by 1916 to an admission, at least in some of his writings, that the war with Britain was primarily a war for independence. By insisting contrary to his own evidence that colonial society was undemocratic and class-ridden, Becker created the impression that this society was not one that good men and true could look back upon with pride. If progress is indeed the essence of history, obviously one should not demonstrate that the colonial period was a golden age of economic opportunity and freedom. And by placing great emphasis on class conflict in the eighteenth century, Becker could demonstrate the need for class consciousness in the twentieth. The business of history, as he had said, was to arouse an intelligent discontent and to foster a fruitful radicalism.

By 1916, the promising young scholar who had left Wisconsin in 1898 had clearly defined the direction of his career. His first published article in 1899 on nominating conventions proved to be his last real scholarly work on American history, whatever may be said about his writing on European history. Influenced by progressivism and the subjective relativism of men such as Turner, Robinson, John Dewey, and others, Becker abandoned scholarship, where the historian tested his generalizations by the logic of his evidence, and became a publicist or propagandist who virtually eliminated objective facts in the interests of a progressive cause. As he had said,

[73] Review of H. R. Eckenrode, *The Revolution in Virginia*, in *Political Science Quarterly*, December, 1916.

history was a pack of tricks to be played on the dead, tricks that were justified if they served useful social purposes.

During this period, two other progressive historians would write books on the Revolutionary era which both helped to perpetuate the Becker thesis and also exposed some of the inconsistencies and contradictions in the progressive interpretation. In 1913, Charles A. Beard published his famous book on the Founding Fathers and the Constitution, *An Economic Interpretation of the Constitution of the United States,* which was significant not so much for Becker's influence on Beard, although Beard cited Becker's work, as it was for the fact that the interpretations of early American history by these two men came to be accepted by many students and professors as part of the same fabric of history. The second book, *The Colonial Merchants and the American Revolution* by Arthur M. Schlesinger, Sr., published in 1918, grew out of progressive historiography and made its way as an important cog in the Becker-Beard interpretation.

Like Becker, Beard did not portray the foundation of the American nation as a golden age to which Americans could look with pride. Instead of a document based on principles of democracy and justice, Beard portrayed the American Constitution as a conservative conspiracy by upper-class capitalists to line their own pockets at the expense of the people. The Constitution, Beard contended, was an economic document designed to benefit certain personal property interests — money, public securities, manufacturing, commerce, land speculators — rather than Americans in general, and it was put over on the people undemocratically in an undemocratic society, for the mass of the people opposed ratification but were disfranchised by property requirements. Published in 1913 at the crest of the Progressive Movement, Beard's book carried the message that a constitution which had been adopted to check democracy and benefit one class could as easily be amended to foster democracy and benefit another class.[74]

[74] Charles A. Beard, *An Economic Interpretation of the Constitution of the United States* (New York, 1913). See especially pp. 324-25 for a summary of the Beard thesis.

Becker and Beard provided the essential framework for Schlesinger's *Colonial Merchants and the American Revolution*. Starting with Becker's concept of an undemocratic colonial society, Schlesinger insisted that a ruling aristocracy of northern merchants and debt-ridden southern planters used the unfranchised classes to forestall British imperial reforms after 1763, but had no intention of extending to these lower classes the rights and privileges which they claimed for themselves. The lower classes had other ideas, however, and when the merchants realized that they had instigated a social revolution which they could not control, many merchants became loyalists while others attempted to remain neutral or to guide the Revolution into conservative channels. Schlesinger assumed that Becker's internal class revolution was successful in democratizing American society and politics. Then Beard took over, for according to Schlesinger, the merchants who were not loyalists became an integral part of Beard's conservative counterrevolution to thwart the democratic aims of the radical revolutionists.[75]

Schlesinger acknowledged fully his debt to Becker as one of the founding fathers of his own thesis. In addition to individual citations, he commended Becker's work on several occasions, noting that he was following "the modern treatment of Becker," that in his accounts of New York politics he had "frequently and gratefully consulted Professor Becker's *History of Political Parties*," and that he relied on Professor Becker's discussion and references.[76]

Essentially, however, the Becker, Beard, and Schlesinger theses were all internally inconsistent and mutually contradictory. We have already seen that Becker's evidence affirmed a democratic colonial society while his own generalizations denied this, and the same was true of Beard and Schlesinger. Both offered evidence that the Revolution and Constitution

[75] Arthur M. Schlesinger, Sr., *The Colonial Merchants and the American Revolution* (New York, 1918), especially pp. 27, 28, 31, 32, 34-36, 38, 39, 66, 90-93, 104, 105, 135, 180, 189, 240, 254, 255, 258, 262, 306, 308, 309, 432, 435, 541, 591-93, 603-06.

[76] *Ibid.*, pp. 90, 92, 291 and note 3, 329-30, 544.

emerged from democratic societies, although both theses rest on opposite assumptions.[77] In addition, if the social revolution for democracy was successful, as Becker implied and Schlesinger assumed, then Beard's thesis, based on an undemocratic society, was not valid. Conversely, if the social revolution for democracy never occurred, as Becker's evidence proved and Beard's thesis assumes, there was really no need for a conservative counterrevolution against democracy, for there was no democracy to revolt against. And if, as Schlesinger assumes, the social revolution was successful, why would the lower classes contribute to a sixty-five per cent landslide victory for a constitution that was intended as a check on the very democratic rights that they had won in eight years of revolution?

Beard and Schlesinger will both return to our story of Becker as it progresses, but these were the essential inconsistencies and contradictions that would dog the footsteps of the progressive interpretation of the Revolution and Constitution down to our own time. And perhaps more than anything else, Becker's philosophy of subjective relativism, by freeing the historian from any obligation to evidence and logic, was responsible for these inconsistencies and contradictions.

[77] For Beard, see *Economic Interpretation of the Constitution*, pp. 24, 71, where Beard never reconciles statements that a "mass of men" was disfranchised, that the extent of disfranchisement cannot be determined, that mechanics and tradesmen voted in the towns, and that in a country which was ninety-five per cent rural, the wide distribution of real property created an extensive electorate and gave the legislatures a broad popular basis. Schlesinger has mechanics and tradesmen electing representatives in Philadelphia, has over 4,000 voters in New York City, and quotes Thomas Hutchinson that the lower classes controlled the Boston Town Meeting. See Schlesinger, *Colonial Merchants*, pp. 27, 28, 223, 256, 279.

V. DISILLUSIONMENT AND THE BECKER THESIS, 1917-1922

> "There is nothing you cannot find in the past — except the truth: a truth you can indeed find; any number of truths are there ready to be picked out, and perfectly indifferent to the process. Such facts as the mind is predisposed to select as interesting or important will come out and 'speak for themselves.' The trouble is, they don't care what they say; and with a little intelligent prompting they will speak, within reason, whatever they are commanded to speak."
>
> — CARL BECKER, 1921

THE period of war and peace, 1917 to 1922, might well be used to demonstrate the validity of the one law of history, the law of continuity and change. Becker, as we shall see, clung to some of his previous ideas, yet abandoned others, in part because of a disillusionment with mankind over involvement in war, the failures of the peace, and the conservative reaction following the war. Physically, there was also change of great moment to Becker's later career. From Kansas, where he had been a professor of European history in spite of his degree with Turner, he moved as a professor of European history first to Minnesota in 1916, then on in 1917 to Cornell University with which his name is most closely associated and which gave him a more influential position in the world of history than his previous positions had accorded. There, within a period of four years, he was to publish three more books — all on American history.

The offer of a position at Cornell resulted in perhaps as good a characterization of Becker, by himself, as anyone could have given. In the correspondence, Becker said that he was somewhat diffident about his ability to fill the position, a diffidence that was certainly well-founded, for the position was in modern European history and at the time Becker had written nothing substantial in the field. But then he went on to say that his forte, if he had any, was "in having thought a good deal about the meaning of history rather than in having achieved erudition in it." [1] This would seem to indicate that he looked upon himself more as the philosopher than as the historian.

In the realm of economics, some of Becker's later hostility toward capitalism and business became evident in 1917. William E. Dodd, who was editing the *Chronicles of America* to which Becker was contributing a volume, had bought some land. Becker chided Dodd on this fact, warning that the first thing Dodd knew he would "get the property point of view and go over to the enemy" — a dangerous thing for a democrat like Dodd.[2]

Relativism, subjectivism, and progressivism were also still very much in evidence. In a book review Becker made the following statement: "It would be interesting to inquire whether Mr. Powers [the author] derives his philosophy from the facts he looks at, or whether the facts he looks at so intently are determined by his philosophy." Becker also referred to the "disastrous assumption that man cannot by taking thought shape his own destiny" — a fundamental tenet of progressives — and that Powers had "faith in progress toward human unity." [3]

In fact, by 1918 Becker had reached the point of virtually eliminating evidence and scholarship as factors in history. The vehicle for this approach was another book, *The Eve of the Revolution,* which the professor of European history again wrote on American history. The most important part is the preface, which not only reveals how far Becker had

[1] Becker to George Lincoln Burr, January 4, 1917, Burr Papers, Cornell University.
[2] Becker to William E. Dodd, May 22, 1917, Becker Papers.
[3] *The Dial,* August 15, 1918.

departed from the accepted canons of scholarship, but also indicates Becker's contempt for those who followed these canons. So important is this preface to an understanding of Becker's philosophy that I have quoted from it at length.

"In this brief sketch I have chiefly endeavored to convey to the reader, not a record of what men did, but a sense of how they thought and felt about what they did. To give the quality and texture of the state of mind and feeling of an individual or class, to create for the reader the illusion (not *delusion,* O able critic!) of the intellectual atmosphere of past times, I have as a matter of course introduced many quotations, but I have also ventured to resort frequently to the literary device (this, I know, gives the whole thing away) of telling the story by means of a rather free paraphrase of what some imagined spectator or participant might have thought or said about the matter in hand. If the critic says that the product of such methods is not history, I am willing to call it by any name that is better; the point of greatest relevance being the truth and effectiveness of the illusion aimed at — the extent to which it reproduces the quality of thought and feeling of those days, the extent to which it enables the reader to enter into such states of mind and feeling. The truth of such history (or whatever the critic wishes to call it) cannot of course be determined by a mere verification of references." Becker also referred to his book as "an enterprise of questionable orthodoxy" with which reputable historians would not wish to be associated.[4]

These are strange words indeed for a scholar to utter, even a "scholar" with Becker's sense of humor, yet not so strange if one does not consider Becker as a historian. How can anyone, for example, convey a sense of what men thought and felt about what they did without going to the evidence to find out what they thought and felt about what they did? If the truth of history cannot be determined by a verification of

[4] From Carl L. Becker, *The Eve of the Revolution: A Chronicle of the Breach with England* (V. 11, THE CHRONICLES OF AMERICA), preface. By permission of the United States Publishers Assn., Inc.

references, how, one might ask, can it be verified? Then there is the astonishing misuse of the word "illusion." Did Becker really mean what he actually wrote — that he was attempting to create false and deceptive ideas about history? It is quite true that he did do this, but was this what he meant to say? Later Becker claimed that his aim was the "truth and effectiveness of the illusion" — an impossibility, for by definition an illusion cannot reflect truth even though it might be effective. Furthermore, anyone who traffics in what some imagined spectator or participant *might have thought or said* is a novelist, not a historian. Historians are limited to what men of the past actually thought or said, provided they can uncover this information. It seems quite evident that here Becker did not consider himself as a historian nor his literary production as history.

The remainder of the book, whatever its literary merit, is worse than worthless as history. The truth is that Becker could not possibly recapture the state of mind or feelings of colonial Americans because he did not place them in their own milieu or climate of opinion. Occasionally he revealed that eighteenth-century American society was mobile and democratic, but when the chips were down, he always reverted to his class-conflict approach. Becker almost made the Revolution a personal war brought on by a clash of petty interests between Samuel Adams and Thomas Hutchinson, but Becker never really understood that Samuel Adams was popular because he exposed himself to dire consequences in the interests of a democratic society while Hutchinson was despised for exactly the opposite reason. Logically, Samuel Adams should have been Becker's hero, but if anything, Becker sympathized with Hutchinson and the British, a reflection, perhaps, of the influence of the imperial historians at that time.[5]

Curiously enough, if Becker failed to make a progressive

[5] Imperial historians, such as George Louis Beer and Charles McLean Andrews, were attempting to foster better relations between the United States and Great Britain by playing down British responsibility for the American Revolution. See especially Beer, *The English-Speaking Peoples* (New York, 1917).

hero out of Samuel Adams, as he could easily have done, he still found many elements of progressivism to emphasize. He pictured Patrick Henry of Virginia as a "tribune of the people," a "leader and interpreter of the silent 'simple folk,' " "one of those passionate temperaments whose reason functions not in the service of knowledge but of good instincts and fine emotions; a nature to be easily possessed of an exalted enthusiasm for popular rights and for celebrating the virtues of the industrious poor." Henry considered it his mission to stand forth boldly as the "champion of liberty and the submerged rights of mankind." [6] Henry was also a slaveowner, but to a man who was interested in "illusions" as Becker was, this fact presented no serious problems. Henry, if he had lived in 1918, obviously would have been a good progressive, and one cannot but feel compassion for the common man in reading Becker's account.

If Becker had a tongue-in-cheek attitude when he wrote *The Eve of the Revolution* — if he knew that his work was unorthodox, that his use of what some imagined character *might* have thought or said was open to criticism, and that some people might suspect that his work was literature, not history — it is equally true that uninitiated readers could and did accept his account as authentic history.

The reaction of Frank Hodder, a former colleague at Kansas, indicates how one progressive might well interpret the writing of another progressive. Hodder called *The Eve of the Revolution* a "charming book" but he did not see that Becker's point of view was very "heretical." The mode of presentation might not have been orthodox, Hodder continued, but the substance was what Hodder used in class, even though he did not say it "within a thousand miles" of Becker's style. Said Hodder: "I would come right out and say that Sam Adams was a dead beat or that Teddy [Roosevelt] was a Prussian. If I had camouflaged that Prussian business I might not have got into trouble." [7] Obviously neither Hodder

[6] Becker, *Eve of the Revolution, passim.*
[7] Frank H. Hodder to Becker, March 23, 1919, Becker Papers.

nor Becker understood the liberalism of Samuel Adams, and the statement about Roosevelt suggests how far Roosevelt had fallen from the good graces of progressives by 1919 because of his advocacy of American entrance into World War I.

The extent to which a reader could be misled when he did not know either the facts of early American history or Becker's philosophy of relativism and subjectivism appears in a letter from an admirer. Archibald MacMeehan of Dalhousie College expressed pleasure on reading *The Eve of the Revolution,* then remarked that Becker's knowledge, skill at narrative, and "ironical detachment" from his theme combined to make the book a masterpiece.[8] And this about a man who did not believe that detachment was either possible or desirable!

It remained for a reviewer to capture the relativism, subjectivism, and New History progressivism inherent in *The Eve of the Revolution,* while at the same time placing a stamp of approval on the book as legitimate history. Walton H. Hamilton referred to Becker's "creative touch" but also declared that "the honesty, workmanship, and artistry" of the author were beyond question. There was "no quarrel over facts," he declared. But, he continued, Becker knew, "that facts tell different stories for different men" — that there is something back of the facts that we may call "a conception of history." A judgment on Becker's new adventure in history writing would depend on who made the judgment, for there were many historians and thus "no reason why anyone should not have the past of America arranged according to his liking." Hamilton declared that "the 'new history' of which Mr. Becker's book is so valuable a type" would find readers. It would appeal to those who had acquired "modern notions" of human motives and conduct and what is meant by cause in history. The book contained statements not found in any document, he concluded with approval, and one could not "escape the conviction that there is quite a bit of Mr. Becker in the episode of the past which he has remade"[9] — as indeed there was.

[8] MacMeehan to Becker, January 11, 1926, Becker Papers.
[9] *The Dial,* February 8, 1919.

If Becker allowed quite a bit of his own self to enter into his creative writing, however, he did not permit the same freedom to other historians. In reviewing Norwood Young's *Frederick the Great,* Becker had this remark: "If Mr. Young's Frederick is mostly enigma, when it is not caricature, it is due largely to the fact that he judges a man whom he neither likes nor understands by standards that were foreign to the age in which he lived." [10] Yet Becker was the man who said that the facts do not exist until they are created by the historian, that into every fact that he creates some part of his own being must enter, and that while we explain a man's actions by the standards of his own time, we judge him by the standards of our time. Apparently it depended, as Hamilton said, on who did the judging.

The Becker thesis received an additional boost in 1920 when again the professor of European history wrote another book on American history. *The United States: An Experiment in Democracy* was based on class structure, class conflict, and the struggle of the lower classes to democratize American society. The early settlers were content to establish European class division; a small group of wealthy families formed a ruling aristocracy; the "humble folk" comprised of small farmers, artisans, and mechanics were sharply differentiated from this ruling aristocracy; assemblies composed of property owners "passed laws mainly in the interest of the classes that controlled them;" and the Revolution was a dual movement in which the unfranchised "humble folk" were demanding political equality. "In fact," Becker repeated, "the American Revolution was not only a movement for national independence from Great Britain: it was also a movement for the democratization of American society and politics — a movement which has continued from that day to this and which is the central theme of our history." In fact, the class-conflict aspect was the aspect of the Revolution which gave it its

[10] *New Republic,* November 12, 1919.

"chief significance for modern democracy." [11] Becker, who earlier had appeared to be turning away from the internal class revolution in favor of an emphasis on a war for independence, now returned to his original interpretation.

Even British mercantilism and imperialism took on the trappings of class conflict in Becker's estimation. He said that the burden of the trade laws fell chiefly on the poor of both England and the colonies, "since the mercantile system was designed not so much for the advantage of England at the expense of the Colonies, but rather for the special advantage of the upper classes in both countries, the merchants and landowners in England and the colonies alike." [12] This interpretation of mercantilism would have come as a great surprise to both Englishmen and Americans.

Becker also saw the American and French Revolutions as major episodes in the eternal struggle of mankind to better itself. In America, radicals rested their claims on the rights of man, not just the rights of Englishmen, and their aims were "the abolition of class privilege, . . . the democratization of American politics and society, . . . the inauguration of an ideal state." The Declaration of Independence listed specific grievances against the king, which no one remembers, Becker said, but everyone remembers "We hold these truths" which states the rights of man. Thus the American Revolution had universal appeal because it rested on the proposition that all men are created equal and that government rests on the will of the people. In France, American ideals of liberty and human welfare elicited great popular support, for over the years men such as Voltaire, Montesquieu, and Rousseau, "by trenchant criticism and corrosive satire and passionate denunciation of corruption, hypocrisy, and injustice," had destroyed the moral foundations of the monarchy. Frenchmen and Americans dreamed of a new era, a regenerated society, in which en-

[11] Carl L. Becker, *The United States: An Experiment in Democracy* (Harper and Brothers, New York, 1920), pp. 7-8, 11, 12, 24-25, 36-41, 45-52. All quotations used by permission of Harper & Row, Publishers, Incorporated.   [12] *Ibid.*, p. 12.

lightenment would banish ignorance, vice, selfishness, and brutality, and generous and humane instincts of natural man "would find expression in law and customs designed to establish and perpetuate the general welfare." [13]

Time and again, however, Becker, as he had done in his previous three books on American history, contradicted himself and refuted his own thesis. Although in most places in this book he emphasized the internal revolution, at one point he conceded that "the American Revolution was thus primarily a struggle between the Colonies and Great Britain over the question of self-government," which reversed his earlier statement that the Revolution was almost entirely a class affair. Becker obviously recognized that to Europeans, America was not class-ridden but a "new land of promise where every citizen was a free man, where the necessities of life were the sure reward of industry, where manners were simple, where vice and crime had almost disappeared, and where native incapacity was the only effective barrier to ambition!" [14] These two statements, which can be documented from the sources, add up to the proposition that the Revolution was a war for independence and that American society contained few ingredients essential for class conflict, yet Becker did not see these inconsistencies.

It was in this 1920 book that Becker revealed the useful social purpose which justified in his own mind the playing of tricks on the dead. What he wanted was the adoption in the United States of a system of collective democracy to replace democratic or laissez-faire capitalism. In his "Kansas" article, Becker had warned that anyone who wanted socialism must use other terms, for socialism carried connotations of some kind of foreign system which Americans would reject. Actually, Becker distinguished from this point on between collective democracy, which would entail only regulation of capitalism, and socialism, which meant government ownership of the chief means of production.

[13] *Ibid.,* pp. 47-52, 58-60.
[14] *Ibid.,* pp. 6-7, 9, 10, 17, 26, and especially pp. 12, 61, 65-70, 158.

Becker's argument for collective democracy centered, as did Turner's, in an erroneous account of the impact of the frontier on American institutions. Becker contended that voting rights were restricted in 1789, but there were men who had more faith in people than in wealth, and because of the democratizing influence of the frontier, restrictions on the suffrage were gradually abolished. The election of Jackson was the culmination of a "great democratic movement," for Jackson had profound faith "in the worth, the integrity, and the sound sense of the average man." [15] Becker saw that the frontier "made impossible the establishment of rigid class distinctions" and that it created conditions under which a man could go as far as his ability and ambition would take him. The equality of the frontier was not an equality of rewards and possessions, but an equality of opportunity and reward according to merit. The frontier developed respect for ability but not deference in the sense of servility.[16] Becker's failure, as far as his thesis was concerned, was in not realizing that this democratizing influence of the frontier had been operative long before 1789.

Becker then went on to demonstrate how the frontier from 1790 to 1890 had created something approaching his ideal of what society should be. Liberty and equality were well suited to the United States, he declared, for it had freedom of government, speech, religion, and contract from the earliest days. No violent revolution was required, as in France, to establish these principles in practice. Liberty was not inconsistent with equality, for an agricultural community in which workers could easily get land "prevented the formation of any defined or persistent class inequalities." Where the poor could look forward to a better tomorrow, where the son of a laborer could become an employer and the son of a farmer could go to college, people lived for the future and the better things it could offer. Said Becker: "Thus it is that for a hundred years, thanks to an abundance of land, a settled democratic habit of mind, and a people in whom resourcefulness and self-

---

[15] *Ibid.*, pp. 86-87.   [16] *Ibid.*, pp. 165-73.

confidence have come to be almost acquired characteristics, the United States preserved an equality of opportunity and of conditions quite unknown in Europe." [17] As Becker was to admit late in life, these very same things were also true about American society in the eighteenth century.

Following Turner again, Becker insisted that the passing of the frontier at the close of the nineteenth century now made mandatory a collective rather than an individualistic democracy. With the passing of the frontier, he said, the economic opportunity which fostered equality and democracy disappeared, to be replaced by an industrial society in which government aided industry. Freedom resulted in inequality, and the situation was approaching when free competition and individual initiative would perhaps not be among the inherent rights of man. Social philosophers were now turning, as in Europe, from production of wealth to distribution of wealth, which might well mean modification of our ideas and government. The United States had stood for democracy, he continued, but democracy means nothing if it does not mean equality of opportunity and well-being. Therefore, it might be necessary for government to interfere with individual liberty in order to retain equality — to curtail property rights in the interests of human rights. Becker believed that the issue might well be individualism versus collectivism. If it is proper to equalize opportunity and well-being with free land and free schools, he declared, it is also proper to achieve the same result by equitable distribution among the people of the wealth, which is the product of their labor, and the resources which belong to them. [18]

Becker even used eighteenth-century France as an example of the need for more collective democracy in the interests of the common man. French progressives believed that the wretched state of the masses was due to environment rather than to heredity, and that the way to improve men was to abolish arbitrary government and class privilege — to confer

[17] *Ibid.,* pp. 307-10.
[18] *Ibid.,* pp. 311-22. For similar views by Turner see *The Frontier in American History,* pp. 266-67, 277, 281, 285, 305, 307, 319-24, 336.

personal, political, and industrial liberty which would enable every man to make the most of himself. There would still be inequalities due to inheritance and a better home environment, so it should be the duty of the state to remove these inequalities, especially by establishing free schools as a sure foundation for democracy and progress toward human perfectibility. Inequalities in eighteenth-century France were maintained by law, and thus the aim of the philosophers was to remove restraints that prevented equality.[19] What Becker did not say was that these same French progressives looked upon eighteenth-century America as the society which had already achieved the very characteristics that they desired for France. Becker later elaborated on his ideas of French progressivism in a book, *The Heavenly City of the Eighteenth Century Philosophers,* with the "heavenly city" a secular, equalitarian society on earth.

Becker was obviously moving beyond the liberal democracy of the eighteenth and nineteenth centuries — beyond the equality of opportunity but not necessarily equality of ability and possessions provided by the frontier — to an equality of everything under a collectivist society. The industrial revolution had changed the conditions under which representative democracy had developed, he said, bringing with it a conflict between capital and labor rather than sectional conflicts. As a result, our political machinery was no longer adapted to our economic organization. Capital wanted to keep government as it was, for the divine right of the state and the absolutism of the majority were now controlled by the capitalist class. Labor wanted change, however, and tomorrow a "proletariat" might be in control. Either alternative was dangerous, for each desired a strong government which would further its ends. Becker warned that the American people must face realities if this country was to be in the future what it had been in the past, "a fruitful experiment in democracy." His solution, of course, was social democracy or democratic collectivism.[20]

19 Becker, *The United States,* pp. 275-76, 296-98.
20 *Ibid.,* pp. 322-30.

Becker's appeal for social democracy was not lost on liberals who were prone to be sympathetic with his views. The historian, David Muzzey, who with Becker was later accused of being procommunist and whose high school textbooks were widely used, characterized *American Democracy* as "Bully!" The last chapter, in which Becker especially advocated collectivism, was "magnificent," Muzzey declared, as he made this significant comment: "This book is a *call to the uncommitted* if ever one was sounded." [21] Muzzey certainly had no illusions about Becker's detachment or the progressivism of his history.

Becker's debt to Turner in this book appears in a letter of 1920, written shortly after both men had published books. Turner had collected a group of his articles and papers into book form under the title *The Frontier in American History,* and these items, taken together, reveal Turner's development from individualism to collectivism as the impact of the closing of the frontier became apparent. Becker, who had just received a copy of Turner's book, assured Turner that Turner had a large share in Becker's stock, for whatever it was worth. Becker said that everything he had written on American history showed the influence of the ideas expressed in Turner's book. Then he made this confession: "In my last book, as you will see if you look at it, I have appropriated your interpretations without scruple, without fear also, without reproach I hope, and certainly without research." [22]

Becker also acknowledged that it was Turner in particular who had directed him into the life of a scholar. Becker said that he had always wanted to write, and from the age of twelve he had had "writer's itch." But his models were cheap fiction writers who did not represent the "best that had been thought and said in the world." He had in him the makings of a scrubby journalist and a third-rate literary fellow, and while the literary fellow was still around, Becker hoped that he had kept him in his place. What Becker got from Turner and Haskins was a "kind of grip on the idea of scholarship," a

[21] Muzzey to Becker, October 16, 1920, Becker Papers.
[22] Becker to Turner, October 24, 1920, TU, Box 30.

holy fear of the dishonest, of words without sense, of easy generalizations unballasted with knowledge.[23] We have already seen, and shall see again, how much Becker violated these ideals in practice.

World War I wrought a profound change in Becker, for the war, which he envisioned in Wilson's terms as a crusade to save the world for democracy, turned out to be only an illusion for liberals. From this time on, Becker seems to have been two different persons, one who at times continued to advocate progressivism and a belief in the perfectibility of man, yet in other instances, usually in his private correspondence, one who expressed a grave doubt about progressivism and the ability of the common man to achieve the good society through rational thought and action. It often appeared that the Becker who spoke with his heart was at odds with the Becker who spoke with his mind.

Some of this conflict within Becker appears in two reviews of books written by the redoubtable historian, Henry Adams, who had died in 1918. Becker looked upon Adams' *The Education of Henry Adams* as the story of a historian who had failed because he had never found a philosophy of history that would enable him to direct the course of human development. Adams had a good mind, Becker said, but he was an aristocrat whose own writings led nowhere and explained nothing. The world would have been exactly what it was if Adams had never lived, for he was never able to impress himself powerfully upon his own time. Adams died without determining the lines of force that attract the world, concluded Becker, and this is the problem of all history.[24]

More particularly, however, Becker attempted to counteract the antiprogressivism inherent in Adams' philosophy. Adams denied ultimate progress because of the physical nature of the universe, for science, the creator of democracy, teaches the degradation rather than the increase in vital energy. Science shows that the universe must ultimately be exhausted of energy, and therefore the millennium promised by democracy

---

[23] *Ibid.*   [24] *American Historical Review,* April, 1919.

is a delusion; for man, instead of progressing toward perfectibility, must also experience a degradation toward death and extinction. Historians taught progress toward a more perfect society, but the notion of progress was a delusion to Adams, for if the entire universe, like a clock, was running down, historians should deal with history on this basis. Becker attacked Adams for accepting so naively the dogmas of natural science and for quarreling with historians because they refused to bow down and worship the great god Adams. The ash heap and the millennium were still a long way off, Becker suggested, so there was no urgent need to prepare for them.[25]

In the process of refuting Henry Adams, however, Becker denied that historians were progressives who taught progressive history. Historians did not teach or assume a philosophy of progress, he declared, and he himself did not teach either progress toward or degradation from democracy. He taught history, he said, as a series of "changes in configuration," attempting to understand, not in terms of physics but of human needs, how these came about. "Whatever its ultimate end or its absolute value may be, or whether we know the ultimate end or the absolute value," Becker concluded, "human life will remain essentially what it has been, and will have the same finite and human values and meaning. It is the function of history, as I understand it, to deal with this meaning and these values as they are revealed in the thought and acts of men." [26] This review came out almost simultaneously with *American Democracy,* which advocated progress toward collective democracy and which Muzzey characterized as a *"call to the uncommitted."*

In a letter to William E. Dodd in 1920, after the impact of World War I and its results began to be apparent, there was much more of degradation in Becker's outlook than Becker indicated in the Adams review. Becker confessed that he had always been susceptible to the impression of the futility of life and always easily persuaded to regard history as no more than the meaningless resolution of blind forces which struggl-

[25] *Ibid.,* April, 1920, pp. 480-82.   [26] *Ibid.*

ing men, good and bad, do not understand and cannot control. The war and the peace "(God save the mark!)" had immensely deepened his pessimism. The war was inexplicable on any ground of reason, a most desolating and repulsive exhibition of human power and cruelty. If the war represented thousands of years of human progress, Becker declared in unconscious agreement with Adams, "what in Heaven's name would retardation be!" The world was not divided into good and bad men, but all men, with their principles, faith, and ideals, were unknowingly at the service of complex and subtle instinctive reactions and impulses. This was the meaning, if it had any, Becker said, of *The Eve of the Revolution,* particularly the chapter on Samuel Adams and Thomas Hutchinson.[27] Although it is doubtful that most readers placed this interpretation on *The Eve of the Revolution,* the philosophy expressed here by Becker is hardly that of a good progressive.

In the same letter to Dodd, Becker also expressed disillusionment about men's political and business activities. Politics he called a business of self-deception and dishonesty compared with the honesty and genuineness of all good art, scholarship, craftsmanship, and other human activities — activities designed to create something beautiful or useful, to discover some truth (strange words from a man who used "truth" as he did), or to do something helpful for others. But most politics and much business were aimed, not at the ideal of helping humanity, but at the gaining of some private advantage. There was a taint of dishonesty about politics and business that warped the minds of their followers. Politics demonstrated to Becker the truth of the old saying that "the human heart is deceitful above all things, and desperately wicked." World War I, purportedly fought for justice and liberty but actually for the spoils of victory, convinced him of the futility of a new international order founded on nationalism, and if he voted at all in the 1920 election, he said, he would vote for Eugene Debs, the Socialist.[28] Becker might

[27] Becker to Dodd, June 17, 1920, Becker Papers.
[28] *Ibid.*

111

have added that this evaluation of politics could also raise questions about the desirability of collective democracy.

That Becker remained primarily interested in the future rather than the past and that he would use history to improve the future there can be no doubt. In one review he said, "Let us at least dwell on the past for the purpose of searching out, and correcting if we can, the general conditions, for which we are all in our different ways responsible, which made the misery and the sin possible." [29] He criticized Montesquieu as a historian because he had *"more often been occupied with finding the reasons for that which is than with seeking that which ought to be"*[30] — a true New History goal. And he praised a book, not because it was original or scholarly, but because it would be widely read, popular, and found interesting. "With histories, that is after all the main thing," he declared, for Voltaire came close to the truth when he said that "history is only a pack of tricks which we play on the dead." [31]

Increasingly the relativity of historical facts engrossed Becker's thinking. In castigating John Spencer Bassett in 1921 for failure to interpret his facts about World War I, Becker declared that letting facts speak for themselves was a worthy but unattainable ideal, for facts were so wretchedly complacent, so indifferent, so neutral, that they speak several languages. It is all one with them, for they care not what they say. Indeed, it is not the facts that speak for themselves; it is the author who speaks through the selection and arrangement of facts.[32] Then in a review of H. G. Wells' *Outline of History*, a clarion New History call for socialism, Becker again virtually abandoned facts altogether in favor of the subjective historian. Said he: "There is nothing you cannot find in the past — except the truth: a truth you can indeed find; any

[29] Review of Viscount Haldane, *Before the War*, in *The Nation*, May 22, 1920, pp. 692-93.

[30] Becker Notes, Box 7, File Drawer 16, Becker Papers.

[31] *New Republic*, July 14, 1920.

[32] Review of John S. Bassett, *Our War with Germany*, in *The New Republic*, February 23, 1921, pp. 382-83.

number of truths are there ready to be picked out, and perfectly indifferent to the process. Such facts as the mind is predisposed to select as interesting or important will come out and 'speak for themselves.' The trouble is, they don't care what they say; *and with a little intelligent prompting they will speak, within reason, whatever they are commanded to speak.*" In other words, he said, "each age reinterprets the past to suit its own purposes," and he repeated the Voltaire quip that, after all, history is only a pack of tricks we play on the dead.[33]

The review of Wells' book did signify that there was still a faint struggle in progress between Becker the historian and Becker the propagandist. There was no doubt that Becker approved of Wells' aims even though he was scholar enough to recognize that Wells was not really writing history. Anticipating his own later book, *The Heavenly City*, he said that the French philosophers looked for those ideas and events in the past which would serve as guiding principles in the pressing task of social regeneration. Now the New Historians were "calling for a reinterpretation of the past in the service of social reform." James Harvey Robinson was one of those who desired "a history which would not be content to relate the past just as it happened, but which will, on the contrary, exploit the past in the interest of advance." Wells, Becker continued, knew for a certainty what history ought to be doing, that is, move toward a federal world state that was democratic, educated, inspired by a religion of brotherhood, directed by science, and devoted to the exploitation of the material world for the benefit of mankind. Wells' aim, in short, was a heavenly city on earth, and it was not the past but the present that had imposed this splendid ideal upon Wells. Then Becker admitted that possibly Wells had read the past too close to his own desires, but if what he wrote was not history, perhaps it would help to make history.[34]

[33] Carl Becker, "Mr. Wells and the New History," *American Historical Review*, July 1921, pp. 641-66. Italics added. Reprinted in *Everyman His Own Historian: Essays on History and Politics* (New York, 1935), p. 169.
[34] *Ibid.*

Becker's review of Wells brought a word of praise from his old mentor and preeminent New Historian, James Harvey Robinson, who by now had left the conservative ivory towers of Columbia to found the ultra-liberal New School for Social Research. Saying that he approved of Becker's review, Robinson declared that Wells needed help from the "few of us" who really sympathized with his enterprise. From the standpoint of the public, Wells could do more than "anyone of us," Robinson continued, but it was shocking to see how few "of us" really saw the point of Wells' work. Robinson also said that a book of his, *The Mind in the Making*, was just being published and he hoped that Becker would review it in the *American Historical Review*. Should Robinson or Becker approach J. Franklin Jameson, the editor? Then Robinson concluded by saying that he and Charles Beard were starting a history of modern times, written "according to our own lights without regard to conventional standards, something as you did in your admirable book on the U.S." [35]

The Mind in the Making, which Robinson wanted Becker to review, marked a significant change in Robinson's ideas of the way to achieve the good society. In *The New History*, he had stressed one pathway to knowledge, the study of history, which would reveal man's accumulation of knowledge over the centuries and which demonstrated the inevitability of progress. World War I seems to have caused a reversal in Robinson's ideas of progress, for now he advocated the study of history as the best way to understand the present deplorable condition of the world, which obviously to him did not signify progress. Instead of history as the path to the good society, he turned to the second method of acquiring knowledge, logic, and *The Mind in the Making* was an appeal to readers to use logical reasoning or the best powers of the mind in solving the world's problems. [36]

The shift from history to logic also entailed other changes

---

[35] Robinson to Becker, November 16, 1921, Becker Papers.

[36] James Harvey Robinson, *The Mind in the Making: The Relation of Intelligence to Social Reform* (New York, 1921).

in Robinson's philosophy. For one thing, he abandoned democracy and the common man in favor of the elite few who were capable of creative thought. Most men, he said, substituted reverie for thinking and rationalization for logical reasoning, basing their decisions on prejudice and "good" reasons rather than "real" reasons. But while few men are capable of creative thought, some can at least distinguish it from inferior brands and accord it the esteem it merits as the greatest treasure of the past and the only hope for the future. Civilization is not the product of the many but of a small number of restless and adventurous spirits, Robinson continued, and most men are not progressive animals but merely want to get by and reproduce their kind. The great mass of humanity has never had anything to do with the increase of intelligence, he declared, except to act as a medium of transmission and perpetuation.[37] At this time, Robinson and Becker seemed to be thinking along parallel lines — lines which did not accord the common man a very prominent place in the wave of the future where elitism would replace democracy.

Robinson's new solution for the world's social problems was the application of scientific method to the social sciences. The sciences, having freed themselves from restraints of ignorance, tradition, and vested interests, could examine all scientific problems completely. But social scientists still just "muddled through," as the recent war demonstrated. There must be a reconstruction of the mind — a careful, critical, dispassionate examination of the facts as the basis for conclusions and philosophy rather than acquiring a philosophy first and finding facts to support it later. Robinson suspected that future generations would brush aside as mere rationalization what now passed for social science, and he urged men to lessen respect for the past so that we no longer take the wisdom of the ages as a guide to reform.[38]

In effect, Robinson was repudiating both his philosophy of history and his historical method. His statement that the

[37] Ibid., pp. 41-44, 61-62, 73.   [38] Ibid., pp. 28, 38.

historian should draw his conclusions logically from his facts rather than search for facts to bolster a philosophy suggests a disillusionment with the philosophy of progress on which he had apparently imposed the facts. And his advocacy of scientific method meant that relativism and subjectivism were no longer adequate tools for the study of the social sciences.

Although Becker approved of Robinson's *Mind in the Making,* he did not follow Robinson's admonition that historians return to a careful, critical, dispassionate examination of facts as a basis for conclusions and philosophy. Quite the contrary. In 1922, the professor of European history lengthened his bibliography of works on American history with another book that was due to become famous, *The Declaration of Independence.* Throughout the book, which was based on subjective relativism and the Becker class-conflict thesis, Becker was mainly concerned with the emergence and later demise of the liberal natural-rights-of-man philosophy on which the Declaration was built.[39] Becker's *Declaration of Independence* has been so widely acclaimed that it deserves some analysis in depth.

Throughout the first chapter, Becker leaves the reader with the impression that the Declaration was much more a propaganda document than it was a true statement of existing conditions. This thesis appears in several different ways. For example, he said that the list of grievances against the king, which justified revolution, were "not quite the same as those which a careful student of history, seeking the antecedents of the Revolution, would set forth." [40] Becker later emphasized his doubt about the validity of the grievances when he referred to them as "facts" on four different occasions, and each time "facts" was in quotation marks, implying doubt that they were real facts.[41] And finally he said that when the historian uncovered each particular charge against the king, he was

---

[39] Carl L. Becker, *The Declaration of Independence: A Study in the History of Political Ideas* (New York, 1922). Copyright 1942 by Alfred A. Knopf, Inc. Quotations used by permission of Alfred A. Knopf.

[40] *Ibid.,* p. 6.   [41] *Ibid.,* pp. 10, 14-15.

"likely to think the poor king less malevolently guilty than he is made out to be." [42]

The truth, of course, was that Becker did not do the research on each grievance to discover whether or not it was valid or mere propaganda. In fact, he confessed that it was not his intention to search out the particular measures of the British government which served in the mind of Jefferson and his colleagues as validation for each particular charge against the king. But this was just the trouble. Robinson's admonition to the historian to do his critical and dispassionate research before he drew his conclusions was exactly what Becker had to do before he could write an authentic account of the Declaration, yet this was precisely what he failed to do. If he had done so, he would have found that not only Jefferson and his friends, but the great bulk of the American people, believed that these were just grievances. Careful research would have disclosed that these were precisely the issues over the years that had antagonized the American people. And if one can occasionally be permitted an unhistorical suggestion, it would be that Becker himself, if he had lived in 1776 and had been true to his professed principles, might well have considered British measures as tyrannical.

Becker also implied that the Declaration was propaganda by assuming that it was really a minority document representing only a small fraction of the American people. He said that the Declaration asserted the right of "the people" to revolt, but that there were many difficulties "concealed" in the words "the people," implying by the quotation marks that "the people" did not really mean the people. Then Becker made his implication explicit as follows: "But it is sufficient to note in passing that a large part of the people in the colonies, not being convinced that the British government had as yet become destructive of their liberties, or for some other reason, were either indifferently or strongly opposed to separation." The leaders of the Revolution, who were committed to in-

[42] *Ibid.*, p. 23.

dependence, found it politically expedient to act on the assumption that the opposition was negligible.[43]

Careful research, however, would have revealed quite a different situation. An interpretation of the Declaration as propaganda and "the people" as not the people fits the Becker class-conflict thesis, for according to this thesis, the upper classes were not interested in extending the rights they were demanding from the British to the lower classes, and the lower classes were more intent on democratizing American society than they were on separation from Great Britain. But if the entire Becker thesis was erroneous, as Becker's own evidence from sources suggested, then an interpretation of the Declaration as propaganda by a minority cannot be valid. Dispassionate research would have revealed to him that "the people" really meant the people, and that even most of those men who were reluctant to declare independence would have accepted reconciliation only on terms of what they interpreted the rights of Englishmen to be. But Becker at this stage of his career was not convinced, as he would be later, that history should be based on the dispassionate search for truth.

There is a further hint that the Declaration was propaganda in Becker's analysis of the omission of "Parliament" and the "rights of Englishmen" from the Declaration. Throughout the 'sixties and early 'seventies, he said, the main issues had revolved around the rights of Parliament and the rights of Englishmen, yet the Americans trained their guns on the king rather than on Parliament in the Declaration and grounded their rights in universal rights of man rather than specific rights of Englishmen. The Declaration was "superficially" concerned with the causes of the Revolution, Becker stated, but in reality it was solely concerned with a theory of government in general and of the British Empire in particular.[44]

Once again careful research would have revealed more accurate reasons for the omission of Parliament and the "rights of Englishmen" than Becker gave. At least from 1661 when Massachusetts declared that acts of Parliament were

[43] *Ibid.*, pp. 8-9.   [44] *Ibid.*, pp. 18-19.

confined by the four seas around the British Islands and did not extend to America, colonials in their legislatures had attempted to maintain the practice that an act of Parliament was not valid in a colony until it had been validated by a colonial act. For a long time, also, the colonists had considered the British Empire as a commonweath of nations. Each member had its own legislature for internal affairs, with the whole held together by the king. And while it is true that Americans for awhile conceded to Parliament the right to regulate empire trade, that concession gradually broke down when Parliamentary regulation began to hurt American interests. By 1776, most Americans had been pushed to the point of denying the right of Parliament to legislate for the colonies. Finally, since Americans already had "more than English liberties," and since their pleas for English liberties had fallen on the deaf ears of some Englishmen who had declared that English rights did not follow people around the world, there is no mystery about the omission of "rights of Englishmen" from the Declaration.

Fortunately, Becker unknowingly confirms this interpretation of the omissions in the Declaration. The words of the Declaration, as Becker shows, say that the king had joined with others, meaning Parliament, to subject Americans "to a jurisdiction foreign to our constitution and unacknowledged by our laws," and that the British had been warned "of attempts by their legislature to extend an unwarrantable jurisdiction over us." [45] Since the colonists had long attempted to confine Parliamentary acts to England, unless acknowledged by colonial laws, why would they recognize the authority of Parliament now that they were justifying separation from Britain? As for the "rights of Englishmen," Becker shows in his quoted statement from James Otis that Americans interpreted "rights of Englishmen" either as rights that Americans had or rights that Englishmen ought to have. When the English pointed out that the cities of Manchester and Sheffield were not represented in Parliament, Otis declared: "If these

[45] *Ibid.*, p. 19.

now so considerable places are not represented, they ought to be." [46] In short, to Americans the "rights of Englishmen" were what Americans already had and what Englishmen ought to have had.

Having used a chapter to develop the thesis that the Declaration was something of a propaganda piece which truly reflected neither the "facts" of the case nor the extent of American support for the American cause, Becker unwittingly repudiated his interpretation in the second chapter. This comes out in a controversy between John Adams and Thomas Jefferson over the content of the Declaration. Adams claimed that there was not an idea in the Declaration that had not been "hackneyed in Congress for two years before." Becker said that this was true, but it was an irrelevant criticism, for "the strength of the Declaration was precisely that it said what everyone was thinking." And Jefferson, himself, declared that the purpose of the Declaration was "to place before mankind the common sense of the subject" and to make the document "an expression of the American mind." [47] If these three statements by Adams, Becker, and Jefferson are accurate, then "the people" and the "facts" must really have been the people and the facts. There is no hint here that the grievances listed in the Declaration were not the ones accepted by the people, or that the Declaration was the work of a minority.

In addition to refuting his previously-developed interpretation of the Declaration, Becker, in discussing the impact of John Locke on the natural-rights philosophy of that document, also emasculated his thesis that the Revolution was primarily a class war to democratize American society. Becker said that "most Americans had absorbed Locke's works as a kind of political gospel" that governments exist for men, not men for governments, for all governments derive their just powers from the consent of the governed. Later Becker continued with this significant statement: "It was Locke's conclusion that seemed to the colonists sheer common sense, needing no argument at all. Locke did not need to convince

[46] *Ibid.*, p. 133.   [47] *Ibid.*, pp. 24-26.

the colonists because they were already convinced; and they were already convinced because they had long been living under governments which did, in a rough and ready way, conform to the kind of government for which Locke furnished a reasoned foundation. The colonists had never in fact lived under a government where 'one man . . . may do to all his subjects whatever he pleases.' They were accustomed to living under governments which proceeded, year by year, on a tacitly assumed compact between rulers and ruled, and which were in fact very largely dependent upon 'the consent of the governed.' How should the colonists not accept a philosophy, however clumsily argued, which assured them that their own governments, *with which they were well content,* were just the kind that God had designed men by nature to have!" [48]

"Their own governments, with which they were well content"! How could Becker do this to his famous thesis? How could he declare on the one hand that Americans were sharply divided by class interests over the kind of government to have and that the Revolution was primarily designed to democratize undemocratic American politics and society, and then on the other hand say that Americans were well content with their governments which rested on the consent of the governed? Without recognizing his inconsistencies, Becker was really saying that Americans already possessed a democratic society which they were determined to preserve against British imperial encroachments. In fact, on another page Becker confirmed this by saying that the underlying purpose which conditioned American action "was always the determination to be free. They felt that they had been free in fact, and that they ought therefore to be free in law." [49]

If Becker's Chapter II on natural rights demonstrated that the Becker thesis of class war for democracy was invalid, Chapter III on the theory of the British Empire confirms a thesis that Americans were attempting to preserve liberties that they already possessed, not to acquire new ones.[50] The

---

[48] *Ibid.,* pp. 27, 72-73. Italics added.
[49] *Ibid.,* p. 133.   [50] *Ibid.,* ch. III.

American Revolution was perhaps unique among revolutions, for most liberal revolutions — and the American Revolution was a liberal revolution — have had as their objective the acquisition rather than the preservation of liberal rights. It is what is preserved, not the act of preserving, that determines whether the Revolution was liberal or conservative.

The next two chapters on drafting the Declaration and on its literary qualities, while interesting in themselves and doubtless relevant to Becker's subject as he saw it, do not add much to our understanding of various interpretations of the Revolution. Yet to the extent to which these chapters contribute to any interpretation, they tend to demolish Becker's own thesis. For example, he said that the reader might not believe that all men are created equal, that they are endowed with the rights of life, liberty, and the pursuit of happiness, and that governments are established to protect these rights; but Jefferson and his contemporaries believed these things.[51] Jefferson and his contemporaries, it should be added, believed in the strength of the type of society to which they were accustomed, and except for slavery, it was not the class-structured society that Becker depicted.

There is also in these two chapters evidence that the Revolution was designed to preserve a social structure rather than to transform it in the direction of democracy. Jefferson, said Becker, built the Declaration around the idea that "the colonists were not rebels against established political authority, but a free people maintaining long established and imprescriptible rights against a usurping king."[52] The colonists were rebelling "because the king by repeated and deliberate actions had endeavored to usurp an absolute authority over them contrary to every natural right and to long established custom."[53] And a story, told by Franklin to Jefferson and included by Becker, tells us what kind of a society they were trying to preserve — one in which "an apprentice Hatter, having served out his time, was about to open a shop for himself."[54]

[51] *Ibid.,* pp. 201-02.   [52] *Ibid.,* p. 203.   [53] *Ibid.,* p. 204.   [54] *Ibid.,* p. 208.

Becker was correct in pointing out the hypocrisy in Jefferson's early draft of the Declaration in which he castigated the king for instigating and perpetuating slavery, for as Becker indicated, Jefferson and others owned slaves.[55] Yet even here there is an element of truth in Jefferson's accusations against the king. Doubtless there were colonists who were only too happy to deprive Negroes of *their* life, liberty, and pursuit of happiness by purchasing them as slaves. But there were other colonists who took the long view that the country would benefit more from self-motivated free white workers than it would from unmotivated slaves. What the colonists would have done about extinguishing slavery had they been free to do so is a moot question, but it is true that they attempted legislation to stop the importation of slaves and that this legislation was negatived by the king.

Becker's final chapter, "The Philosophy of the Declaration in the Ninteenth [sic] Century," tells us more about Becker and his misunderstanding of the American Revolution than it does about the Declaration of Independence. The general tenor of the chapter is that the Declaration gave the United States a foundation that was indissolubly tied to a human-rights theory of politics which, if valid at all, was valid not only for Americans but for all men. But the sad aspect in Becker's eyes was that no sooner had this human-rights philosophy been declared than it began to be eroded away to nothing by other philosophies and practices. The natural-rights philosophy, he said, is to be found in the early state constitutions but not in the Federal Constitution. Then successively came the idea that *free white* men only had natural rights, that rights were something to be earned rather than inherited, that men had historic rights rather than natural rights, that the might of the majority determined human rights, and that social Darwinism or the survival of the fittest fixed men's position in society. All of this added up, Becker said, to the gradual extinction of the liberal natural-rights-of-

[55] *Ibid.,* pp. 212-13.

man doctrine which is the foundation of the Declaration of Independence.[56]

Becker rightfully made much of the natural-rights philosophy as the cornerstone of the Declaration, but here it seems that both Jefferson and Becker were in error. Jefferson listed the natural rights as life, liberty, and the pursuit of happiness, which Becker accepted, but these were not the customary natural rights as they appeared to men in the eighteenth century. There are literally thousands of references to natural rights in the sources, but almost without exception these included life, liberty, and property, not happiness. What prompted Jefferson to substitute happiness for property has never been explained, but perhaps Americans associated happiness with property, just as antipoverty people do at the present time. In any event, Jefferson's version of natural rights did not raise any questions at the time, even though many historians seem to have forgotten that property was once one of man's natural rights. Perhaps Becker, who was anticapital in his outlook, preferred Jefferson's version of natural rights to that accepted generally in the eighteenth century, but this tells us more about Becker than it does about the Revolutionary generation.

Jefferson was undoubtedly one of Becker's favorite historical figures, but Becker forgot to indicate that there was not much difference between Jefferson and other Southerners who later interpreted natural rights of man to mean only free white men. As he demonstrated in his *Notes on Virginia,* Jefferson was a mild white supremacist who did not believe that the races were equal in capacity and who, though he opposed slavery in principle, kept his own slaves and desired that freed Negroes should be transported out of the country to avoid racial mixture. Whatever Jefferson said in the Declaration, in the context of the America of 1776, he, too, really meant free white men.

It is equally true, as Becker indicated, that former Massachusetts governor Thomas Hutchinson castigated the Declara-

[56] *Ibid.*, ch. VI.

tion on the ground that Americans proclaimed all men equal yet held slaves, but two aspects of this criticism should be noted. Hutchinson, who had thrown his lot with Great Britain, did not mention British opposition toward any American efforts to eliminate or restrict slavery. Furthermore, Hutchinson's criticism was based on the discrepancy of rights between white men and black men, not between different classes of white men, as Becker had done in his thesis. On many occasions, Hutchinson had pointed out that colonial society, except for slavery and whatever restraints the British could impose, was middle class and democratic, with Americans enjoying far more rights than Englishmen did.

Other points in the Declaration discussed by Becker also tend to refute the Becker thesis. Governor Johnstone, who did not approve of American independence, said in England that the Americans "were driven to the measure by our vigorous persecution of them," thus indicating that the struggle was really for home rule rather than who should rule at home. And Charles James Fox declared that the Americans "had done no more than the English had done against James II," which has similar connotations.[57]

Becker's discussion of French reaction to the Declaration was a further refutation of the Becker thesis. Frenchmen were enthusiastic and as Becker said, "democratic impudence" of the Americans could hardly go further than to ask a French monarch to approve a rebellion based on the theory that governments derive their just powers from the consent of the governed. To Frenchmen looking forward to the regeneration of their own country, "America appeared as a striking confirmation of their hopes, possessing all the importance of a concrete illustration of their imagined state of nature."[58] In short, America in the eyes of Frenchmen was already something of the heavenly city of the eighteenth-century philosophers, and would become even more so after it had cast off its British shackles.

Becker's view, that the "sublime truths enshrined in the

[57] *Ibid.*, p. 228.   [58] *Ibid.*, pp. 229-33.

Declaration of Independence" became "fallacies" and "glittering generalities" to be rejected by later generations, is based on an erroneous interpretation of natural rights. Given the democratic nature of American society in 1776 and the natural-rights philosophy as a basis for government, it was only to be expected that the United States would continue on a democratic course. But the natural-rights philosophy that it used involved both human rights and property rights, if one wants to make the distinction. James Madison believed that men were entitled to life and liberty, but in Federalist No. X he was also adhering to natural rights when he said that men had different abilities which resulted in the acquisition of different kinds and amounts of property, and that one of the important functions of government was the protection of these different capacities of men to acquire property.[59]

Apparently because of Becker's disillusionment due to the war, he deplored the one article of Jefferson's philosophy which Americans have accepted, that government rests on the consent of the governed, and which they have erected into an article of faith in the form of majority rule. He said that "the simplest, the naive, way to justify majority rule was of course to fall back upon force — the majority has the power, and therefore the right." [60] But this appears to be part of Becker's postwar disillusionment with the majority, and certainly a contradiction of his thesis which obviously approved of a revolution to democratize American society. If democracy means something approximating one man one vote, there can be, as Lincoln said, only two kinds of government, minority and majority. Surely Becker was not advocating a return to minority government. If not, then the majority must rule under conditions which set up constitutions, courts, and other checks and balances in an attempt to ensure that what the

[59] *Ibid.*, pp. 233-34. In his *Second Treatise on Government*, Locke contended that the main function of government was the protection of property, but by property he meant life, liberty, and estate.

[60] *Ibid.*, pp. 234-35. Locke also coupled together government based on consent and majority rule founded on natural rights.

majority does is also right for all. Unfortunately for Becker's apparent aversion to majority rule, progressives after 1900 had been the most ardent advocates of the kind of legislation that would make majority rule effective.

In deploring majority rule, Becker tended, I think, to overemphasize the revolutionary aspects of the natural-rights philosophy and to underestimate its democratic aspects.[61] If the Declaration provided a philosophy of government which could justify revolution, it also laid the basis for a democratic government, the chief virtues of which would be that differences could be compromised without resort to revolution. If democracy has any virtues, certainly the one that change can be achieved without revolution must rank high. Becker appears to deplore the fact that as the world became progressively more democratic, it became at the same time increasingly antirevolutionary. But this was only natural, for the chief virtue of democracy is that it permits change by eliminating the need for revolution. In this country the Civil War came, not because democracy had ceased to be valid, but because men were not willing to accept democratic decisions. Given the widespread property ownership and the emphasis on property under the natural-rights philosophy, it is difficult to envision any other solution to the slavery question except compensated emancipation if the democratic process had been allowed to work its way, a solution which would have been better and cheaper than war.[62] But accommodation through democratic processes is just as inherent in the Declaration as is change through revolution, for once government is based on the consent of the governed, change can be effected through concensus.

If the philosophy of the Declaration justified revolution in order that men might establish governments based on the consent of the governed, does revolution have any place in a society which already has a government based on consent?

[61] *Ibid.,* pp. 237-40.
[62] For Becker's discussion of slavery and the Declaration, see *ibid.,* pp. 240ff.

This question arose in Shays' Rebellion, it involved aboli-
tionists and southern secessionists at the time of the Civil War,
and of course it is still with us in the form of demonstrations
and draft-card burning. With the disintegration of society into
complete individualism, what happens to men's natural rights
of life, liberty, and property — or even the pursuit of happiness? How can there be government "based on the consent of
the governed" if each individual is allowed to judge the
validity of measures passed by this government? Does the
reactionary have the same right as the radical to flaunt majority decisions and resort to violence, and if so, what happens
to the democratic system? One must always remember that
the Declaration of Independence came into existence as a
protest *against an arbitrary government,* not against one based
on the consent of the majority.

Unlike the revolutionary French Declaration of the Rights
of Man, the American Declaration of Independence never had
to survive a baptism of extremism and the resulting conservative reaction. Already a country which internally measured up to a great extent to the natural-rights philosophy,
which had governments that rested on the consent of the
governed and with which the people, as Becker once said,
"were well content," the Americans did not experience the
blood and fire of the Jacobin Reign of Terror, the guillotine,
and Napoleon. If the Declaration influenced other countries,
as it did Latin America, it was not carried there by American
armies as the French Declaration of Rights was carried to
other European countries. Approved by men of many religions
because many religions already existed together peacefully in
this country, the Declaration of Independence never had to be
defended against charges of atheism and anarchy.[63]

Unlike the Declaration of the Rights of Man, also, the
Declaration of Independence was not a "standing invitation
to insurrection and a persistent cause of anarchy." Insurrection could occur only under certain conditions when government violated man's unalienable rights, but always the as-

[63] *Ibid.,* pp. 256-58.

sumption was that there would be a government, not anarchy. Government was established initially to protect man's natural rights, government violation of those rights justified revolution, but then the people were to set up a new government to guarantee their safety and happiness. Nowhere does the Declaration imply that anarchy is to replace government. And it should be noted that the Declaration was primarily one of independence, with rights of man thrown in as a justification, not one setting forth the rights of man.[64]

Once more Becker emphasized the importance of history in fostering or retarding social change. On many occasions, he had pointed out that men would not look forward to the good society of the future as long as they were looking backward toward the golden age of the past. To Becker, of course, the aim of history was the good society of collective democracy in the future, for he had once said that the aim of history was the fostering of a fruitful radicalism. Here he noted the reverse: "To prevent the world from changing too rapidly, nothing is more effective than to look with admiration on the past." [65] Until the last few years of his life, when circumstances greatly altered his attitude toward American democracy, Becker was not one to look back with admiration on the past.

Becker closed his discussion of the Declaration with the expression of a social philosophy which explains why he was the darling of the Old Left and still has something to say to the New Left. Disillusioned by what he believed to be the demise of the liberal natural-rights-of-man philosophy as expressed in the Declaration, he saw the liberal gradually being smothered under the social philosophy of historic rights which "left the individual more diminished than ever, and more helplessly bound." As a result, he said, militant socialists had abandoned the old revolutionary doctrine to be found in the Declaration of Independence and the Rights of Man. In its place they found a new higher law "in natural law reconceived in terms of Marxian doctrine of the class conflict." [66] Becker's account

[64] *Ibid.,* p. 257.   [65] *Ibid.,* p. 266.   [66] *Ibid.,* pp. 276-77.

of the decline or demise of the once laudable natural-rights philosophy from 1776 to the present left little of value in Robinson's idea of history as progress.

What, then, was left for the liberal? If society had abandoned his cause for historic rights and social Darwinism, the individual must make peace with his own conscience and act accordingly, regardless of democracy and majority rule. Said Becker: "To ask whether the natural-rights philosophy of the Declaration of Independence is true or false is essentially a meaningless question. When honest men are impelled to withdraw their allegiance to the established law or custom of the community, still more when they are persuaded that such law or custom is too iniquitous to be longer tolerated, they seek for some principle more generally valid, some 'law' of higher authority, than the established law or custom of the community. To this higher law or more generally valid principle they then appeal in justification of actions which the community condemns as immoral or criminal. They formulate the law or principle in such a way that it is, or seems to them to be, rationally defensible. To them it is 'true' because it brings their actions into harmony with a rightly ordered universe, and enables them to think of themselves as having chosen the nobler part, as having withdrawn from a corrupt world in order to serve God or Humanity or a force that makes for the highest good." [67]

Carried to its logical conclusion, this kind of individualistic philosophy expressed by Becker must inevitably lead to complete anarchy and the disintegration of the democratic system — a system which was itself the goal of the natural-rights philosophy — or to some kind of military dictatorship. The New Left could hardly find a better statement of its philosophy, for such a philosophy leaves little room for any kind of government, democratic or otherwise.

The original Declaration, however, cannot easily be interpreted as the torch of revolution, anarchy, and individualism that Becker implies. It justified to the world why Americans

[67] *Ibid.,* pp. 277-78.

believed they were entitled to independence, and in doing so, it implied that in a world where some men did not honor the natural rights of other men, war was a necessary recourse. It also said that to secure men's natural rights, which for most people meant property as well as life, liberty, and the pursuit of happiness, governments were instituted, deriving their just powers from the consent of the governed. If government violated these ends, *the people* could alter or abolish the government and set up a new government, "laying its foundation on such principles, and organizing its powers in such form" as seemed most likely to promote their safety and happiness. The implication was that the process was not an individual one but something that "the people" did collectively, and that once established by "the people," the government would be obeyed until "the people" wanted to change it. Since the term "the people" had always meant in colonial society an expression of the will of the majority, one must assume that this was the process by which majority will would be determined. There is nothing in Jefferson's statement that each individual could decide whether to obey the government, although again there is the implication that the individual had a right to win the majority to his point of view if he could.

Reviews of *The Declaration of Independence* did little to clarify what Becker had done and failed to do in the book. One reviewer applauded the fact that a book on American history was written "by one whose university chair is European history," apparently without realizing that all of Becker's many books had been written on American history and none as yet on European history. The review merely summarized without criticism, ending with Becker's conclusion that the natural-rights philosophy as found in the Declaration was a humane and engaging faith, advocating toleration instead of persecution, good will instead of hate, peace instead of war.[68] James Truslow Adams, who followed Becker's interpretation of early American history, said this of Becker and the New History: "Among the leaders of the new school none has done

[68] Caroline E. Margill, *Post Literary Review,* October 4, 1922.

more valuable work in bringing its harvest before the public than Professor Becker. Always readable and always scholarly, his books are justly entitled to the widest of audiences." [69]

At times the Becker who emerged from World War I gave the impression of being two distinct characters not always in harmony with each other. Disillusioned with the idea that progress was inevitable and that the instrument for its achievement would be the common man, he nevertheless looked forward to a heavenly city on earth in the form of a collective democracy whose chief beneficiary would be the common man. If the vehicle for progress shifted from the common man to an elite, as it apparently did with both Becker and Robinson, the better world of the future would presumably benefit the common man at the expense of the elite. At the same time World War I, if anything, strengthened Becker's philosophy of subjective relativism to the point where he virtually eliminated facts in history. And finally, he believed that the better world of social democracy would be achieved, to the extent that the historian had any influence, through the use of a subjective relativism which would emphasize the evils of the past that men would look to the heavenly city of the future.

Two books, published in 1922 at the end of this period of Becker's disillusionment, gave further indication, as James Truslow Adams had put it, that the "harvest" of the new school (even, we might add, including its contradictions) was reaching an ever-widening audience. Step by step the Becker-Beard-Schlesinger interpretation was inching its way into the mainstream of American history.

The first book, *New Viewpoints in American History* written by Schlesinger himself, merely summarized the New History or progressive interpretation of the Revolution and Constitution by Becker, Beard, and Schlesinger. Taking the Becker thesis that the main thread of American history was the democratization of American society and politics, Schlesinger pictured the colonial society that produced the Revolution as something that good liberals would not approve. Social

[69] *New Republic,* November 22, 1922.

and political life was dominated by the "well born," the "ruling class," an aristocracy of birth and manners resembling the aristocracy of England, with a restricted electorate and disproportionate representation their chief weapons. Said Schlesinger: "As a result of these practices, the mass of the population was excluded from participation in the government, to the great glory of the aristocracy."[70]

But when he reached the Revolution, Schlesinger, who had apparently accepted Becker's social revolution in his earlier book, *The Colonial Merchants* (1918), was undecided as to whether or not that social revolution had really materialized. As the Revolution approached, he said, the rule of the privileged orders was being seriously threatened, for town artisans and mechanics, though legally excluded from the franchise, "were galvanized into group-consciousness" and played a role in mass meetings. Then came this curious interpretation of the Declaration of Independence. The Declaration was the first great official denunciation of aristocratic rule in American history, said Schlesinger, implying that it was part of the social revolution. Almost immediately, however, he changed his mind and declared that the aristocrats who joined the revolutionary movement had no intention of surrendering their special privileges simply because they had joined the "unlettered masses" in opposing Great Britain. In fact, Schlesinger insisted, the signers of the Declaration had no notion of setting forth a program of domestic reform. Neither at that time nor for many years later were all persons equal before the law. Slaves and women were inferior, while a "great majority" of white men were excluded from political participation and educational advantages. The American aristocracy could take pride in the fact that it retained its privileged position amidst a people who, notwithstanding fetters and handicaps, possessed at that time greater freedom than any other people in the world.[71]

[70] Arthur M. Schlesinger, Sr., *New Viewpoints in American History* (New York, 1922). pp. 73-75.
[71] *Ibid.,* pp. 75-78.

Indecision and contradiction about social revolution also marked Schlesinger's discussion of the Confederation and Constitution. Aristocrats continued to dominate during the Confederation, he declared, even though events gave them moments of fear, and the net result was the vindication of the wellborn to positions of leadership and public trust. State constitutions, despite the philosophy of the Declaration, were based on the principles that governments derive their just powers, not from the consent of the governed, but from taxpayers and men of property, for these constitutions imposed property restrictions on voters and even higher restrictions on officeholders. On second thought, however, Schlesinger said that the chief manifestation of antiaristocratic feeling was the abolition of entail and primogeniture, and "in a number of states the party of the masses gained control of the government and assailed wealth" through passage of paper money and debtor laws. Events demonstrated to the aristocracy "the incapacity of the masses for self government," and with a zeal animated by despair, the aristocracy turned every energy to recovering its lost ascendency in public affairs — an ascendency that he previously said was never lost.[72]

Schlesinger then out-Bearded Beard in his view of the Constitution. In spite of saying that the people of this country enjoyed greater freedom than any other people in the world, and regardless of numerous quotations from the Constitutional Convention debates to the effect that American society was very democratic, Schlesinger insisted that the Constitution was "calculated to keep the plain people in a subordinate place and to assure political power to men of substance and quality." Those aristocrats who had not defected to the British, he declared, were later instrumental in restoring the "caste" idea in American life through the adoption of the Constitution.[73] Schlesinger never explained how a "caste" could exist among the freest people in the world.

The second book, *The Causes of the War of Independence* by Claude H. Van Tyne, included the progressive interpreta-

---

[72] *Ibid.*, pp. 79-80.   [73] *Ibid.*, pp. 78, 80-81.

tion but did so seemingly as an afterthought. For more than four hundred pages, Van Tyne pictured colonial America as a land of great opportunity, middle class and democratic, with few ingredients for class conflict and many reasons for British-American friction. But then Van Tyne suddenly reverted to such phrases as mob rule, radicals, leaders of the masses, and voteless laborers and artisans. The colonial masses "could no longer be controlled by reverence for the high born," he declared, and the upper classes "could no longer rule without question their social inferiors. . . . Thus, in 1774, came the climax in the struggle between rich and poor, East and West, those with the vote and those who were voteless, between privilege and the welfare of the common man." Merchants might welcome lower-class support against Britain, "but the price, a right to vote and to hold office" was too great, Van Tyne continued, and such merchants "were forced to abandon the colonial cause rather than try to win at the cost of the loss of privilege." [74]

Without ever recognizing the contradiction, Van Tyne, as Schlesinger had done, presented the paradox of bitter class conflict among a people who were the freest in the world. In fact, Van Tyne's last chapter was entitled "The Freest Peoples Were the First to Revolt," but the freest people in the world revolting against the restrictions of British imperialism which would have eliminated much of that freedom is quite a different proposition from the freest people in the world engaged in internecine class warfare. Van Tyne was right about the freest people being the first to revolt, but he was right for the wrong reasons. Instead of condemning the British for attempting to restrict American liberties, Van Tyne, who was a strong Anglophile, said that the American Revolution was really "one of the glories of British history rather than a blot upon her fair political record," and that Britain should be praised rather than blamed because Englishmen in America

[74] Claude H. Van Tyne, *The Causes of the War of Independence* (Houghton Mifflin Company, New York, 1922), pp. 424-26. Quotations used by permission of Houghton Mifflin Company.

insistently demanded full enjoyment of those liberties which England had fostered beyond any other country in the world. The truth was, however, that people in America looked upon themselves as Americans more than as Englishmen, and believed that their "more than British liberties" had been gained in spite of, rather than because of, Great Britain. Few Americans in 1776 would have interpreted the American Revolution as Van Tyne did in 1922.[75]

Thus the class-oriented but contradictory progressive history of Becker, Beard, and Schlesinger was gaining momentum, with the impetus in this period being provided especially by Becker, with the help of Schlesinger and Van Tyne.

[75] *Ibid.,* ch. XVIII.

VI. TRIUMPH OF SUBJECTIVE RELATIVISM, 1922-1932

> "We are thus of that ancient and honor-
> able company of wise men of the tribe,
> of bards and story-tellers and minstrels,
> of soothsayers and priests, to whom in
> successive ages has been entrusted the
> keeping of the useful myths. Let not the
> harmless, necessary word 'myth' put us
> out of countenance. In the history of
> history a myth is a once valid but now
> discarded version of the human story, as
> our now valid versions will in due course
> be relegated to the category of discarded
> myths."
>
> — CARL BECKER, 1931

THE ten years following publication of *The Declaration* witnessed the rise of Becker and his philosophy of history to
a position of preeminence among American historians. It was
not a productive period in terms of books, for Becker published
no books during this time except a high school textbook in
European history, but there was a maturing of his thinking
which can be found in his letters, book reviews, and papers.
A conservative period of prosperity which ended in the stock
market crash and depression also culminated in Becker's selection as president of the American Historical Association and
his famous presidential address, "Every Man His Own Historian." Three threads are clearly discernible — a skeptical
attitude toward the abilities of the common man, confused
thinking about early American history, and by far the most
important of all, a complete surrender to subjective relativism.

In print, Becker continued to appear as the liberal advocate
of progress for the common man, even though he did not have
much confidence in the masses. In a favorable review of Charles

Beard's *Cross Currents in European History,* Becker called Beard an exasperated cynic and warm-hearted friend of humanity, a hard-headed idealist and sworn foe of all that is stupid, selfish, disingenuous, soft, comforting, or merely well-intentioned. Beard was not tender, Becker continued, toward people who were wrong-headed in the right direction or right-headed in the wrong direction; and though he was perfectly aware of human folly, he never quite lost faith in human nature.[1]

In his private correspondence, however, Becker might easily have been mistaken for a conservative in his attitude toward the common run of men. To William E. Dodd, a fellow progressive, Becker expressed the view that the masses did not think consistently about important ideas — few people think with their heads; most think with their emotions. Becker did not see history quite as much in terms of conscious class struggle of conflicting economic interests as Dodd did, for people thought little of social and political ends and their minds were "far too muddled to carry on any such struggle for more than a short time." [2]

Becker still seemed to be caught between the dictates of his heart and his head. In a letter of praise for Felix Frankfurter's stand on the Sacco-Vanzetti case, he said, "I admire your valiant championship of the oppressed, your courageous defense of lost causes, and only wish I had the generous spirit and intellectual optimism which inspires your actions." [3]

Becker was undergoing some of the same difficulties experienced by his old mentor, James Harvey Robinson. The problem was how to remain a "friend of humanity" without having much respect for most of humanity's members. Progress implied the perfectibility of man, but at this juncture of their careers, neither Becker nor Robinson expressed much confidence that the common man, the mass of humanity, could be perfected to any great extent. While still concerned about

[1] *The Nation,* November 22, 1922.
[2] Becker to Dodd, c. 1922, in *Detachment,* pp. 79-81.
[3] Becker to Frankfurter, c. 1927, Becker Papers.

the good of humanity, both Becker and Robinson looked to the elite as the only way to realize the heavenly city on earth.

Robinson's views, which continued to influence Becker, are to be found at this time in *The Humanizing of Knowledge,* published in 1923. The big problem, according to Robinson, was how to free men's minds in all fields through application of the scientific method, yet how to humanize knowledge when scientific method had achieved its position precisely because it had become dehumanized. Science provides the most accurate and best authenticated information that we have, Robinson declared, but while scientific information is accepted in material things, it immediately encounters fierce opposition from tradition, religion, and folklore when applied to human affairs. Attitudes toward evolution and birth control were only two of many outstanding examples.[4]

But there was also the problem of the masses and the elite that had previously troubled Becker. Apparently Robinson had abandoned his earlier idea that most of what we call human nature is due to environment rather than to heredity. Like Becker, he now believed that progress could be achieved only by the elite, the few curious minds, the creative men who widened the gap between men and animals. The masses, on the other hand, were generally indifferent to scientific truth, took many mysteries for granted, believed things that would not stand scrutiny, or accepted whatever suited them without regard for the "truth." Since scientific information affected the lives of the masses, however, it was dangerous to allow the masses to retain their old beliefs in the face of new knowledge. Somehow the masses had to be dragged into the modern world.[5]

Robinson's solution was general education which would both humanize science for the good of mankind and permit scientific methods to be applied to humanistic studies. One of the biggest problems was the elimination of the road block of

[4] James Harvey Robinson, *The Humanizing of Knowledge* (New York, 1923), pp. 1-61.
[5] *Ibid.*, pp. 62-63.

religion and its replacement by human intelligence as the most profound and secure source of knowledge. But any attack on religion would involve conservatives who controlled the establishment, excluded controversial topics from class-rooms, and placed restraints on teachers and writers, forcing them to use subterfuge in their teaching if they wanted to discuss liberal or controversial topics.[6]

Although Robinson appeared as the advocate of scientific method in the study of human problems, he was still not willing to abandon subjective relativism. He cited H. G. Wells' *Outline of History* as an example of humanizing the past, but if Robinson really believed that his heavenly city on earth should be founded on *truth,* the subjective relativism of Wells was hardly the place to begin. Robinson also thought that scholars should study some phase of human interest rather than a field of scientific investigation, and he suggested topics such as the theory of human conduct called "behavior-ism" or the theory of knowledge called "pragmatism." [7] Thus Robinson would accept subjective relativism, behaviorism, and pragmatism as the philosophical foundation of his own heavenly city. Both Robinson and Becker during this period were experiencing difficulties in finding an acceptable basis for their utopias of the future; and one of the intriguing aspects of the Becker story, as we shall see, was his final solu-tion of the problem.

As for the Becker thesis about the Revolution, Becker con-tinued the contradiction of asserting it on the one hand and denying it on the other. The colonialist, Charles McLean Andrews, had raised some questions about Becker's use of "democracy" in his books. Did the people themselves mean "democracy" when they spoke of government by the people? Andrews planned to write a book with a different view, but Becker did not believe that Andrews had anything new. Then Becker went on to say that Andrews' discussion about whether the people really wanted democracy in 1776 struck Becker as

[6] *Ibid.,* pp. 65-67.
[7] *Ibid.,* pp. 85-87, 114.

futile because it missed the point that democracy and aristocracy, like war, were not objects in themselves which people
want or do not want.[8] Yet the Becker thesis was based on the
very assumption that democracy was exactly what the people
wanted in 1776, a fact which made the Revolution primarily
an internal class conflict.

The contradictions of the Becker thesis also appeared in
Becker's analysis of George Bancroft as a historian. In a review
of one of Bassett's books, Becker first branded Bancroft as a
bad historian because his militant patriotism and enthusiasm
for democracy led him to interpret the facts in a "glaringly
prejudiced way." Professional historians well understood that
Bancroft's history was interesting to read but unsafe to follow,
Becker continued, for Bancroft was a prejudiced historian
whose chief defect was his lack of ideas, or at least lack of
fresh and novel ideas. Bancroft was now read, not for his
history, but for his style. But then Becker reversed himself by
insisting that Bancroft's style was abominable while his chief
merit was his scholarship. Bancroft's careful investigation and
exceptional accuracy made his books still useful to students of
the American Revolution, said Becker, for Bancroft had
learned from Heeren that "the first duty of the historian is to
be sure of his facts." [9]

This seeming paradox of Bancroft as both a poor and a
good historian actually stemmed from the contradictions in
the Becker thesis. Bancroft's evidence and interpretation added
up to a unique American colonial society characterized by a
great deal of economic opportunity, political democracy, and
religious freedom. To Bancroft, British imperialism and
British tyranny threatened this democratic society, the Revolution was a fight to preserve democracy, not to achieve it,
and thus the issue was really "home rule" rather than "who
should rule at home." Becker's evidence, when he used evidence, substantiated Bancroft's interpretation, but of course

---

[8] Becker to Dodd, c. 1922, in *Detachment*, pp. 79-81.
[9] Review of John Spencer Bassett, *The Middle Group of American His-torians*, in *Everyman*, pp. 132-42.

Becker had imposed a class-ridden society and class conflict on evidence which did not support his interpretation. Becker himself would eventually come around to Bancroft's point of view, and certainly anyone who adhered to subjective relativism should not have condemned Bancroft for being prejudiced, for Becker assumed that all written history could be nothing else but a reflection of prejudice.

In fact, Becker's very next attempt to write American history proved that Bancroft was right and Becker was wrong. In "The Spirit of '76," a purely fictitious concoction similar to the literary device used in *The Eve of the Revolution,* the main character, Jeremiah Wynkoop, was "of that considerable class of substantial men" who did as much as any other class of men to enable the colonies "to maintain their liberties against British tyranny." Becker also pictured the thirteen colonies as "the most fortunate and the freest countries in the world — thirteen communities living in peace and content, happily without kings, neither burdened with an idle aristocracy nor menaced by a depraved populace, with a press uncensored, and many religious faiths deprived of the power of persecution and long habituated to the spirit of toleration." The New York assembly was "chosen by the free suffrages of the people" and Wynkoop denied that Britain had any right "to legislate in restraint of American liberties." [10]

Having introduced "evidence" that contradicted his thesis, Becker, still using the novelist's license, reversed himself by attempting to impose class conflict on his open and free society. After previously showing that popular antagonism was directed against British measures which threatened American freedom, Becker now injected violence due to class antagonism. Livingston and Colden were pictured as men of substance and standing and thus the populace or people aimed at the "class privileges," as one character said, of the class that always had, and he trusted always would, govern the province. And again one of his actors dragged in the dual revolution by saying that "we must keep the province loyal to the cause, and we must

<hr />

[10] "The Spirit of '76," *Everyman,* pp. 48-56.

prevent the leveling ideas of the New Englanders from gaining the ascendency here." [11] Becker did not point out that Livingston, ostensibly one of the "aristocrats," was, in fact, one of the popular leaders in the American cause, and, with Jefferson, John Adams, Benjamin Franklin, and Roger Sherman, one of the architects of the Declaration of Independence.

For the most part, however, Becker wrote little history during the ten-year period, concentrating his efforts mainly on the meaning of history. By 1925, he was placed on a list of "New Historians," which included Robinson, Turner, Beard, Schlesinger, Dodd, and many others, but he rejected this label. In doing so, he cited Robinson's admonition to the historian to "turn on the past and exploit it in the interest of advance," called the universities "those entrenched citadels of conservatism," and declared that what the historian needed was intelligence, literary ability, experience with men and things, insight into human conduct, and knowledge of the subject matter first of all.[12] It was good advice except for the fact that it ran counter to Becker's often-stated concept that history really centered in the historian.

Turner also continued to exert an important influence on Becker's thinking during this period. Becker was writing an essay on Turner, and when a former Turner student, Allyn A. Young, spoke at a retirement dinner at Harvard for Turner in 1925, Becker asked for a summary of Young's remarks. Young said that Turner was a presentist — every historian worthy of the name is a student of the present as well as the past, and the past has no meaning or significance for us except as a background or as an integral part of the present. Turner, he said, was much interested in the social life of his own generation, and thus his history was not only past politics but present politics, present economics, present sociology. Turner made large contributions to American history because

[11] *Ibid.*, pp. 56-57, 72.
[12] Review of Harry Elmer Barnes, *The New History and the Social Studies*, in *Saturday Review*, August 15, 1925; also in *Detachment*, pp. 35-40.

he asked new and significant questions, a process which required genius.[13]

Young also used Turner as an example of the idea that the historian is an artist rather than a scientist. Out of the infinite number of sequences of events that run back into the past, the historian selects and portrays those which seem to him significant. His history is a matter of values, not mechanics, for he paints and reconstructs the past as he sees it. His problem is not so much that of recording and articulating as it is of selecting, valuing, and coloring. Turner was "a very great artist," said Young, for he conceived the pageant of our national history in a new way and recorded it in new colors. It convinced scholars, not through the process of reason, but in precisely the same way that a great novel or picture is convincing.[14]

That Turner and Becker were thinking along similar lines can be seen from a paper, "What Are Historical Facts?" which Becker gave at the American Historical Association meeting in Rochester in 1926. In this paper, Becker emphasized the present as the only vantage point for the historian and again virtually eliminated objective facts from history.[15]

Becker began his paper by pointing out that people, including historians, have an erroneous notion of what historical facts are. They have the idea that historical facts, like bricks, are something that the historian digs out, either to use himself or for some sociologist or economist to use. But the historical fact, like cause, liberty, or progress, is a word, a symbol, not something hard and concrete like a brick. Historical events themselves are gone, never to be repeated or recovered, so the historian can deal only with statements or evidence that the event actually occurred. It is the affirmation about the event, not the event itself, said Becker, that constitutes the historical fact.[16]

---

[13] Allyn A. Young to Becker, October 3, 1925, Becker Papers.

[14] Ibid.

[15] "What Are Historical Facts?," in Detachment, pp. 41-64. Quotations used by permission of Cornell University Press.

[16] Ibid.

Taking the philosophical idealist's point of view that reality exists only in the mind, Becker answered the question of where historical facts are by saying that they are in the historian's mind, or in somebody's mind, or they are nowhere. Historical facts that lie dead in the sources cease to be historical facts and can do no good or evil in the world. They become historical facts, capable of doing work, of making a difference, only when someone brings them alive in the mind by means of images of the actual occurrence. Said Becker: "For this reason I say that the historical fact is in someone's mind, or it is nowhere, because when it is in no one's mind it lies in the records inert, incapable of making a difference in the world." [17]

And finally, to the question of when is the historical fact, Becker answered: "If the historical fact is present, imaginatively, in someone's mind, then it is now, a part of the present." Men have thought of the world of history as part of the external world and of historical facts as actual events, but "In truth, the actual past is gone, and the world of history is an intangible world, re-created *imaginatively,* and present in our minds." [18]

Thus a combination of presentism, pragmatism, relativism, and subjectivism made anything like objective scientific history impossible. As Becker said, he had taught for twenty years that there was no possibility that a historian could "present all the facts and let them speak for themselves." One historian will necessarily choose certain affirmations and relate them in certain ways while rejecting other affirmations and ways of relating them. Other historians "will necessarily make a different choice." Why? Said Becker: "The purpose he has in mind will determine that. And so the purpose he has in mind will determine the precise meaning which he derives from the event. The event itself, the facts, do not say anything, do not impose any meaning. It is the historian who speaks, who imposes a meaning." The historian "cannot eliminate the

---

[17] *Ibid.,* p. 49.
[18] *Ibid.,* pp. 50, 52. Italics mine.

personal equation," for the universe speaks to us only in response to our purposes, and the constructions we put on things are "only such as are found most convenient for some human need or purpose." [19]

For all of these reasons, according to Becker, historians, unlike scientists, could never agree on the meaning and significance of historical facts. The personal equation meant that the history of any event was never precisely the same for different people, and thus "every generation writes the same history in a new way and puts upon it a new construction." The actual event contributes something to our image of the past, but there is always "our own present purposes, desires, prepossessions, and prejudices," all of which enter into the process of knowing history. Historiography, the history of history, is thus the story "of what successive generations have imagined the past to be like." [20]

For Becker, the personal element also meant that present, past, and future all become inexorably intermingled. Just as the present influences our idea of the past, so our idea of the past influences the present. If it is true that the present is the product of all the past, it is equally true to say that the past is the product of all the present. We built our conceptions of the past partly out of our present needs and purposes, but since purposes involve the future, the past becomes a kind of screen upon which we project our vision of the future.[21]

And finally, Becker brought his philosophy of history down to the common man. Since our knowledge of the past and our hopes for the future guide our actions, he declared, everybody uses history. But unfortunately, unlike the results of science, men cannot benefit from the study of history unless they do the studying themselves. But whether or not they study formal history, Becker contended, the kind of history that has the most influence on the life of the community and the course of events is the history that common men carry around in their

[19] *Ibid.*, pp. 54, 55-56.
[20] *Ibid.*, pp. 57-58.
[21] *Ibid.*, pp. 58-59.

heads. Whether people read books or not, they picture the past in some fashion, true or false, and this picture helps to determine their ideas about politics and society. It is thus imperative that they read history, and also imperative that historians write history in such a way that it will be read. Proof of all of this was World War I, which governments and people rushed into "with undiminished stupidity," and which was "the most futile exhibition of unreason, take it all in all, ever made by a civilized society." [22]

Additional evidence of the Turner influence on Becker appeared in 1927 in a beautifully written chapter by Becker on Turner in Howard Odum's *American Masters of Social Science*. Becker first related the process by which he came under Turner's influence, which I have given earlier, then indicated how Turner had contributed to Becker's philosophy of presentism, pragmatism, and subjective relativism.[23]

Turner seems to have implanted in Becker the notion that fact and interpretation in history are somehow different entities. Turner gave Becker the feeling that the end of research was not knowing the facts, but that behind the facts lurked some problem concerning humanity that awaited solution. There was the implication that students might turn over the "dead facts" once more and find something that others had missed. Becker watched Turner "playing freely with facts and ideas," handling problems of history that turned out to be problems of life itself. He waited for ideas to be born (not gained from the evidence apparently) and secret meanings and convenient hypotheses to be discovered, lurking under the dullest mass of drab facts ever seen.[24] Becker did not seem to see that the aim of research is facts — facts explaining both what happened and why it happened — for no one can think without facts, and if one does not find the facts to explain the "whys" as well as the "whats," one's interpretation is merely unreliable inference.

[22] *Ibid.*, pp. 62-63.
[23] Becker, "Frederick Jackson Turner" in Odum, *American Masters of Social Science*.
[24] *Ibid.*, pp. 277-82.

Although this article on Turner was highly laudatory and presumably indicated the great influence that Turner had exerted on Becker, in actual fact it really showed how far Becker had deviated from the teachings of Turner — assuming, of course, that Becker's evaluation of Turner was accurate. Becker emphasized that Turner, above all, was detached, objective, but without being indifferent, even to the point of convincing Becker that detachment did not necessarily signify indifference. Turner was so objective that one could not tell whether he was a protectionist or a freetrader, a Democrat or a Republican. In characterizing Turner, Becker gave an interesting definition of social philosophies: "Above all is he a conservative, satisfied with the evils we have? Or a liberal, willing to substitute for them others which formerly existed? Or a radical, eager for the shock of new ones never yet tried?" [25] The association of "evils" with conservatives, liberals, and radicals, seems to signify a pessimism that no social group can really achieve the good society. If Turner indoctrinated Becker with the idea of detachment, Becker had long since parted company with his noted mentor, for no one more than Becker had emphasized the fact that the historian cannot possibly be detached, for if he has a detached mind, it is a dead mind.

There is the bare hint in Becker's account of Turner that perhaps Turner was not as objective as Becker depicted him. Becker said that as a citizen, Turner left no doubt that he knew what was right and wise. If this was true, he could hardly escape being a conservative, or a liberal, or a radical, and he doubtless voted for Republicans or Democrats on the basis of whether they agreed with his philosophy. As for philosophy, Turner also said that history was the self-consciousness of humanity, implying that a knowledge of history would make men aware of the good and evil of the past that they might adopt the good and avoid the evil in the future. Furthermore, Turner had said that "the question is not whether you have a Philosophy of History, but whether the

---

[25] *Ibid.*, pp. 286-87, 290-92.

philosophy you have is good for anything," a suggestion that perhaps Turner was not as detached as Becker implied.[26]

In discussing Turner, Becker also gave a different answer to the question of the nature of historical facts from the subjective one contained in his paper on historical facts in 1926. To explain why Turner would never write a "great work" on history, Becker said this: "The factual substance is there, inexhaustible, lying conveniently under the hand, needing not to be invented or imagined, needing only to be carefully searched out and verified." Here the "fact" appears, not as something that the historian has "created" or something that is in his mind as Becker previously contended, but as something apart from the historian, something "out there," perhaps in the documents, something that can be "carefully searched out and verified" by any number of historians.[27]

There was also some of the same presentism in Turner that appears in Becker. Becker said that to Turner the past was dead except as he could see it living in the present, and that Turner was always occupied with the present. His great concern, of course, was what happens to a democracy which developed out of the economic opportunity of the frontier after that frontier ceases to exist. Presentism is also implied in Becker's statement that Turner wrenched his facts loose from their natural setting in time and place in order to assemble them again in support of some idea that occurred to him.[28]

Although he had lost faith in the common man as a result of the war, Becker seems to have taken some of his emphasis on the importance of the common man in history from Turner. Said he: "Turner seems to take it for granted that common place people, acting in common place ways, somehow or other, unconsciously for the most part, determine the social process and shape the course of history." Thus historians must consider "what people did and why they did it," the latter something that had long concerned philosophers

[26] *Ibid.*
[27] *Ibid.*, p. 313.
[28] *Ibid.*, pp. 302, 308, 313.

but not historians.[29] Becker would have more to say later about the common man in history.

Once again Becker demonstrated the weakness of the Becker thesis. He said that Turner emphasized the differences rather than the similarities between American and European institutions, and that "America was important, not because it resembled Europe, but precisely because it was different." As Goethe had said, "America has the best of it," although this was not chiefly because of economic resources but because America brought something new and original to the world — "the ideal of democracy developing under conditions unlike those of any other age or country."[30] The agent was the frontier, but as Becker would acknowledge eventually, the frontier had brought both the ideal and the reality of democracy to America long before the American Revolution.

Continuing his praise, Becker attributed to Turner the characteristics of a successful historian that eventually would have to be applied to Becker himself. "For my own part," he said, "I do not ask of any historian more than this, that he should have exerted in his generation a notable influence upon many scholars in many branches of humanistic study."[31] No one would deny that Turner and Becker were both successful according to this definition.

It was in his presidential address before the American Historical Association in 1931, however, that Becker reached the high point of his historical philosophy of presentism, pragmatism, and subjective relativism. The title of the paper was "Everyman His Own Historian," and since this pronouncement of a philosophy of history became so influential, it is worthy of a study in depth.[32]

[29] *Ibid.*, pp. 297-98.
[30] *Ibid.*, p. 300.
[31] *Ibid.*, p. 317.
[32] "Everyman His Own Historian," *American Historical Review* (January 1932), pp. 221-36; also in *Everyman His own Historian*, pp. 233-55. The following page numbers are from the latter. Quotations by permission of Appleton-Century-Crofts.

Becker began his paper by pointing out that there were really two histories — the actual series of absolute and unchanged events that occurred, and the ideal and relative series of events that we affirm and hold in our memories. The first, history as actuality, cannot be known directly and thus cannot be tested by repetition as the scientist tests a hypothesis. The second is only what we know about the past, which changes in response to increased or refined knowledge. The real event *was;* the affirmed fact about the event *is now.* Ideally, the function of the historian is to make the two histories correspond as closely as possible, but we must remember, he said, that the actual series of events exist for us only in terms of the ideal series which we affirm and hold in memory. Therefore, as Becker defined it, "history is the memory of things said and done." [33]

Becker then emphasized the pragmatic nature of history by showing how history helped Mr. Everyman in his day-by-day living. Everyman has his own "specious present" composed of the present fleeting moment, the remembered events of the past which he must have to orient himself in his world, and the anticipated things to be said and done in the future. Without this combination of past and anticipated events, today would be aimless and tomorrow would have no significance. To Everyman, history that lies dead and inert in the sources does him no good. So he consults his sources, his memorandum book, which in this instance tells him that he purchased some coal in the past and must pay for it in the future.[34]

Naturally, Mr. Everyman's use of history involved subjectivism. The future refuses to be excluded from the past, Becker continued, but which comes first, which is cause and which is effect? Do our memories construct a pattern of past events at the behest of our desires and hopes for the future, or do our desires and hopes spring from a pattern of past events imposed upon us by experience and knowledge? Becker sus-

[33] *Ibid.,* p. 235.
[34] *Ibid.,* p. 235ff.

pected that memory of the past and anticipation of the future went hand in hand, for it was impossible to divorce history from life. Memory of things said and done running hand in hand with things to be said and done allowed us to judge intelligently what we are doing in the light of what we have done and what we hope to do. In this sense, all living history is contemporaneous.[35]

But since the ideal series of events that we know is so intimately associated with what we are doing and what we hope to do, living history cannot be the same for everyone at any given time or from one generation to another. Hence subjective relativism. History "is rather an imaginative creation, a personal possession which each one of us, Mr. Everyman, fashions out of his individual experience, adapts to his practical or emotional needs, and adorns as well as may be to suit his aesthetic tastes." Mr. Everyman does not wish to learn the whole truth or arrive at ultimate causes: he wishes to adjust to a practical situation and is a good historian precisely because he is not disinterested. His picture of the past does not need to be either complete or completely true; it is essential only that it be useful for what he is doing and hopes to do.[36]

Thus Mr. Everyman resembles the creative artist and his history becomes art rather than science. As Becker said, it "will inevitably be an engaging blend of fact and fancy, a mythical adaption of that which actually happened," part true, part false. Mr. Everyman does not wish to deceive himself or others, but he never suspects how malleable facts are, "how easy it is to coax and cajole them." [37]

Essentially the professional historian differed little from Mr. Everyman in his presentism, pragmatism, and subjective relativism. As is true for Everyman, so also for the historian "the pattern of remembered things said and done will be woven, safeguard the process how we may, at the behest of circumstance and purpose." Then Becker administered the

[35] *Ibid.*
[36] *Ibid.*, p. 243.
[37] *Ibid.*, p. 245.

coup de grace to the historian as a scholar and to history as a scholarly discipline: "We are thus of that ancient and honorable company of wise men of the tribe, of bards and storytellers and minstrels, of soothsayers and priests, to whom in successive ages has been entrusted the keeping of the useful myths. Let not the harmless, necessary word 'myth' put us out of countenance. In the history of history a myth is a once valid but now discarded version of the human story, as our now valid versions will in due course be relegated to the category of discarded myths." [38]

Becker did pay lip service to the importance of "facts" in history, but this was obviously only a meaningless gesture toward historical scholarship. He said that the aim of history was always a true story, that the historian's "first duty is to be sure of his facts, let their meaning be what it may," and that "to establish the facts is always in order, and is indeed the first duty of the historian." But then Becker said that to suppose that the facts, once established in all their fullness, would speak for themselves was an illusion. Instead, "the history written by historians, like the history informally fashioned by Mr. Everyman, is thus a convenient blend of truth and fancy, of what we commonly distinguished as 'fact' and 'interpretation.' " [39]

Therefore any attempt to write objective history, according to Becker, was doomed to failure. The younger generation, he declared, was eager to believe that the quest for objective history, if one of perfection, was equally one of futility. Even the most disinterested historian has at least one preconception, the fixed idea that he has none. Left to themselves, the facts do not speak, do not really exist, since for all practical purposes there is no fact until someone affirms it: "It is thus not the undiscriminated fact, but the perceiving mind of the historian that speaks." The historian is conditioned by his own "specious present," he is not the same person at all times, and thus the significance of his remembered events "will vary with

[38] *Ibid.*, pp. 246-47.
[39] *Ibid.*, pp. 248-49.

the time and place of the observer." Like Mr. Everyman, the historian will be played upon by all the diverse, unnoted influences of his own time.[40]

In the end, Becker insisted, historians would have to adapt their history to Mr. Everyman's necessities or Mr. Everyman would abandon the historian. Research must be converted into common knowledge, for it is living history, true or false, not history that lies inert in unread books, that does the world's work. Each generation must understand the past and anticipate the future in the light of its own restricted experience — "must inevitably play on the dead whatever tricks it finds necessary for its own peace of mind." Mr. Everyman thus imposes his version of history on the historian, forcing him to view history in terms of the present. The function of the historian is not to repeat the past but to make use of it, to correct and rationalize for common use Mr. Everyman's mythological adaptation of what actually happened. The historian must be as honest and intelligent as human frailty permits, Becker declared, but success would be in conforming to the temper of Mr. Everyman which historians seem to guide only because they are so sure, eventually, to follow it.[41]

Having emasculated both the historian and history, it was small wonder that Becker had little respect for the discipline or its practitioner. He referred to history as "an indispensable even though not the highest form of intellectual endeavor." But true to his subjective relativism, he confessed that his approach to history was imposed on him by his own climate of opinion and thus was sure to be supplanted in the future.[42]

The many accolades which Becker received as a result of his presidential address attest to his tremendous and growing influence among historians. "Among the many shouts of joy that your presidential address must have brought you through the mails," wrote one enthusiastic admirer, "this is one of the loudest and most delighted." It made beautifully clear and

[40] *Ibid.*, pp. 251-52.
[41] *Ibid.*, p. 253.
[42] *Ibid.*, p. 254.

inevitable some ideas that he had been groping for, but it was too artistic, for the very art of Becker's presentation concealed the profound and devastating quality of his ideas. He suspected that few in the audience who had applauded so long at the meeting were aware of the dynamite in his message. Becker was so dexterous that they smiled as he took out their appendices — no, their backbones and other vital parts; he had destroyed the most valuable part of their work. It was sacrilege against the deity, Scientific History, so long enthroned; it was treason against the profession; it was glorious; it was grand. The wonder was that Becker was not tied to a stake and pelted with heavy tomes full of actual, self-expressing facts. Noting that his letter did not call for a reply, this admirer said, "Its purpose is merely to lay at your intellectual feet the tribute of _____." [43]

Becker did answer the letter, and his answer made more explicit his philosophy. He agreed that there was some dynamite in his paper, but also believed that there were a good many younger men in the Association who thought as Becker did but who had not clearly formulated their own ideas. It was pretty well admitted by all that every generation has to write its history anew, yet many who admit this often seemed quite unaware of the implications. They appeared to think that history must be rewritten because of the appearance of new material or a more expert technique, so that they still believed that historiography presents a steady onward and upward march of progress in knowledge and sound interpretation. Of course, Becker continued, the implications of his address were far more radical than that. Many outside the historical profession would appreciate and understand better than some within it. Becker understood that Dodd of Chicago considered the address as an argument for the futility of history couched in ironical form, and misunderstanding could hardly go further than that.[44]

[43] To Becker, January 13, 1932, Becker Papers.
[44] Undated letter, Becker Papers.

In answering Dodd's criticism, Becker further clarified his presidential address and what he intended to achieve by it. In a letter to Dodd, Becker denied that his presidential address advocated the futility of historical research under a thin guise of irony. He was simply trying to answer the frequent question, "What is the good of history?" Much historical research was simply "a dreary waste" of the meticulous determination of unimportant facts — plagiarism if taken from one book, research if taken from many. All people seem to have a universal need for a history, and what Becker did was to point out that "it is simply the need of a conscious creature, who has memory and who can anticipate the future, to enlarge his present perceptions by remembering things that happened in the past." Critical history was simply the instinctive and necessary exercise of memory, tested and fortified by reliable sources. But while the facts may be determined with accuracy, the interpretation of the facts will always be shaped by the prejudices, biases, and needs of the individual, and these, in turn, will depend upon the age in which the individual lives. Hence, history must be rewritten by each generation, for even if the facts are the same, the slant on the facts will be different. Becker said that his address was intended to find a natural and necessary basis in the nature of the human animal for the study and writing of history, to prove that history is a fundamental and most important branch of knowledge, to show that Mr. Everyman has and will have his history, true or false, and that one function of the historian is to keep Mr. Everyman's history, as far as possible, in reasonable harmony with what actually happened.[45]

Whatever Dodd's original reaction, another historian at Chicago, Ferdinand Schevill, greeted Becker's address with unfeigned rapture. He did not see how any historian who analyzed his own work could get around Becker's theory "that history is nothing other than an artificial extension of memory." He believed that historians should feel proud that their work has tremendous social significance for the living genera-

---

[45] Becker to Dodd, January 27, 1932, Becker Papers.

tion. The next generation would "require another version of the recited facts," but so what? The scholars who sat at Becker's feet at Minneapolis were all evolutionists, yet they had so long fooled themselves with the hokum of scientific method and scientific truth that they were deeply offended when Becker "blew these aside as so much chaff." Said Schevill: "I did not think I should live to see the day when a president of the Am. Historical Association would make so clear an analysis of this business of history and lay his hammer to so many idols of the market-place. You positively have thrown me into a mood of religious thanksgiving: Now can my spirit depart in peace!" Schevill planned to use Becker's address as the basis for a talk to the graduate history club at Chicago, and he said that he would treasure the offprint that Becker sent as a source of strength and clarity when his mental outlook became blurred.[46]

A few days later, Schevill wrote that his Becker-based talk, "Agitated Historians," had been a great success with the graduate students but not with most of the faculty. The "faculty brethren," who attended in force, indicated their lack of conviction in the familiar faculty manner by sitting glumly without comment. But the graduate students in the main rose to the occasion with almost enthusiastic affirmation. Schevill said he chose his title because social scientists, who had adopted the methods of natural science, had relegated historians to the undertakers. Historians took their punishment lying down, for when a natural or social scientist appeared on the scene, "our bewildered colleagues" dropped flat on their stomachs and registered their awe by striking their foreheads on the floor. Strangely enough, Louis Gottschalk, a student of Becker's, told Schevill privately that he did not believe one word of Schevill's bunk, but Schevill hastened to add that Gottschalk referred to Schevill's bunk, not to Becker's.[47]

A few weeks later, Dodd wrote that Becker was making a strong impression on graduate students at Chicago. There had

[46] Schevill to Becker, February 9, 1932, Becker Papers.
[47] Schevill to Becker, February 18, 1932, Becker Papers.

been a student meeting, with some faculty present, to discuss Becker's presidential address, and Dodd reported general appreciation and enthusiasm in the audience for the kind of appeal that Becker was making. He said that Andrew McLaughlin and Schevill had a lively discussion about whether history should have an avowed objective. Curiously enough, Dodd said, Schevill and Becker fell on one side while McLaughlin and Beard fell on the other.[48]

If Gottschalk at Chicago did not appear too enthusiastic about Becker's ideas, at least as they were presented by Schevill, another Becker student, Leo Gershoy, made up for the deficit. He said that Becker's offprint and his own copy of the *American Historical Review* containing the address were in great demand among advanced history students at Long Island University. Another professor referred his young hopefuls to the address, and prospective teachers in Gershoy's courses "must swear by it." He said that the address had a fine symphonic character, a fine quality of symphonic music or architecture — a harmony in which each thought played a discreet and beautifully determined part.[49]

Chicago and Long Island were by no means the only schools to feel the impact of Becker's address. A former student said that there had been many discussions at Ohio State over his paper, which had caused "no end of confusion" among the "scientifically minded" there, and as he imagined, elsewhere. Many of these men forgot that what Narcissus saw in the water was not the water but his own image. History could not be scientific because it did not lend itself to control and repetition, and because it must be refracted in a mind psychologically conditioned by its past experience. This man said that his own attitude dated back to Cornell and had its origins in Becker's two early articles, "Detachment" and "Some Aspects of the Influence of Social Problems and Ideas

[48] Dodd to Becker, May 21, 1932, Becker Papers.

[49] Gershoy to Becker, February 11 [1932], and an undated letter, Becker Papers.

Upon the Writing of History." [50] Another wrote that he had heard no end of complimentary comments since the Minneapolis meeting, and that Arthur C. Cole had used "Everyman" and "What is Historical Fact" in a talk at the University of Iowa on "The Historian's Philosophy of History." [51]

The plaudits continued to flow in from all sides. Turner, retired from Harvard and then at the Huntington Library, read Becker's address "with intense pleasure." Not only was it fine writing, but Turner agreed with Becker's ideas and declared that one of the real pleasures of his life was to have been associated with Becker. [52] A former student, Herbert Snyder, said that Becker's speech was apparently "a new and refreshing idea" to the editor of the *New York Times,* who had written an editorial on it. But to the fortunate one who had sat in Becker's seminars, the reflection that history was usually subjective was familiar. Students were "skillfully led to see the truth of many things." [53] Another correspondent called the paper a "lovely piece of analysis," and contended that pedants could not answer it except by misunderstanding Becker. Calling Becker a philosopher, this writer declared that "Everyman His Own Historian is literature in perfection and the 'nothing more beyond' of good sense." [54]

The philosopher, T. V. Smith, not only approved of Becker's address but also appeared to consider Becker as something of a fellow philosopher. Calling the address a "grand speech," he said that the assimilation of history to the march of culture makes an interesting point of comparison with the pragmatic movement. John Dewey had been saying the same thing about philosophy, although he did not wave aside the metaphysical issue as easily as Becker did. Smith said that pragmatism on the metaphysical side left him out simply because it was not willing to face the implication of Becker's common sense dualism. He referred, of course, to the two

[50] Sidney Ferr (or Terr) to Becker, December 18, 1932, Becker Papers.
[51] G. G. Andrews to Becker, Ferbuary 14, 1932, Becker Papers.
[52] Turner to Becker, January 14, 1932, Becker Papers.
[53] Herbert Snyder to Becker, January 16, 1932, Becker Papers.
[54] R. D. O'Leary to Becker, February 7, 1932, Becker Papers.

histories — the actual events that were absolute and the image which was relative. It warmed Smith's heart to see a historian debunk his subject without surrendering self — or even subject — respect. He had been trying to say the same thing of philosophy — it was common sense ashamed neither of its commonalty nor its sense, but willing to submit both as reduced to the lowest terms.[55]

Men of the law also added their voices to the chorus of praise. Felix Frankfurter wrote that his wife had said of Becker, "Why that man is not merely a scholar and thinker; he's a poet." [56] Arthur M. Schlesinger, Sr., quoted Frankfurter as saying the address was the "swellest" piece of writing in many a moon. "How truly human he makes scholarship! And how he deflates it of all its pompous bunk." If Schlesinger was not enthusiastic, Frankfurter said he was through with him, and given this imperative, Schlesinger said he could not afford to disagree.[57] And Oliver Wendell Holmes, who received an offprint from Becker, declared: "I have heard you called the finest historian in the country." [58]

One of the most laudatory of Becker's admirers was one of his own colleagues at Cornell, Preserved Smith, who praised Becker both as a man of literature and as an outstanding purveyor of subjective relativism in history. Wrote Smith: "You are the most interesting of all living historians. Your presidential address not only far surpasses all those within my memory, but will add to your fame and live long, with your other essays, in world literature. You have disposed once for all of the *voranssetzungclose Geschichtswissenschaft* once lauded by the 'objective' historians. You have killed the notion that facts have any meaning in themselves apart from that shed upon them by our own minds. They are dark ob-

[55] T. V. Smith to Becker, February 2, 1932, Becker Papers. Smith's daughter-in-law, Charlotte Watkins Smith, would later write one of the biographies of Becker.
[56] Frankfurter to Becker, February 4, 1932, Becker Papers.
[57] Schlesinger to Becker, February 9, 1932, Becker Papers.
[58] Holmes to Becker, February 7, 1932, Becker Papers.

jects, invisible and intractable until they shine and effloresce in the rays cast upon them by our ideas." [59]

Such lavish praise must have been heady wine indeed for the former Iowa farm boy, and certainly "Everyman" marked a high point in his career as an exponent of presentism, pragmatism, and subjective relativism. To be called the foremost American historian and the most interesting of all living historians was a mark of distinction aspired to by all but achieved by few. Charles Beard wrote that he had heard on good authority that Becker was no historian — nothing but a man of letters. Beard said that this made him jealous — he wished God (or what is it) had also made him a man of letters.[60] If there were doubters, there were also many in high places in the profession who not only considered Becker a man of letters, but in addition, the country's outstanding historian.

Adulation, however, was not the only reward. The accolades for Becker and his subjective relativism were accompanied by a spectacular triumph of the Becker-Beard-Schlesinger interpretation of the American Revolution and Constitution that almost matched Becker's own rise to preeminence as a historian. Now the class-struggle approach of the progressives, which was already gathering adherents, took on something of the aspects of an avalanche that swept all before it. There are many examples, but the writings of five men — James Truslow Adams, Allan Nevins, J. Franklin Jameson, Charles Beard himself, and Vernon Louis Parrington — will suffice to indicate the vastly-enhanced influence of the progressives.

One need read only the preface of James Truslow Adams' *Revolutionary New England,* published in 1923, to see that Adams had taken over the Becker thesis completely. Adams, whose works were widely read during the 'twenties and 'thirties, and, in fact, are still used by college students, based his entire approach on the "dual revolution." Because of recent scholarship, he declared, people were now "far more acutely aware of the double nature of the struggle as at once

[59] Smith to Becker, January 15, 1932, Becker Papers.
[60] Beard to Becker, September 26 [1932?], Becker Papers.

a political contest between colonies and mother country, and a social revolution in the colonies themselves." Adams planned to trace "the origins of radical thought" in order to understand "the domestic social revolution," to note the endeavors of the upper classes to control the life of the colonies for their own advantage and the demands of the less fortunate for an increase in power and the betterment of their position, and to point out the concentration of wealth, the increasing obstacles placed in the paths of the poor, the growth of radical discontent, the slow slippage of political power from the higher to the lower social class, and the steady growth of lower-class self-consciousness. Later Adams cited Becker's statement that "to the question of home rule was added that of who was to rule at home." [61]

When he followed his evidence, however, Adams did what all the others did — he depicted a middle-class, democratic society, not one that was class-ridden. As he said, the great bulk of the population consisted of "a property-owning, agricultural class" which enjoyed liberty "to a greater degree than anywhere else in the world." Instead of a declining opportunity for the poor, as he had previously stated, Adams found a steady advance in the standard of living and it was this steady improvement which fostered discontent "among the less favored classes." He recognized that frontier conditions provided unequaled economic opportunity and that economic opportunity carried with it liberty, democracy, and equality. Yet Adams still insisted on a class-conflict dual-revolution interpretation in which "the revolution in the colonies broadened into a war for independence against the mother country" while at the same time declaring, as Van Tyne did, that Americans had far more liberty than Englishmen and that it was this liberty which propelled them toward independence. [62]

In 1926, Adams published another book, *New England in the Republic, 1776–1850,* which projected the class-conflict

[61]James Truslow Adams, *Revolutionary New England* (Boston, 1923), preface, 322.

[62] *Ibid.*, pp. vi, 4, 5, 6, 9, 11, 15. For contradictions on opportunity and the franchise, see pages 31, 35, 71, 107-09, 115, 116, 160, 161, 192, 253, 256.

interpretation of the progressive historians through the Revolution and Constitution periods. In the preface, Adams defined the main theme of the book as the continual struggle of the common man to realize the doctrines of the Revolution in the life of the community. Increasing self-consciousness among the lower classes brought a gradual demand on their part for a growing share in political power. Leaders, he said, influenced the people through popular propaganda which stressed the rights of man and the sovereignty of the people, but having achieved a revolution, they then endeavored to stop the revolutionary movement from proceeding further and altering class relations or the structure of American society.[63]

Allan Nevins also perpetuated the myth of class society and social revolution while at the same time presenting evidence of a democratic society and evolution by concensus. In *The American States During and After the Revolution,* Nevins pointed out the lack of revolution within the states as the states tended to retain the general pattern of life that had developed under the British. Nevins referred to the "fierce democracy" in Massachusetts and quoted Jefferson on absence of revolution, yet he ended with this interpretation: "Almost everywhere the Revolution opened up a hope of political participation to men who had been denied it." [64]

The important social revolution aspect of Becker's dual-revolution thesis received book-length treatment in 1926 with the publication of J. Franklin Jameson's *The American Revolution Considered as a Social Movement.* Reversing the order implied by Becker and explicitly stated by J. T. Adams that the War of Independence grew out of the internal social conflict, Jameson declared: "But who shall say to the waves of revolution: Thus far shall we go and no farther? . . . The stream of revolution, once started, could not be confined within narrow banks, but spread abroad upon the land. Many

[63] James Truslow Adams, *New England in the Republic, 1776–1850* (Boston, 1926), preface.

[64] Allan Nevins, *The American States During and After the Revolution* (New York, 1924), pp. 1-14, 18, 22, 42, 44-45, 51, 61, 75-85, 89, 91, 95, 96, 97, 114, 117, 119, 128, 133, 148, 182, 420, 444-45.

economic desires, many social aspirations were set free by the political struggle, many aspects of colonial society profoundly altered by the forces thus let loose." To Jameson, it was the war for political independence which let loose the social revolution, not social class conflict which brought on the war.[65]

Unfortunately for the Becker and Jameson theses, however, virtually all of the changes which Jameson saw in American life as a result of the Revolution can be explained simply by the fact that restraints imposed by Great Britain were removed. Often what appears as social change, such as checks on the importation of slaves, a widened franchise, and equitable representation, had been attempted by colonial legislatures before 1776 only to be vetoed by the British. Some states placed restrictions on importation of slaves after 1776, but slavery itself and the stake-in-society philosophy of government continued with little alteration after the Revolution. Americans could eliminate entail and primogeniture as forms of landholding and inheritance where it existed, but these were relatively insignificant in a country with an abundance of free land where an equal share for all children was the most common rule and where entails were easily broken. Commerce and manufacturing were naturally freed from British mercantile regulations, land policy fell under American management, and the Church of England lost its foothold, but these were all the result of independence, not social revolution.

The validity of the Jameson thesis rests on the question of whether class relationships in the colonies were what Jameson said they were and whether the Revolution changed these relationships. He insisted that the American Revolution, like the French Revolution, was a "popular revolution," and popular revolutions, unlike palace revolutions, have social consequences. Jameson defined a popular revolution as one in which there was a transfer of power from the hands of a

[65] J. Franklin Jameson, *The American Revolution Considered as a Social Movement* (Princeton University Press, Princeton, N.J., 1926), p. 9. Quotations used by permission of Princeton University Press.

smaller into those of a larger mass of the people or from one great sector of the population to another. Believing as he did that the American Revolution was "popular," Jameson said it was "clear that in most states the strength of the revolutionary party lay most largely in the plain people, as distinguished from the aristocracy," and that "in the main we must expect to see our social changes tending in the direction of levelling democracy." [66]

As other historians had done, Jameson placed great emphasis on voting rights as a barometer of social revolution. He stressed "the expansion of the suffrage" and the fact that "the right of suffrage was much extended" as a result of the Revolution. Naturally "the elevation of whole classes of people to the status of voters elevates them also in their social status," he declared, while democracy was further enhanced by the fact that "multitudes of squires had been driven into exile or dethroned from their high position of dominance over the community." Because of the internal revolution, "the legislatures were in the hands of the radical revolutionaries, or extreme Whigs," and thus social democracy and political democracy progressed together in legislation of the period respecting the suffrage. And as a result of these changes in the suffrage, "the people" who established the Constitution "was a much larger and more democratic body" than the people who acquiesced in the Declaration of Independence.[67]

Having said these things, however, Jameson completely confused the issue of democracy as an indication of social revolution. At times he showed that American society was already democratic before the Revolution so that there was no need for a social revolution. In this country, which was "almost absolutely rural" and where the franchise was based on land, Jameson declared, the "right to vote had nowhere been narrowly restricted" in colonial times and "in a country so wholly given up to agriculture a real-estate qualification excluded few men." Then having shown that the Revolution resulted in a

[66] *Ibid.*, pp. 7-11, 18.
[67] *Ibid.*, pp. 18, 19, 36, 39, 40.

significant widening of the franchise, which by his own admission was almost inclusive already, he reversed himself with
the statement that at the end of the Revolution the electoral
franchise "fell far short of complete democracy," that "political democracy came among us somewhat late, certainly long
after the Revolution in most states," and if manhood suffrage
is taken as a criterion, democracy did not arrive until 1840.[68]
Certainly this is an amazing display of logic.

The progressive interpretation, with all of its glaring contradictions, was given a tremendous boost in 1927 with the
publication of the widely-used college textbook, *The Rise of
American Civilization,* by Charles and Mary Beard. Statements
about "servile" labor, indentured servants who were little
better than slaves and became a hopeless body of poor whites
— "proletariat of the countryside" — and free artisans and
laborers with a brand of inferiority stamped upon them,[69]
marched hand in hand with other statements about great
economic opportunity which allowed anyone to become an
independent farmer or enter a trade, broke the rigidity of class
status, permitted rapid movement up and down the scale, and
resulted in the "comfort of the free masses in contrast with
the awful beggary of Europe." [70] In political affairs, ruling
classes, slave-owning barons, and aristocratic merchants dominated,[71] yet Britain developed agencies "to check and control
the swelling authority of colonial democracy," uneducated
yeoman in wretched huts were voters and constituted the
majority of the "popular party" which usurped all power
through the "popular" assembly, and Britain feared the
" 'democratical' pretensions of America." [72] Property was widely
distributed (implying a broad electorate), the Beards declared, but still limitations on the suffrage excluded a large

[68] *Ibid.,* pp. 18, 27, 28, 39, 40.
[69] Charles A. and Mary R. Beard, *The Rise of American Civilization* (The
Macmillan Company, New York, 1927), pp. 103, 104, 105, 131, 132. Quotations used by permission of the Macmillan Company.
[70] *Ibid.,* pp. 82, 108, 137, 138, 145.
[71] *Ibid.,* pp. 109, 118, 125-27, 129.
[72] *Ibid.,* pp. 112, 130-31.

proportion of the population — just how large could not be determined.[73]

Just as the Beards could not decide whether American society before the Revolution was democratic or undemocratic, so also were they equally confused about whether the Revolution was a social movement. At one time, the "directors who engineered the Revolution at the top contemplated no drastic alteration of arrangements at the bottom," [74] but then the Revolution appeared as a move by Britain against the "popular" assembly which had become almost sovereign and which was controlled by a "popular party" where uneducated yeomen were the majority.[75] Later the same ruling classes who engineered the Revolution at the top became "radicals," a term with social connotations, and the Articles of Confederation, placing all power in the states, "corresponded with marked fidelity to the ideas of the radicals who had engineered the Revolution." [76] This interpretation was to be more fully developed later by Merrill M. Jensen. The Beards implied social revolution by saying that the new states differed as much from the colonial provinces as the France of Louis Philippe differed from that of Louis XV, yet half a century passed before the leveling democracy of Jefferson's Declaration of Independence came flooding into power, and in the savage contests between conservatives and radicals, the conservatives were victorious and wrote their views of property rights into the first state constitutions. But then the Beards, quoting Jameson, reverted to the social revolution by insisting that the Revolution "was in truth an economic, social, and intellectual transformation of prime significance." [77]

Finally, the Beards' account of the Constitution was equally confusing. The title of their chapter on the Constitution, "Populism and Reaction," suggested an agrarian democratic social revolution that was nipped in the bud by a conserva-

[73] *Ibid.*, p. 110.
[74] *Ibid.*. p. 257.
[75] *Ibid.*, pp. 113-18, 130-31, 203.
[76] *Ibid.*, p. 291.
[77] *Ibid.*, pp. 291, 292, 296.

tive counterrevolution in the form of the Constitution. State legislatures, with farmers in the majority, they said, were supreme as radicals rid themselves of outside interference by structuring the Articles of Confederation to suit their interests. Yet with most men farmers and with these farmers in control of state legislatures, the Beards contended that the Constitution was "bitter medicine to a large part of the public." [78] What is confusing is why ordinary farmers, who could so overwhelmingly control state legislatures, adopted a Constitution that was "bitter medicine" and that was designed according to Beard to protect personal rather than real property. Confusion is compounded when we discover that the Constitution received a sixty-five per cent majority in a country dominated by small farmers — a landslide greater than that of Lyndon Johnson in 1964.

If the Beards reached a vast audience of history students through *The Rise of American Civilization,* Vernon Louis Parrington perpetuated the progressive interpretation to an equally vast audience of students of American literature in his *Colonial Mind,* also published in 1927. Parrington warned his readers with engaging frankness that he was a subjective relativist who wrote from a progressive point of view. Dedicating his book to J. Allen Smith, the progressive political scientist who had anticipated Beard's *Economic Interpretation of the Constitution,* Parrington wrote as follows: "The point of view from which I have endeavored to evaluate the materials, is liberal rather than conservative, Jeffersonian rather than Federalistic, and very likely in my search I have found what I went forth to find, as others have discovered what they were seeking." Parrington especially acknowledged his debt to those historians who, over the past score of years, had worked with such fruitful results in the Revolution and Constitution periods. Then he incorporated their findings into his book, ringing the changes on class conflict and social revolution

[78] *Ibid.,* pp. 297, 304, 310, 328, 329, 335.

while at the same time citing evidence that contradicted the entire interpretation.[79]

With the publication of these books from 1923 to 1927, and especially those of Adams, the Beards, and Parrington which reached untold thousands of college students and, in the case of Adams and Parrington, are still being read in history and literature classes, the progressive interpretation of the Revolution and Constitution became widely disseminated in intellectual circles. At the very time that progressivism in politics and economics was under the cloud of the conservative reaction of the 1920's, progressivism in ideas was gaining momentum with each passing year.

[79] Vernon Louis Parrington, *The Colonial Mind* (Harcourt, Brace & Company, New York, 1927). Quotations used by permission of Harcourt, Brace & World. For class conflict, see pp. i, 3, 19-21, 171, 176, 177, 180-83, 187, 191, 198, 217, 245, 246, 274, 283. For evidence of democracy, see pp. 126, 127, 133, 137, 139, 140, 142-46, 185, 191, 198-204, 216, 241, 243, 268, 275, 282, 290, 291.

VII. LIBERALISM AND THE THIN ICE OF COMMUNISM, 1932-1937

> "They did not ask how society had come
> to be what it was, but how it could be
> made better than it was."
> — CARL BECKER, 1932

IF World War I raised doubts in Becker's mind about progress and the capacity of the common man to achieve the good society, the Great Depression after 1929 led to a more intense questioning of capitalism as a functioning economic system. Long a critic of the capitalistic system, Becker now became more convinced than ever that some better economic organization must be found. How close his liberalism led him toward the thin ice of Communism becomes apparent in the following pages. And withal, presentism, pragmatism, and subjective relativism continued as the philosophical foundation of his quest for the good society.

All of these elements are present in the only "scholarly" work on European history that the professor of modern European history was to write — *The Heavenly City of the Eighteenth Century Philosophers.* In this volume, Becker not only retained his philosophy of history, but he also interpreted the eighteenth-century French philosophers as twentieth-century progressives whose main aim was to create the good society not in heaven but on earth.[1] Since this book on European history had some relevance to Becker's philosophy about American history, it is worth an analysis of considerable length.

---

[1] Carl L. Becker, *The Heavenly City of the Eighteenth Century Philosophers* (Yale University Press, New Haven, 1932). Quotations used by permission of Yale University Press.

Aspiring as he did to the reputation of philosopher, which he considered several rungs above that of historian, Becker used the first chapter to deplore the elimination of philosophy from history. Each age can be understood only in terms of its "climate of opinion," Becker declared, and in the thirteenth century, theology, philosophy, and logic explained man and his universe. Bertrand Russell destroyed the religious orientation of society with the result that today we have little use for theology, philosophy, and logic. We ask what and how, not why; the historian is no longer a philosopher, and his climate of opinion includes history and science, not theology and philosophy. By the eighteenth century, a clear-cut philosophy of history had degenerated into an amiable and gentlemanly "philosophy teaching by example." [2]

Unfortunately, Becker continued, neither history nor science really explains the world. Historians merely note what happened just as it happened. "No respectable historian any longer harbors ulterior motives; and one who should surreptitiously introduce the gloss of a transcendent interpretation into the human story would deserve to be called a philosopher and straightway lose his reputation as a scholar," Becker said, with tongue in cheek. Mankind is committed to the historical approach to knowledge, which includes most knowledge; but the other approach to knowledge, science, has taught us the futility of troubling to understand underlying agencies. Scientific method, once expected to banish all mystery from the world, actually leaves the world more inexplicable than ever.[3]

Then Becker turned to a progressive explanation of the eighteenth-century philosophers. The "philosophes" were really not philosophers but men of letters who wrote books designed to shape the future. By no means, he declared, were they disinterested or objectively detached. Their leading light, Voltaire, was a defender of causes, a crusader pledged to recover the holy places of the true faith, the religion of human-

[2] *Ibid.*, pp. 1-18.
[3] *Ibid.*, pp. 18-24.

ity. No skeptic himself, Voltaire wrote to convey the truth that would make mankind free; and the eighteenth century was preoccupied with human welfare, with projects to improve human happiness. There was a humanitarian impulse to set things right, to free men from the bondage imposed by medicine men and priests, and the key words were nature, natural law, first cause, reason, sentiment, humanity, and perfectibility.[4]

If St. Augustine's "City of God" was a heavenly city, Becker declared, that of the philosophes was a humanitarian "Heavenly City" on earth. In place of God, they substituted nature and the law of nature. Ideas, customs, and institutions of men, if they were to attain perfection, must be in accord with laws which nature reveals at all times to all men. Men continued to worship, but the object was different: "Having denatured God, they deified nature." Locke demonstrated that the mind owed nothing to heredity or innate ideas and everything to environment. Having demolished the Christian doctrine of total depravity, Locke made it possible for men to believe what they wanted to believe, namely, that since man and the mind of man was shaped by nature which God had created, it was possible for men, by using their natural faculties, to bring their ideas, conduct, and institutions into harmony with the universal natural order. To the question of why there was evil in the world, the philosophes gave the progressive answer that the world was neither a completed drama nor a perfected machine, but something to be finished and perfected in the future.[5]

According to Becker, the agency by which the philosophes expected to achieve the better world of the future was the proper study of history. Having undermined the foundations of Christian morality, the philosophes turned to the study of history, economics, and politics. Increasingly, thinking men were concerned with questions of political and social reform: "The amelioration of society was the very thing Philosophers

[4] *Ibid.,* pp. 33-42.
[5] *Ibid.,* pp. 63-69.

had most at heart." They had to identify the qualities that were common to all men so that they could determine what ideas, customs, and institutions were out of harmony with the universal natural order. Abstract reason had to be supplemented with experience, and thus the philosophes needed a " 'new history' . . . that would be philosophy teaching by example." [6]

The New History of the eighteenth century, like that of the twentieth, was grounded in subjective relativism. Said Becker: "The 'new history' is an old story. Since history is not an objective reality, but only an imaginative reconstruction of vanished events, the pattern that appears useful and agreeable to one generation is never entirely so to the next. There is thus a profound truth in Voltaire's witticism, 'History is only a pack of tricks we play on the dead.' " The tricks do no harm to the dead, Becker continued, and certainly they do us much good; at best they help us to master our difficulties; at worst, they allow us to endure by nourishing the hope of a better future. Twenty years earlier, Robinson had urged historians to "turn on the past and exploit it in the interests of advance," but Robinson was not the first. St. Augustine's new history, "The City of God," was one of the most ingenious and successful tricks ever played on the dead. Since then, humanists had exploited the past in the interest of classical learning, patriots in the interest of national or royal prestige, Protestants in the interest of the new religion, and Catholics in the interest of the old faith.[7]

In particular, the New History would help to promote the good life of the future by pointing out how bad the old life of the past had been. Diderot once said of Voltaire: "Other historians relate facts to inform us of facts. You relate them to excite in our hearts an intense hatred of lying, ignorance, hypocrisy, superstition, tyranny; and this anger remains even after the memory of the facts has disappeared." As Becker said, public happiness was something to be attained in the

[6] *Ibid.*, pp. 83-88.
[7] *Ibid.*, pp. 88-89.

future. It could not be attained without breaking with the past, but in order to induce men to break with the past, it was first of all necessary to show them how bad the past was.[8]

To the philosophes, as to Becker, the study of history had as its purpose the future rather than the past. Their interest was in change rather than stability. "They did not ask how society had come to be what it was, but how it could be made better than it was." They saw society as irrational, oppressive, unjust, and needing to be set right quickly. What they wanted to know was how it could be set right, and they looked to the past for light, not on the origins of society but on its future state — for ideas, customs, and institutions embodying constant and universal principles of human nature upon which to establish a more equitable regime than that which existed. Condorcet censured Montesquieu for finding reasons "for that which is" when he should have been "seeking that which ought to be." [9]

Quite naturally the New History of the philosophes was necessarily predicated on the perfectibility of mankind. They studied history, not to discover something new, but to substantiate what they already believed about the nature of man. To them, man was not natively depraved; the end of life was the good life on earth rather than the beatific life after death; man, guided by reason and experience, could perfect the good life on earth; the good life required the freeing of men's minds from the bonds of ignorance and superstition and their bodies from the arbitrary oppression of constituted social authorities. In short, man was natively good, easily enlightened, and disposed to follow reason and common sense. He was generous, humane, and tolerant, and more easily led by persuasion than compelled by force. Becker admitted that these philosophes deceived others as well as themselves, for "mankind" was simply their own image and the principles

[8] *Ibid.*, pp. 91-94.
[9] *Ibid.*, pp. 97-101.

they sought were the ones they started with. This was the trick they played on the dead.[10]

The philosophes were thus progressives and their New History was progressive history. As did Wells, Becker said, Voltaire wrote the kind of history that made the great events of the world scarcely more than a history of crimes. In *The Spirit of the Laws,* Montesquieu was not so much concerned with what the laws were as he was with what they should have been, and his book furnished ammunition for eighteenth-century reformers. Imbued with the idea of progress, the philosophes saw the present as much better than the past and they believed that the future would be better than the present.[11]

True to his concept that the specious present involves past, present, and future, Becker tied the past with the heavenly city of the eighteenth century as well as with the hoped-for heavenly city of the twentieth. He repeated the now-familiar statement that to be oriented to the present, man must use the past and be prepared for what is coming by anticipating the future. The future refuses to be excluded from the present, and the more of the past we drag into the present, the more a hypothetical, patterned future crowds in also. The specious present, then, involves memory, perception, and anticipation, both for individuals and the climate of opinion; and to the eighteenth century, the past was bad, the present better, and the future would be better still.[12]

To achieve reform, however, the philosophes had to present a different interpretation than the accepted Christian version of past, present, and future. This Christian version, which was designed for the common man, furnished a happy ending by substituting a golden age to come in place of a helpless, hopeless world. Christianity announced with authority that the common man had significance, that the golden age lay in the future, and that the common man could be

[10] *Ibid.*, pp. 102-04.
[11] *Ibid.*, pp. 110-15.
[12] *Ibid.*, pp. 120-22.

among the chosen. The golden age of Christianity would come, however, not in this life, but in the next.[13]

If the eighteenth-century religion of the philosophes, the religion of humanity, was to appeal to the common man, Becker went on, the old heaven of Christianity had to be replaced by a new heaven. Furthermore, this new heaven had to be located somewhere within the earthly life, not after death, since the philosophes believed that the end of life was life itself — the perfected temporal life of man. This better heaven would be in the future, for the temporal life of man was not yet perfected, and it must be attained by man himself, by the progressive improvements made by successive generations of men, not by God. Posterity would complete what the past and present had begun, and the love of humanity would replace the love of God. But the philosophes could not grasp the modern idea of progress until they abandoned ancestor worship and realized that their own generation was superior to any yet born.[14]

Becker said that this vision of a heavenly city on earth naturally led to the creation of imagined Utopias where the philosophy of humanity would be realized in all its fullness. Locke and Condillac taught men that they were the product of their environment, and that a reshaping of the environment in accordance with the laws of nature would speedily accomplish material and spiritual regeneration. In France, where social discontent was most acute, the doctrine of progress became an article of faith in the new religion of humanity. Ideas of Utopia, transferred by the sophisticated to imagined lands, were projected into the life of man on earth and identified with the desired and hoped-for regeneration of society.[15]

To the philosophes, the French Revolution became a milestone in the march of progress toward the heavenly city. Based on a determination to set things right and to create the

[13] *Ibid.*, pp. 125-28.
[14] *Ibid.*, pp. 129-31.
[15] *Ibid.*, pp. 138-39.

better future, the Revolution in its later stages took on the character of a religious crusade. It not only attempted to substitute the religion of humanity for other faiths, but it also had its own God, forms of worship, and sacred principles of liberty and equality. The sustaining force in the Revolution was a mystical faith in humanity and in the ultimate regeneration of the human race.[16]

But when the Revolution failed to achieve Utopia, said Becker, the discontented renounced their faith in democracy in order to follow the prophets of a new religion — the religion of Marx and Engels. Founded on the laws of nature as revealed by science, this new faith, like the old, looked both to the past and to the future — to persistent conflict in the past and to a millennial state in the future. It did not look back to a Garden of Eden nor view the history of mankind as a deliberate and sinister betrayal of good men by bad. Instead, it saw in the past a ruthless and impersonal conflict of material forces functioning through the economic class interests of man. This conflict created a landowning aristocracy in the Middle Ages, replaced it with bourgeois capitalists in the nineteenth century, and would in time destroy the capitalists in the interests of the proletariat. Social revolution would come, not through enlightenment and good will, but through the indefeasible operations of economic forces.[17]

Becker went on to say that the new Utopia, the new heavenly city on earth according to Marx and Engels, would inevitably be a Communist Utopia. The function of intelligence was to understand the terms of these economic forces; the duty of the common man was to adjust to the inevitable process. The stars in their courses, rather than the puny will of man, would bring about the social revolution, the promised land to which the masses could look with faith and hope.[18] Economic forces, working their inexorable will, had replaced rational man as the engine to achieve the good society.

[16] *Ibid.,* p.155.
[17] *Ibid.,* pp. 155-62.
[18] *Ibid.,* pp. 162-63.

Despite their obvious differences, Becker saw many similarities between the French and Russian Revolutions. Like the French Revolution, the Russian Revolution had as its aim the true establishment of liberty and equality. Moreover, its leaders, having received the tables of eternal law, regarded their Revolution not merely as an instrument of political and social reform, but much more the realization of a philosophy of life which, being universally valid because it is in harmony with science and history, must prevail. Its dogmas are the theories of Marx interpreted by Lenin; the days which it celebrates are the great days of the Revolution; its saints are the heroes and martyrs of the Communist faith. And men now feared Communism much as men in 1815 feared the French Revolution.[19]

Finally, Becker arrived at the relevance of these past and present heavenly cities on earth to the future of American capitalistic democracy. Becker had his own heavenly city. He said there was talk — some but not much — of economic planning. This indicated an awareness of the need in our high-powered technological society for less liberty and more control — a less freely competitive and a more consciously regulated economy. Within a hundred years, a regulated economy (Communism or collective planning), he declared, might be recognized throughout the western world as the indispensable foundation of social order, peace, prosperity, and the welfare of mankind. And he ended with the query as to whether the Russian Revolution was but another stage in the progress of mankind toward perfection or just more of the same old stuff.[20]

Historians of the Enlightenment must determine the validity of Becker's analysis of European history, but it seems safe to say that, in line with his whole philosophy, he was using history as a screen on which to project his own vision of the future — a collectivist democracy. And given the state of health of democratic capitalism in the United States in 1932,

[19] *Ibid.*, pp. 163-64.
[20] *Ibid.*, pp. 167-68.

it is hardly surprising that Becker's analysis of Communism was not too unfavorable.

The *Heavenly City* met with a mixed response. On the plus side, one admirer called the book a gem, a work that lived up to his expectations of what he thought that Becker at his best could write.[21] The *New York Times* reviewer caught the point that the philosophes aimed at "the amelioration of society" through creation of the heavenly city on earth, and that they believed in the perfectibility of man in this life. This reviewer also recognized that the philosophes were really romanticists who hid their emotions behind frigidity, barbed wit, and polished hardness, yet had a deep interest in man and hearts that beat fervidly for him.[22]

The *New York Times* characterization of the philosophes seems also to have been a fairly good analysis of Becker himself, but some of the reviewers failed to get his message. For example, the *Herald-Tribune* reviewer said that there was dynamite in Becker's little volume, but that he was using it "for the purpose of inculcating an all-embracing skepticism." To him Becker was saying that the philosophes merely substituted a new set of delusions for old ones which they had discarded, and that this process is the only one possible today and forever. He accused Becker of ostensibly examining the ideas of the philosophes but actually defending in his own aloof way the chilly doctrine of Eternal Recurrence.[23] What the reviewer failed to see was that Becker, like Voltaire, used skepticism and cynicism to arouse in his readers a conviction that man was capable of something better than the repetition of fruitless delusions. This reviewer, in fact, had risen nicely to the bait.

Somewhat more serious, but equally unperceptive, was the review in the *Philadelphia Public Ledger*, especially because of its implications about Communism. Calling Becker a philosopher as well as a historian, this reviewer said that Becker

---

[21] Undated Letters, Becker Papers.

[22] *New York Times*, June 8, 1933.

[23] Joseph Wood Krutch in *The New York Herald Tribune*, December 18, 1932.

"seems to be engaged in the undoubtedly pleasant but certainly unfruitful pursuit of reflection for its own sake, intellectualization without a goal, the kind that leads to what has been called reflective paralysis." (Becker without a goal? How wrong could a reviewer be!) He saw that the heavenly city was to be an earthly Utopia for the perfectible common man. But then, he continued, Becker lets the reader down when he leads him to the threshold of the present. What is the end of it all? To Becker it seems possible that a hundred years from now the world will be celebrating the dates of the Russian Revolution "as a happy turning point in the history of human freedom." But then this reviewer missed Becker's cynicism and skepticism by saying that Becker, from his ivory tower, dismisses it all with the cynical suggestion that nothing better will emerge in the future.[24] What the reviewer did not understand, of course, was the general tenor of Becker's thinking over the previous thirty years.

Having skated close to the thin ice of Communism in the *Heavenly City,* Becker almost immediately backed off because of the threat to liberty which Communism posed. In an article, "The Dilemma of Liberals in Our Time" (1932), he recognized the almost untenable position of the liberal who believed in both liberty and equality. Unrestrained liberty had led, not to equality, but to the concentration of wealth in the hands of the few. The masses, exploited in the name of liberty, turned to Marxism which would restrain the rich in the interests of the poor. Liberals thus found themselves crushed between these two extremes, placed in a position where they must choose between liberty and equality. They admired Russian efforts to achieve equality, but they shuddered at the fate of liberty in Russia; they were humane lovers of the masses, but were also individuals who prized liberty, including the liberty not to belong to the masses they loved. Becker would have both liberty and equality if it were possible, but if he had to make the choice, it would be for liberty rather than equality, for he much preferred American

[24] Saul Carson in the *Philadelphia Public Ledger,* July 15, 1933.

liberty with all its flagrant inequalities to Russian equality with its lack of liberty.[25]

What Becker really wanted was a collectivist democracy which would regulate the economy to bring about a more equal society yet at the same time retain individual liberty in noneconomic matters. What was needed was less liberty and more control over the economy, but he did not spell out just how far controls over liberty should extend. He wondered whether this country was headed toward a more consciously regulated economy, whether this regulation could be achieved by methods other than those used in Russia and Italy, or whether intelligent regulation would be defeated by the demands of liberty.[26]

That Becker was no Communist is attested by a letter explaining a contribution to defend free speech for a Communist who did not really believe in free speech. Becker said that he could never understand how a Communist, on his own principles, could claim the right or expect the grant of free speech. Communism preached social revolution, the suppression of certain classes by force, and elimination of all free speech for those who opposed Communism. Communists were therefore asking for free speech in order to establish a system that would deny free speech. Becker could understand why Communists resisted oppression, but not why they resented it, for what Hitler was doing to Communists was exactly what Communist would do to Fascists if Communists had the opportunity. If Becker, as a liberal, wished for Communists to have free speech in this country, it was not to advance their cause, but because he believed that Communists would be weaker if let alone than if they were repressed.[27]

In the political arena, Becker quite obviously did not believe that the election of Franklin D. Roosevelt in 1932 would

---

[25] *Detachment*, pp. 188-213.

[26] *Ibid.* See also "Liberalism — A Way Station," *Everyman*, pp. 91-100.

[27] Becker to Norman Spitzer, May 10, 1933, Becker Papers. For a "radical" criticism of Becker's position, see Arthur M. Allen to Becker, March 20, 1933, *ibid.* Allen believed that Becker, liberal as he was, was much too far to the right.

usher in the heavenly city. He asked Dodd at Chicago whether he was one of the three million people who voted for F.D.R. in the belief that they were voting for Teddy. As for himself, he had voted for Norman Thomas, the Socialist, because he knew that Thomas could not be elected and because he did not want to be responsible in any way for the people who ran things in Washington.[28] Given Becker's emphasis on collectivism, one wonders whether his own explanation was his only reason for supporting Thomas. In a review of Charles Beard's *The American Leviathan,* Becker came to the conclusion that both political parties stood for the same thing, and that the real leviathan was society itself, which used politics as a device for getting from government all it could.[29]

For the most part, Becker was afraid that Roosevelt would not go far enough with economic regulations to cure the maladies of American capitalism. Again expressing doubt that the average man was capable of achieving great social changes through deliberation and rational reflection, Becker declared that the N.R.A. (National Recovery Administration) was a good beginning in the right direction but it was not good if it was *only* a beginning. The country would have to go much further, particularly in the distribution of profits that would enable the people to buy the goods that they produced. But then came the difficulty for Becker the liberal. He hoped that regulation could be achieved without the suppression of the traditional right of discussion and criticism, for if it could not, the country would have lost the best thing it had.[30] It was this same threat to freedom that caused him to balk at the threshold of Communism.

That Communism and Becker's philosophy of subjective relativism were closely associated became apparent in 1933 when the American Historical Association held its annual meeting in Urbana, Illinois. In part because of his reputation, and in part because of his philosophy of history, Becker was

[28] Becker to Dodd, November 29, 1932, Becker Papers.
[29] *Everyman,* pp. 81-90.
[30] Becker to Rodky?, November 27, 1933, Becker Papers.

asked to participate on the program. Conyers Read, executive secretary of the Association, and Charles A. Beard, its president in 1933, were planning a "revolutionary" session on historiography in which written history would be considered "as a record of the historian and his times rather than as a record of the times of which he writes." Read said that Becker had harped on this string in his own presidential address, "Everyman," and throughout the *Heavenly City*. It was imperative, Read continued, that they "should bring this conception of historical writing forcibly before the rising generations of historians." [31]

For reasons of health, Becker did not participate in the session on historiography, but the Urbana meeting did have repercussions of some significance to Becker's later philosophy of history. This was the meeting at which Charles A. Beard delivered his famous address, "Written History as an Act of Faith," which denied objectivity in interpretation of historical facts and projected the notion that the historian would be judged not on his account of the past, but on his correct anticipation of the future.[32] Beard was later answered by Theodore Clark Smith, who insisted that subjective relativism did not necessarily lead to the collective democracy that Beard, Becker, and their followers wanted. Smith pointed out that this philosophy had, in fact, been used to promote Fascism and Communism in Europe, and he urged historians to abandon subjective relativism in the interests of scholarly history.[33] Smith's suggestion that Fascists and Communists could manipulate society through subjective relativism would later come home to Becker with devastating force.

Although Becker refused to embrace Communism, his position on the left continued to merit the approval of socialists and liberals. One George N. Falconer, well up in the hierarchy of the Socialist Party and obviously friendly to Becker,

[31] Read to Becker, May 9, 1933, Becker Papers.

[32] Charles A. Beard, "Written History as an Act of Faith," *American Historical Review*, January, 1934, pp. 219-29.

[33] Theodore Clark Smith, "The Writing of American History in America from 1884 to 1934," *American Historical Review*, April, 1935, pp. 439-49.

wrote that "Bolshevism was Socialism with its working clothes on; Communism was Socialism with its dress suit on." He also quoted an old Russian proverb, "Do not spit in the well — you may have to drink the water," which he said was well suited to the critics of Socialism and Communism.[34] Merle Curti, whose admiration for Becker was almost unbounded, sent a copy of *Social Frontier* with a paper Curti had written on the disappearance in public thought of the idea of the right of revolution. Curti wanted Becker's criticism of his forthcoming book, *The Social Ideas of American Educators,* which Curti characterized as a rather radical kind of book that many historians might look upon as too Marxist. Curti said that he had avoided as much as possible a too close adherence to the Marxist pattern and hoped that he had succeeded somewhat.[35]

In spite of the depression, Becker himself seemed to prosper under the capitalistic democracy which he criticized and which, he insisted, must work justly for all or perish.[36] When he was approached by Felix Frankfurter about a Harmsworth professorship in England, Becker declined on the excuse that he really knew very little of the essential details of American history which he had never taught (an enlightening statement from one who had written five books on American history). Furthermore, he could not afford to accept, he said, because he now had a higher standard of living than that provided by a Harmsworth professorship. In fact, he was about to depart for California to lecture at Stanford and the University of California, lectures which would augment his income substantially.[37] A royalty account for 1934 showed that Becker for that year realized $3,171.43 on his high school textbook *Modern History.*[38]

[34] Falconer to Becker, June 5, 1934, Becker Papers.
[35] Curti to Becker, January 1, 1935, Becker Papers.
[36] "Freedom of Speech," *Everyman,* pp. 101-12.
[37] Becker to Frankfurter, January 10, 1935, Becker Papers.
[38] Silver, Burdett and Company Royalty Account, April 1, 1935, Becker Papers. Becker had published *Modern History: The Rise of a Democratic, Scientific, and Industrial Civilization* in 1931.

When he arrived on the west coast a few weeks later, Becker found many kindred spirits among the younger men at both California and Stanford. He said he had talked to the graduate students at Berkeley and would do the same at Stanford. At both institutions the hard times had made quite an impression on young instructors and graduate students; they both appeared to have been jarred out of their complacency and were quite as alert and "advanced" as the Cornell bunch.[39]

In 1935, both Becker's philosophy of history and his interpretation of early American history were given additional publicity with the appearance of another book, *Everyman His Own Historian*. In reality, the book was a collection of papers, reviews, and articles that Becker had written at one time or another, but since these were scattered in various publications, they could not exert the full impact that they could as a collected publication. In essence, the format followed that of James Harvey Robinson's book, *The New History*, and took its title from Becker's presidential address, "Everyman His Own Historian." Two chapters, one on Communism and a second on the American Revolution, are of particular interest here.[40]

Among the essays in *Everyman* was one entitled "The Marxian Philosophy of History" which explained why Becker could skate so close to Communism yet never make the final breakthrough. Communists, he said, insisted that he should either refute the Marxian philosophy of history or honestly support Communism. Becker's answer was that one could accept a Marxian interpretation of the past without embracing the Marxian prognostication for the future. A law of history based on class conflict in the past, he declared, could not possibly be valid in predicting the classless society of the future. And in addition, while Becker sympathized with the Communist desire to make a better world for the masses, he had

[39] Becker to Willis ?, May 3, 1935, Becker Papers.

[40] Carl L. Becker, *Everyman His Own Historian: Essays on History and Politics* (New York, 1935). As previously noted, quotations are used by permission of Appleton-Century-Crofts.

no faith in the use of force and the suppression of all critical opinion as the primary means of achieving the good life.[41]

The second article, a fictitious concoction entitled "John Jay and Peter Van Schaack," was first published in 1919 as an expression of Becker's disillusionment about World War I. But it was still a valid reflection of his views when it was re-issued in 1935, and shows why Becker appealed to the Old Left of his own day and to the New Left today. Although built around an episode in the American Revolution, the main thrust of this quasi novel was the liberal's concern over the questions of the individual versus the state, of freedom versus compulsion. The episode involved the question of why John Jay and Peter Van Schaack, friends with similar upper-class backgrounds, would choose the patriot or loyalist side in the Revolution.[42]

In Becker's eyes, however, the "real issue between the two friends was indeed something more fundamental than the opposition of a man who supported Britain to a man who supported America." It was an aspect of the old controversy between the one and the many, of the state against the individual, of personal liberty opposed to social compulsion, of might versus right. Jay believed that America was right, identified America with the organized power of government, and affirmed the duty of the individual to submit "to this right which was might, or this might which was right." But Van Schaack thought that America was right "only in so far as she could win the approval of Americans," and he gave his first allegiance, not to force, but "to reason and conscience." Van Schaack the loyalist was declared a traitor by Jay the patriot, but, concluded Becker, "Whether all things considered, Jay or Van Schaack was the better American, the better friend of mankind, who shall say?"

Becker's technique in using an episode of the Revolution as a vehicle for his liberalism is also significant. First he introduced class conflict through a quotation from a contempor-

[41] *Ibid.*, pp. 113-31.
[42] *Ibid.*, pp. 284-98.

ary, Gouverneur Morris, but did not show any connection between Morris's views and those of Jay or Van Schaack. Then
he injected the question of "who shall rule at home" by de-
picting a struggle between the property holders who governed
the country and "the unfranchised mechanics and artisans
who made up the chief strength of the Sons of Liberty." But
having done these two things, Becker really demonstrated that
neither had any part in the controversy, which was strictly a
British-American conflict over "home rule." And throughout
the article he used the literary device, as he had done in *The
Eve of the Revolution,* of attempting to project what Jay or
Van Schaack might have thought about their actions.[43]

Obviously Becker could not really capture the "essence of
the Revolution," as Carl Van Doren credited him with doing,[44]
for his whole "climate of opinion" was in error. There were
no unfranchised mechanics and artisans in New York, or if
they were, they were violating the law which made freemanship mandatory, and, as we have already seen, freemanship
carried the right to vote. Furthermore, Jay and Van Schaack
came from almost identical backgrounds, yet one was a patriot
and the other a loyalist, a phenomenon difficult to explain on
a class basis, as Becker admitted.

As for which was right, Jay or Van Schaack, Americans in
1776 knew and Becker ought to have known. If, as Becker's
own evidence so often proved, American society was already
democratic and the American Revolution was designed to
preserve the kind of society that Americans approved, there
should have been no doubt in Becker's mind. In effect, Jay
was championing the most nearly equalitarian and democratic
society that the modern civilized world had seen, while Van
Schaack was throwing his lot with a monarchistic imperialism
that would have greatly reduced both equality and democracy.
In particular, Becker should have realized from his evidence
in the *Heavenly City* that eighteenth-century America had

[43] *Ibid.*
[44] Van Doren to Becker, May 2, 1935, Becker Papers.

already achieved the kind of ideal society for which the French philosophes struggled.

Everyman brought both criticism and praise for Becker and his work. On the adverse side, a critical reviewer castigated Becker for his subjective relativism in saying that all "valid" versions of history must eventually be relegated to the ash heap of discarded myths, and for his "wobbly view of life" because of his approval of H. G. Wells and Voltaire.[45] Malcolm Crowley, editor of *The New Republic* and certainly no conservative, criticized Becker on the ground that he had "classangled" his subject in the first article, "Everyman," without realizing that everyman was a small capitalist and that history might appear differently to a factory work or a farmer.[46]

There was praise as well as censure, however, for *Everyman* and its author. As already noted, Carl Van Doren called the Jay-Van Schaack article "the essence of the Revolution," an indication of the impact of the Becker thesis. One of Becker's students, Robert R. Palmer, only regretted that Becker had omitted "Facts of History" ("What Are Historical Facts?") a document which, for combative reasons, he said, "we Beckerites" ought to have readily available.[47] A liberal English friend, commenting on the book, predicted that if a dictator or a Communist came into power, both he and Becker would be suppressed.[48] And from the University of Iowa came word that Andrews, Pelzer, Root, Pierce, Livingston, and Shafer were all pro-Becker, while Iowa graduate students were "absorbing your stuff in large doses and apparently without injury." [49]

It remained for Merle Curti to show the real purpose of Becker's resort to cynicism and skepticism in his writings. Curti had reviewed *Everyman* very favorable in the *American Historical Review*, and in a reply to Becker's note of thanks for

[45] R. Corrigan, *The Historical Bulletin,* May 1935.
[46] Crowley to Becker, May 20, 1935, Becker Papers.
[47] Palmer to Becker, April 5, 1935, Becker Papers.
[48] Charles G. Crump to Becker, May 8-12, 1935, Becker Papers.
[49] Andrews to Becker, April 5, 1935, Becker Papers.

the review, Curti expressed gratitude for the extent to which Becker had influenced his colleagues, especially younger men of Curti's own generation. Then Curti went on to express the revealing opinion that those who criticized Becker on the belief that his work resulted in mere negative skepticism were on weak ground, for skepticism, he said, is not necessarily negative. Curti believed that Becker's skepticism had been effective in making liberalism a force in clarifying social issues and in furthering the goals that social radicals desired.[50]

Promoting goals that social radicals desired was the obvious intent of Becker's 1935 lectures at Stanford which appeared as a book, *Progress and Power,* in 1936. The acquisition of material power made possible the idea of human progress, he said, for without power there was no progress. Men came to see themselves within a predictable outer world that could be controlled and within a developing social world that changes for the better. The idea of progress, with its hope for the material heavenly city on earth, replaced the declining Christian doctrine of the spiritual heavenly city after death. Becker's own values for measuring progress were liberty, equality, fraternity, humanity, toleration, and reason; his antipathies were authority, compulsion, obedience, regimentation, uniformity, and standardization.[51]

But the heavenly city on earth had failed to materialize, not because man had not acquired sufficient power, but because the fruits of that power had not been distributed equitably. Some men, Becker said, looked back to a golden age of the past, but "nostalgia for the past deprives man of confidence in the future." Wealth, created by the efforts of all society, came to be controlled and enjoyed by the few at the expense of the many. Instead of the heavenly city, the result had been class struggle and war, and man would never realize his dream

[50] Becker to Curti, October 12, and Curti to Becker, October 19, 1935. Becker Papers.
[51] Carl L. Becker, *Progress and Power* (Palo Alto, 1936), pp. 4-15.

of a heavenly city until he devised a system which would result in equitable distribution of the world's material goods.[52]

Becker was undoubtedly promoting the goals that social radicals advocated. He looked upon the doctrine of progress as the most effective, revolutionary, and dislocating invention ever made by Europeans, for it liberated men's minds from the restraints of tradition, located perfection in the future rather than in the past, and disposed men to consider change as sufficient validation for conscious revolutionary activity.[53]

In addition to promoting goals that social radicals advocated, Becker made a significant alteration in his philosophy of subjective relativism. He said that in order to view the broad sweep of human history, the historian must take a vantage point of detachment, a position which he had long denied and one which, of course, ran counter to subjective relativism. Fortunately, he declared, "it is not altogether impossible to do this. One of the tricks man has picked up on his way is the power to hold himself at arm's length in order to observe himself as an object from the outside." Becker said that he was choosing the Olympian Heights, the home of the Greek gods.[54] But whatever his vantage point, and assuming that he really meant what he said, this statement marked a change of philosophy which would develop in later years.

As with almost anything else that he wrote, *Progress and Power* brought to Becker the abundant praise to which he had long been accustomed. His colleague at Cornell, Preserved Smith, said, "It is simply one of the greatest historical essays ever written," and contained more fresh thought than many a "polytome" history of the world.[55] Becker's former student, Louis Gottschalk, wrote that he and another student had once discussed Becker's ability to "sit on the moon and unconcerned but interested watch the world go by." Someday he would take the last few pages of the book and by proper

[52] *Ibid.*, pp. 54, 65, 99-103.
[53] *Ibid.*, p. 93.
[54] *Ibid.*, p. 19.
[55] Smith to Becker, May 21, 1936, Becker Papers.

punctuation show all the world that they were in reality free verse poetry.[56] Carl Van Doren considered the book as the work of a historian who was also a philosopher, a wit, and a man of letters.[57] And Moses Aronson, managing editor of the *Journal of Social Philosophy*, asked Becker who would be a proper person to review *Progress and Power*.[58]

Given Becker's repeated criticism of American capitalism and his open advocacy of the Marxian interpretation of history, it was almost inevitable that he would eventually be accused of Communism. Becker's involvement was noted in a letter from a former student who was much surprised to see Becker's name listed with those of Charles A. Beard and David Muzzey in the September, 1935, issue of the *American Legion Monthly* as preaching treason.[59] Then followed a memorandum, submitted to the Board of Education of Washington, D. C., by a Committee of the Federation of Citizens Associations, concerning Communism as it was being taught through textbooks used in the public schools. The Committee requested elimination of Becker's *Modern History* as one of the offending books — the book that Becker had published in 1931.[60]

According to the memorandum, there was no doubt that Becker had left himself open to criticism. In explaining Marx, Becker said that the silent operation of economic forces displaced feudalism with capitalism, and that "just as the feudal nobles were shoved aside by the middle-class capitalists, so the middle-class capitalists will in the course of time be shoved aside by the mass of the people — the 'proletariat.' " Marx had devised a scientific socialism which promised a heavenly city on earth for the struggling masses, "a new philosophy — religion — a religion to console them in their present distress; a philosophy pointing out the good time coming." Lenin was among those great leaders "in the crusade for human freedom"

---

[56] Gottschalk to Becker, March 29, 1937, Becker Papers.
[57] Van Doren to Becker, November 20, 1936, Becker Papers.
[58] Aronson to Becker, June 13, 1936, Becker Papers.
[59] W. B. Townsend to Becker (September, 1935), Becker Papers.
[60] September, 1935, Becker Papers.

who have "united a passionate sympathy for the poor and oppressed with a passionate hatred for those whom they held responsible for poverty and oppression." The memorandum said that Becker was "shown by the records of the Congressional Library to be a well-known communistic writer" who did not include any readings to show Communism's "evil and atrocious aims and purposes." [61]

For a time the situation looked very serious. While Becker had the support of the Washington Board of Education and the high school teachers,[62] and while the *Baltimore Sun* backed him in an editorial,[63] William Randolph Hearst and his *Washington Herald* went after Becker with a vengeance.[64] The publisher of Becker's controversial book prepared to defend him in Washington, pointing out that if the attack were not stopped there, it would spread to schools all over the country.[65] Since $5,890 of Becker's income of $12,238 for 1935 came from royalties on his book, he certainly had a substantial stake in the controversy.[66]

Eventually, however, the charges against Becker were dropped. Becker wrote an open letter to the *Washington Herald* denying that he was a Communist or that he favored the doctrines of Marx and Lenin. As proof, he pointed to a forthcoming review of his book, *Everyman,* by Louis Hacker in the *New Republic* in which Hacker would condemn Becker because he did not subscribe to the Marxian Communist interpretation of history. Becker claimed that his account of Marx, Lenin, and Communism was merely a factual explanation, not a panergyric.[67] In addition, Becker asked for support from

[61] Memorandum, Becker Papers.

[62] Becker to W. Stull Holt, November 7, 1935, Becker Papers.

[63] *Baltimore Sun,* November 22, 1935.

[64] Silver, Burdett and Company to Becker, November 22, 1935, Becker Papers.

[65] Albert L. Hart to Becker, November 22, 1935, Becker Papers.

[66] New York State Income Tax return, 1936, Becker Papers.

[67] Becker to *Washington Herald,* November 26, 1935, Becker Papers. Hacker's review is in *The New Republic,* January 8, 1936.

leading historians in the country, and instead of the twenty-four telegrams he requested, fifty were sent.[68]

In defending himself against the charges of Communism, however, Becker was forced to repudiate to some extent his subjective relativism as a philosophy of history. In his letter to the *Washington Herald,* Becker declared that "the function of the historian is to tell as accurately as he can what happened," and he insisted that in his book he had "studiously refrained from imposing my personal views on students and teachers." [69] Those statements are difficult to square with Becker's often-repeated views that the very function of the historian was to help promote the good life of the future, and naturally one of his aims was to impose his interpretation of history on students and teachers.

Readers of Becker's book might well have been pardoned had they been unable to tell whether Becker's account of Communism was merely an explanation or a panegyric, for apparently even some of his students had difficulty in making this distinction. One of them, who had taken a position interviewing unemployed people in North Dakota, wrote that since she was "wavering between socialism and communism," she would rather return to Cornell and be in the seminar of the man who thought that the Communist Party was "the most intelligent political party in the country" than to converse with people who were as frightened of Socialism as they would be of the Devil.[70]

On final analysis, Becker had indeed skated safely over the thin ice of Communism, but the margin of safety had been drawn dangerously fine.

Given the furor over the charges of Communism, it was probably just as well that an article of Becker's, "New Liberties For Old," did not appear at its scheduled time, October, 1935, and that when it was published in January, 1936, it

[68] Becker to Curti, December 7, 1935, and Irene Gibson (of Silver, Burdett) to Becker, November 2, 1935, Becker Papers.

[69] Becker to *Washington Herald,* November 26, 1935, Becker Papers.

[70] Florence McClure to Becker, February 5, 1936, Becker Papers.

came out in a new and obscure journal, *The Journal of Social Philosophy*. The article was a comparison of the old liberties under liberal democracy and the new liberties promised by Marxian Communism. An uncommitted reader might have experienced some difficulty in deciding which liberty, the old or the new, came off best in the discussion.[71]

In this article, Becker said that both liberal democracy and Communism based their ideologies on "liberty," but both had different concepts of what liberty meant. Herbert Hoover, as a representative of liberal democracy, defined liberty as the right to choose one's own calling, to develop one's talents, to win and preserve a home free from intrusion, to earn, spend, save, and accumulate property for old age and loved ones. The liberties of democracy, however, appeared to the Communist as merely the vested rights of the exploiters. Communists, and others who opposed liberal capitalism, saw democratic liberty in terms of ten or twelve million unemployed who could not under any circumstances do anything that Hoover defined as liberty. Communists would use force to eliminate the evils of the existing regime while Hoover would use force to preserve its benefits. Hoover, wrote Becker, voiced the class interests of the exploiters; Communists voiced those of the exploited.[72]

The failure of liberal democracy, formulated in the eighteenth century to foster freedom, equality, and humanity, had caused the lower classes to turn to Communism, Becker continued. Based on the doctrine of right reason, liberal democracy was expected to promote progress and truth by freeing men from economic and intellectual restraints. But instead of these results, liberal democracy, with the aid of the industrial revolution, brought concentration of wealth into the hands of the few and dispossession of the masses. The latter then became class-conscious, regarded traditional liberties as masked instruments of exploitation, saw that true liberty called for

---

[71] Carl L. Becker, "New Liberties For Old," *Journal of Social Philosophy*, January, 1936. The article was later republished in a collection of essays under the same title (Yale University Press, 1941) pp. 1-43.

[72] *Ibid.*

restriction of individual freedom and extension of social control, and turned to a new radical ideology, Communism.[73]

Becker believed that in their fundamental presuppositions, liberal and Communist ideologies were very much alike, but there were also important differences. Both began as movements to free the enslaved masses from the oppression of the sinister few. But whereas the liberal emphasized reason and sought the emancipation of the individual from social control, the Communist stressed conformity and demanded that the individual be subjected to social control. The triumph of one naturally meant the defeat of the other.[74]

Eventually, said Becker, the liberal concept of right reason as an infallible guide to action became outmoded and was replaced by new concepts for guiding human affairs. Right reason, unconditioned by will or emotion, might be a reliable instrument for distinguishing truth, but when men doubted that reason could distinguish what is true from what is desired, liberal concepts of truth, justice, liberty, equality, and humanity became affected by relativity and lost something of their objective reality and universal relevance. Eventually Darwin provided a theory which made a purely material process adequate to account for biological and social progress. The mind became merely a part of the material process, facilitating adjustment to the environment and enabling men to attain desired ends. Reason could be regarded as a function of activity and truth as an integration of activities that proved successful in attaining desired ends. Applied to social activities, truth was no more than a consistent correlation of the good reasons men were able to find for doing what they wanted to do. Right reason thus was displaced by the relativist conception of reason and truth. In short, the end justified the means.[75]

Relativism thus became an important weapon in the war between liberal democracy and Communism, according to Becker. Marx did not invent the relativist conception of

[73] *Ibid.*
[74] *Ibid.*
[75] *Ibid.*

reason and truth, but he borrowed the dialectic conception of progress, and relativism emerged as an implicit presupposition of a social theory designed to discredit liberal ideology. In seeking a theory of social progress to explain the deplorable condition of the industrial workers, Marx believed that social progress was fundamentally determined by a conflict of material interests rather than by a conflict of rational concepts. Thus ideas and institutions were the results rather than the causes of underlying economic activities. Marx insisted that all economic and ideal structures, since they were inherent in the dialectic, were relatively true and good because they were necessary stages in social progress. But being relatively true, they must be superseded by a higher synthesis, a more advanced form of goodness and truth. The relativist conception of truth was thus indispensible to Communist ideology in condemning liberal capitalism to a lingering death.[76]

But the very nature of relativism blocked Becker's acceptance of Communism as the wave of the future. Relativism justified the workers in using any means to establish Communism, and whatever the means, their goodness and truth would be measured by their success and would emerge as functions of activities inherent in the dialectic. By the same token, however, the workers had no assurance that Communism itself, through the same dialectic process, would not generate its own antithesis and give way to a still higher synthesis. Marx used relativism to undermine liberalism, but then had to discard relativism for absolutism in order to save Communism from the same fate. To Becker, the very dialectic which brought Communism would eventually destroy Communism, but in seeing this, Becker also seemed to have some doubts about the validity of subjective relativism.[77]

In the end, Becker left the final choice of liberalism or Communism to the reader. He obviously approved of the fact that Marx knew what the world ought to be — that it ought to abolish flagrant inequality and shocking injustice by

[76] *Ibid.*
[77] *Ibid.*

socializing private production and private profit. But while he could sympathize with the theoretical goals of Communism, he insisted that in practice, Communism, as had liberal democracy, had failed to live up to its ideals. Nevertheless, looked at in the long perspective, he believed that liberal and Communist ideologies were formulations of the modern doctrine of progress. Both belonged to the category of useful social myths around which men could coordinate perceptions of the present with remembered experiences from the past and anticipated actions in the future. Becker expressed the hope that in time men would increasingly subordinate useful social myths to factual knowledge so that the effective social ideology would take on the flexible pragmatic character of a scientific hypothesis.[78] Used in this context, "factual knowledge" seemed to carry a connotation of truth, something that Becker had long denied in his concept of facts.

The brightness of the Becker star apparently was undimmed by the Communism episode in 1935, for the accolades continued to pour in. In asking about publication of Becker's earlier paper on the nature of historical facts, Harry Elmer Barnes declared that it was "about the most significant paper ever read before the American Historical Association." To Barnes, this paper ("What Are Historical Facts?") occupied about the same place in relation to traditional history that the new physics of Einstein, Planck, and Schrödinger did to physics of the nineteenth century. Its publications would be far more devastating than Beard's reflections on "That Noble Dream." [79] Barnes referred to Beard's rebuttal of the attack on his presidential address of December, 1933, by Theodore Clark Smith in which Beard contended that the objective history called for by Smith was only an unattainable "noble dream." [80] Later Barnes said that the Becker paper was "the

---

[78] *Ibid.*

[79] Barnes to Becker, February 28, 1936, Becker Papers.

[80] Beard, "Written History as an Act of Faith," *American Historical Review*, January, 1934; Smith, "The Writing of American History in America from 1884 to 1934," *ibid.*, April, 1935; Beard, "That Noble Dream," *ibid.*, October, 1935.

most important theoretical contribution to historical criticism since the days of Von Ranke." [81]

That Becker was really still as much the subjective relativist as he was when he gave his paper on the nature of historical facts is also apparent. Becker objected to a statement by a fellow professor in Romance Languages at Cornell, Morris Bishop, who said, "We are rejecting specific testimony on the basis of an *a priori* theory." Becker said that this statement went to the heart of the question as to the value of testimony in establishing historical facts. Our knowledge of history rests on testimony, he said, but testimony shows only that witnesses had a certain experience, not that their interpretation of the experience is correct. But we accept testimony up to a certain point, and that point is reached when witnesses testify to something that conflicts with our settled convictions. Historical knowledge for us, or for any other age, he continued, rests in the last analysis on our general philosophy of the world and how it behaves. Becker agreed with Justice Holmes that "truth is only the system of my limitations." [82]

Letters to Becker continued to indicate the profound influence of his writings on other historians. Marshall Knappen confessed that he was still using Becker's ideas ten years out of graduate school and had them so thoroughly ingrained that "he thinks they are his own." Said Knappen: "That is the supreme form of salesmanship, to give a person not only the idea but the belief that it is his own so that he will go out and fight for his baby." [83] W. Stull Holt confided to Mrs. Becker that in profundity, in keenness of observing human behavior, and in literary artistry, her husband was "without a peer at present in America." [84] Another correspondent reported that "Beckerism" was "seeping into Miami University" through the books of Leo Gershoy and the new Ferguson and Bruun. [85] And Henry Steele Commager sent a

[81] Barnes to Becker, March 21, 1936, Becker Papers.
[82] Becker to Morris Bishop, November 22, 1936, Becker Papers.
[83] Knappen to Becker, November 21, 1936, Becker Papers.
[84] Holt to Mrs. Becker, March 23, 1936, Becker Papers.
[85] O. J. Frederickson to Becker, September 20, 1936, Becker Papers.

copy of his latest book "as an acknowledgment, altogether inadequate, of my debt to you that is long-standing and that grows, like all debts, from year to year. It would be difficult for me to exaggerate the pleasure which I have found in your writing . . . and even more difficult for me to explain the significance that your interpretations of history and of people have had for me." [86]

But whatever Becker's interpretation of American history, it was neither nationalistic nor Turnerian in its implications. A former student spoke of Becker's approach to American history which tried to be fair to the Old Land from which this country received — "well, just everything." She also spoke of the clear, scholarly presentation, and, by implication and illustration, of the prejudice and pitifully contemptible propaganda — a bid for world sympathy — which animated the not overscrupulous Jefferson at the time of the Declaration of Independence. She thanked Becker for his fairness, for many times she had felt the absence of decent respect for the feelings and intelligence of a stranger within these not always hospitable gates. Then to demonstrate how little she understood the real Becker, she said that perchance the "Carl" explained everything, and took one back to the scholarly, unbiased German mind.[87] Becker must have smiled — or winced — at this comparison.

Much more accurate than this student was a characterization of Becker's writing and teaching as directed toward collectivism. Harold Laski, the English Marxist, reviewed a series of books produced under the auspices of the American Historical Association, praising especially the works of George S. Counts (*The Social Foundations of Education*), Merle Curti (*Social Ideas of American Educators*), and C. E. Merriam (*Civic Education in the United States*). The import of these contributions, said Laski, was that the United States needed education with new content and emphasis: "It must be for a life socially controlled instead of for a life primarily motivated

[86] Commager to Becker, April 15, 1936, Becker Papers.
[87] Ada Flockton to Becker, June 22, 1936, Becker Papers.

by individual acquisitiveness." Textbooks should be written and teachers should be trained to achieve this socialization. "At bottom, and stripped of its carefully neutral phrases," Laski continued, "the report is an educational program for a socialist America." As a Marxist, Laski did not believe that the program could be implemented democratically in a capitalist society, but in the review he praised Becker as a great teacher of the doctrines that these books espoused. A friend, who obviously approved of what Laski had to say about Becker, wrote that Laski's review article paid a compliment to Becker.[88]

Apparently Counts, one of the authors reviewed by Laski, agreed with Laski that Becker was a fellow worker in the good cause of collectivism. Becker had written to Counts, praising his last book, and this praise had pleased Counts more than he could say. A favorable comment from Becker meant a great deal, for as Counts said, "I know of no one whose scholarship and social sympathies I respect more highly." [89]

A short time later, Laski had additional praise for both Becker and Beard as apostles of collective democracy. In a joint review of Beard's *Discussion of Human Affairs* and Becker's *Progress and Power,* Laski said that the only difference between his own views and those of Becker and Beard was in method of accomplishment. Becker and Beard were liberal eclectics who believed that collectivism could come through the democratic process, while he was a Marxist who believed that revolution was the only way. But at bottom, their hopes were his hopes, their ultimate goal was his goal; the quality of their gallant service could not be too generously acknowledged. Both books contained much of the liberalism that their authors had sought for nearly forty years to communicate to their students. They were the enemies of conservatism and the vested interests who opposed change,

[88] Harold J. Laski, "A New Education for a New America," *The New Republic,* July 29, 1936; E. R. B. Willis to Becker, July 31, 1936, Becker Papers.
[89] George S. Counts to Becker, October 10, 1938, Becker Papers.

but they shrank from the idea of outright revolution. Laski said that he would be profoundly disturbed if the standards of scholarship of a book of his own elicited the condemnation of Becker or Beard. Nothing was more splendid than the enemies they had been willing to make, enemies who had always united to declare Becker and Beard as dangerous men. There were students to whom Becker's studies of the first generation of United States history had been an epoch in their lives, and one of the most eminent of living French scholars called *The Heavenly City* "the wisest book ever written upon that exciting theme." Laski insisted that young scholars could find no better models than Becker and Beard on which to pattern their own lives.[90]

Laski's praise of Becker's social philosophy as similar to his own brought some significant results. Before publishing the Laski review, Malcolm Crowley, editor of the *New Republic*, asked Becker if he wanted to answer the review, to tell Harold Laski that he was absolutely wrong.[91] Whatever Becker's answer to Crowley, he naturally did not answer the review. Instead, he apparently wrote to Laski praising Laski's latest book, for Laski wrote back that he had written what he had written because he thought it was necessary for his own satisfaction and because two or three of Becker's books had helped him such as no other books had. He also expressed pleasure that Becker liked his latest book.[92]

Yet there appeared to be some ambivalence in Becker's liberalism and social philosophy. His writings reveal collective democracy as his aim, and obviously he conveyed this idea to his students. One of them wrote that she was living in a certain place in New York and someday she would tell him why living there was a "good preparation for a collective society."[93] But shortly thereafter, in a letter to another student, Becker expressed serious doubts about the common

[90] *The New Republic,* September 16, 1936.
[91] Crowley to Becker, August 31, 1936, Becker Papers.
[92] Laski to Becker, October 28, 1936, Becker Papers.
[93] Florence Mishmon? to Becker, October 27, 1936, Becker Papers.

people, such as no good liberal should have had — doubts about the very foundation on which his collective democracy would be built. He opposed Franklin D. Roosevelt's proposal to reform the Supreme Court and signified his lack of faith in the wisdom of the people and the representatives they were likely to choose. Liberals and radicals considered the Supreme Court a nuisance when they had a liberal president and congress, but he wanted to preserve the Court as a check against a reactionary president and congress.[94]

In the public eye, however, Becker continued to be viewed as a liberal. John Dewey headed a commission of inquiry into the charges against Leon Trotsky at the recent Moscow trials "because the truth about the Moscow trials must be established in order to put an end to the controversy that is dividing the labor and liberal movement." Dewey picked Becker as one of the commissioners, along with such well-known liberals as Louis Adamic, John Chamberlain, John Dos Passos, Max Eastman, Louis Hacker, Sidney Hook, Reinhold Niebuhr, Norman Thomas, and W. E. Woodward.[95] When Becker turned down the request to serve on the Trotsky Commission, the Commission wanted a letter from him endorsing the value of the investigation.[96] The managing editor of the *Yale Review* also wrote to Becker for suggestions of liberal writers to write for the *Review*. She already had in mind one writer who was "just as liberal as he can be within the limits of his respect for the law," and another who "expressed a very liberal point of view." [97]

The request for liberal writers for the *Yale Review* brought a new note into Becker's philosophy of history — objectivism. Becker, who was now associated with the *Review*, was looking for someone to write an article on the Spanish Civil War for that journal — someone well grounded in nineteenth and twentieth-century Spanish history to get the war solidly based

[94] Becker to Val Lorwin, February ?, 1937, Becker Papers.
[95] George Novak to Becker, March 23, 1937, Becker Papers.
[96] Felix Morrow to Becker, April 12, 1937, Becker Papers.
[97] Helen McAfee to Becker, March 23, 1937, Becker Papers.

"without being twisted out of shape by either a Communist or fascist, or democratic bias." This was asking a good deal, he knew, and he did not mean that the author should be so objective that he had no opinions. He just wanted a man who would not make his article into a propagandist tract, and he named two writers whom he did not want.[98]

Becker himself fulfilled part of the demand for liberal writers in the *Review* by contributing a liberal article on war. The article, "Loving Peace and Waging War," was an unrelieved condemnation of war as an instrument for settling differences between nations. Becker criticized the writings of Hugo Grotius, the seventeenth-century Dutch statesman, who supported the idea of a just war for defense, for recovery of property unjustly taken, and for righting wrongs. Becker said that Grotius merely made all wars just, because countries always claimed that their wars were just. The best example of the futility of war to promote the interests of any people was World War I, the *reductio ad absurdum,* which had merely helped to make the world safe for dictators. Wars and social injustice both rested on the competitive instincts of men, and before wars could be abolished, economic conflict within nations must be abated. Both war and social justice could be achieved when the people demanded that their governments take action on both fronts. Above all, however, we must not unite such words as right and war, he said, for while we must accept war as a fact, we must strip it of all connotations of right and justice.[99]

There was no doubt in Becker's mind that internal social justice and collectivism went together — something approaching theoretical Communism. To a former student who wrote a paper criticizing democratic capitalism, Becker declared that the objective of Communist ideology, whatever its practice in Russia, was a more equalitarian and democratic society, an ideology not essentially different from American democratic ideology. But Becker warned this writer not to use Communist

[98] Becker to Max [Lerner], April 11, 1937, Becker Papers.
[99] *Yale Review,* June, 1937, pp. 649-68.

terminology if he wanted to achieve collectivism. In twenty-five years, Russia and the United States might well have similar regulated economies, but if so, collectivists must avoid Communist terms and invent new ones. For example, he said, what could be more American and less alarming than the National Industrial Recovery Act? But words such as Soviet, Communism, Marxism, Bolshevism, and dialectic materialism would be rejected. Even the N.R.A. was only a good beginning in the right direction, for the country must go much further in regulating the industrial system and distributing profits fairly. If profits could not be distributed equitably without the suppression of free discussion and criticism, however, the country would lose the best thing it had. How to curtail economic freedom without limiting other freedoms was the big problem.[100]

It is clear to us now that Becker was never a Communist, yet his sympathies with the goals of theoretical Communism were such that he could easily have been mistaken for a fellow traveler. Men did not always distinguish between Becker's acceptance of the Marxian interpretation of history and the humanitarian aims of Communism, on the one hand, and his rejection of Communist methods and prognostications for the future on the other. Certain it is that many of his students believed that he was closer to Communism than he was willing to admit, and it was just as well for him that some of the things which he wrote or which were written about him after 1935 were not in print at the time the charges of Communism were made against him.

The charges of Communism, however, did not appreciably diminish the influence of progressive history during the 1930's, although the gains during this period were not as spectacularly evident as they had been during the twenties. There was no reason, in fact, why they should be, for by this time progressivism had become the accepted mode of interpreting the American past. If progressive history could prosper in the conservative twenties, there was little danger that it would

---

[100] Becker to F. S. Rodkey, November ?, 1937, Becker Papers.

languish under the New Deal, a political philosophy which had at least some of the connotations of the collective democracy that Becker advocated.

Undoubtedly the most convincing indication that the progressive philosophy and interpretation had become established, however, was the extent to which they found their way into history and political science textbooks in the colleges and universities. We have already noted this with the advent of the Beard and Parrington books in 1927, and the trend set by these two writers broadened immeasurably in the thirties. The authors of textbooks, because of the very nature of a textbook, were for the most part following the "specialists" in the field, and the specialists had now become Becker, Beard, Schlesinger, Jameson, Parrington, and others of the progressive school.

More or less typical of the history textbooks which incorporated the progressive interpretation was John D. Hicks' widely-used text, *The Federal Union,* published in 1937. Hicks had the now familiar story of a class-ridden colonial society, a dual revolution for both independence and social democracy, and a conservative counterrevolution in the Constitution to nullify the democratic gains of the Revolution. Removing any doubts about the paternity of his interpretation, Hicks repeated the Becker statement about "home rule" and "who should rule at home," quoted extensively from Jameson's "waves of revolution" characterization of the Revolution, and pointed out that Beard's *Economic Interpretation of the Constitution* had "profoundly affected the thinking of most students of American history" and that the *Rise of American Civilization* gave free rein to "Beard's flare for brilliant interpretation." [101]

That glaring contradiction that we have encountered so often, involving the question of whether the American Revolution really was a social revolution, was also prominent in

[101] John D. Hicks, *The Federal Union* (Houghton Mifflin Company, Boston, 1937). For colonial society, see pp. 73, 77, 132; for the Revolution, see p. 171; for the Constitution see pp. 197 and note, 198, 207-11. Quotations used by permission of Houghton Mifflin Company.

Hicks' account. First there was a social revolution, for the downfall of the colonial aristocracy and the victory of predominantly lower-class patriots over predominately upper-class loyalists "made it possible for men who in colonial times had been regarded as of low degree to hold high office and enjoy important privileges. Common men came naturally to hold themselves in higher esteem and their superiors in lower." [102] But when he got to the revolutionary state constitutions, Hicks decided that there had really been no social revolution after all. These constitutions, which followed aristocratic colonial political practices as closely as possible when they should have reflected radical lower-class social philosophies, placed property restrictions on voters, higher property restrictions on office holders, and contained checks and balances which should have favored the upper classes. It is clear, he declared, that the framers of these constitutions did not include among the natural rights of men the right to vote and to hold office, for probably the adoption of manhood suffrage "would have expanded the electorate fourfold." [103]

Having emasculated the social revolution as suggested by Becker and proclaimed by J. T. Adams, Jameson, and Parrington, Hicks appeared to fall back to Beard's 1913 enigma of a conservative Constitution adopted to thwart a nonexistent democracy. By the end of the Confederation, he said, class lines were clearly drawn between men of property and the common people, the upper classes feared encroachments on their property by the lower classes, and representatives to the Constitutional Conventional were typical representatives of the conservative upper classes who had little faith in democracy. Desiring to construct a government democratic enough to be adopted yet constituting no threat to upper-class control, the delegates incorporated checks and balances in the Constitution to thwart democratic aspirations. There was a great struggle along class lines over ratification, Hicks continued, for suffrage requirements favored upper-class pro-

[102] *Ibid.,* p. 171.
[103] *Ibid.,* pp. 163, 166.

ponents of the Constitution, and ratification did not prove that there was a great popular mandate for the Constitution.[104]

While there were some variations in detail, the general pattern of textbooks followed that of Hicks with considerable fidelity. There appeared to be little inclination in the profession to question the contradictions, for subjective relativism allowed anyone to shape the American past to his own liking, and most historians by this time appeared to like the shape that American history had taken.

Other textbooks, in addition to those on general American history, also followed the progressive interpretation. For example, Oliver P. Chitwood, whose book, *A History of Colonial America,* was widely used during the 1930's, was one of these, although the interpretation was almost lost in the mass of detail that was included without any interpretation whatever. Chitwood often cited J. T. Adams, Parrington, Jameson, Becker, Schlesinger, Van Tyne, and the Beards in footnotes and suggested readings.[105] Then there was the famous "Ogg and Ray," names that became almost synonymous with an introductory course in political science and which stood for the extremely popular *Introduction to American Government: The National Government* by Frederic A. Ogg and P. Orman Ray. It would be impossible to estimate the number of students who were introduced to the progressive interpretation of the foundations of American government through "Ogg and Ray." [106]

There were additional indications outside of textbooks that the progressive interpretation was continuing to spread. One is the work of John C. Miller, who was emerging as a productive scholar in the 1930's. In a 1933 article, Miller interpreted a religious revival, the Great Awakening, and the Massachusetts Land Bank of 1740 in terms of class conflict, contending that the religious revival prevented an economic conflict between

[104] *Ibid.,* pp. 197, 198, 207-11.

[105] Oliver Perry Chitwood, *A History of Colonial America* (New York, 1931), pp. 193, 581-83, 644, 686-88, 702-05.

[106] Frederic A. Ogg and P. Orman Ray, *Introduction to American Government: The National Government* (New York, 1935, 1938), chs. I and II.

upper and lower classes over hard or soft money from turning into a social revolution more than three decades before the American Revolution.[107] Then in 1936, Miller grounded his book, *Sam Adams: Pioneer in Propaganda,* on the class-struggle interpretation of Becker, Beard, and Schlesinger. With Thomas Hutchinson the leader of the aristocrats and Sam Adams at the head of the lower classes, the Revolution became a social revolution in which Adams provoked British-American controversies in order that the radicals could gain power.[108]

Charles A. Beard also continued to underscore progressivism during this time. In the preface to the 1935 edition of his *An Economic Interpretation of the Constitution,* Beard defended his work against charges of Marxism and also put his stamp of approval on his interpretation which had been offered in 1913 as a merely suggestive guide to future research. He pointed out that his was only *An* interpretation, not *The* interpretation, and that he had gotten his inspiration from James Madison and other Founding Fathers rather than from Karl Marx. But Beard did not change the content of the book in any way, an indication that he had come to accept it as definitive just as it was being so accepted by others, and the two minor changes which he said that he might have made had he revised the text would simply have added strength to his original argument.[109]

So by 1937, the seeds of progressive history that had been planted at the turn of the century had produced a bumper crop. Becker's crusade was obviously successful, for as much as any other American historian, he was responsible for the harvest.

[107] John C. Miller, "Religion, Finance and Democracy in Massachusetts," *New England Quarterly,* VI (March, 1933).

[108] John C. Miller, *Sam Adams: Pioneer in Propaganda* (Boston, 1936).

[109] Charles A. Beard, *An Economic Interpretation of the Constitution of the United States* (New York, 1935), preface.

VIII. RETURN OF THE PRODIGAL, 1938-1945

> "The fallacy is to suppose that because truth is in some sense relative it cannot be distinguished from error, or that the margin of error cannot be progressively reduced."
>
> ". . . in the long run all values are inseparable from the love of truth and the disinterested search for it."
>
> — CARL BECKER, 1940

BECKER'S subjective relativism, his critical attitude toward democratic capitalism, and his class-conflict interpretation of early American history were not to prevail in the final accounting. World events would cause Becker to take a hard second look at the climate of opinion which he had labored so long to create, and what he saw assumed a different contour from what it had in the past. The man who emerged from this soul-searching was hardly recognizable as the historian who had influenced countless professors and students of American history during the previous forty years. In the end, the prodigal abandoned history as propaganda, as a pack of tricks to be played on the dead for the benefit of the living. Realizing the harm that his teaching and writing had done, he spent his last years attempting to rebuild what he had so effectively destroyed over a long academic career.

The change in Becker, however, was not immediately evident. As he pursued his goal of the just collective society, Becker's writing continued to be a blend of philosophical creativity and subjective relativism. Both elements are present in an article, "Afterthoughts on Constitutions," published in

1938 as part of the commemoration of the one hundred and fiftieth anniversary of the Constitution.[1]

Becker warned his readers, as he often did, that his writing was much more the result of imagination than of research. He said that a world in which James Madison had a sense of humor would not be the world we know, and since this suggestion catapults us into a world of fantasy, it would not be amiss for one who knew little about the minutiae of particular constitutions to hazard some remarks about constitutions in general. He went on to say that he would dispense with the testimony of independent witnesses not self-deceived, "take a little flight into the blue," and run the risk of going mildly philosophical and visionary.[2]

With these warnings, Becker then developed the thesis that the constitutions which emerged from the Age of Enlightenment were really idealistic attempts by eighteenth-century progressives to draw blueprints for the heavenly city on earth. The aims of revolutionists, he said, were to find answers to the questions of the proper basis of political authority and limits of governmental power, as well as to delineate the fundamental and imprescriptible rights of citizens. Written constitutions were designed to provide answers by delimiting the realms of social compulsion and individual liberty. Becker said that it was taken for granted that when men were free, they would be equal; when they were equal, all would have enough; when all had enough, no one would be unjust or inhumane.[3]

That this notion of eighteenth-century constitutions, as portrayed by Becker, was a "flight into the blue" becomes obvious when one considers the American Constitution. If one concedes that James Madison was the father of the Constitution, one must also admit that the very basis of Madison's constitutional thinking was inequality, not equality. As he revealed so clearly in the convention debates and in Federalist

---

[1] *Yale Review*, March, 1938, pp. 450-62.
[2] *Ibid.*
[3] *Ibid.*

No. X, Madison believed that men were born with differing potentials, that these inherent inequalities would lead to the acquisition of different amounts and kinds of property, and that the function of government was not to make all men equal but to protect those very inherent differences of ability that would result in inequalities of wealth. Madison also believed, however, that constitutions should have checks and balances to prevent the acquisition of privileges by any one group. And one must also remember that the American Constitution implicitly sanctioned the institution of slavery.

Constitutions, Becker continued, resulted from the formulation of the idea of progress. Men came to believe that nature could be made amenable to man's control and that through reason, men could indefinitely improve their lot on earth. Revolution was merely the natural process by which men brought their institutions into harmony with the universal laws of nature; revolution did not need an apology, for it had become a right. All that was necessary, therefore, was to define man's natural rights and then devise a mechanism of government to protect them. Becker listed these rights as life, liberty, and the pursuit of happiness, omitting the natural right so familiar to people of the eighteenth century — the right of property. To Becker, the all-inclusive right was liberty — freedom of thought that truth might prevail, freedom of occupation that careers would open to talent, freedom of self-government that men could not be compelled against their will.[4]

But constitutions did not live up to the optimistic hopes of their progressive supporters, said Becker. Through science, men shaped the outer world of nature to human control, but because man was less tolerant of rational manipulation and control than things were, every effort to shape the world of social relations to humane ends had ended in defeat. The absolutes of the eighteenth century had become the relativities of the twentieth century. Natural law turned out to be only a

[4] *Ibid.*

convenient and temporary hypothesis. Imprescriptible rights depend on perscriptive law for validity, liberty is inseparable from social regulation, and the sharp, definitive lines of reason and truth are blurred. Reason had come to be considered only as a function of the animal organism, and truth was "no more than the perception of discordant experience pragmatically adjusted for a particular purpose and for the time being."[5]

In spite of the reality that constitutions had failed to achieve the good society, and despite the fact that constitutions now appeared as historically conditioned documents, imperfect and temporary products of time and place, Becker was not yet ready to abandon the old faith that man's fate rests with man himself. He still clung to the belief that by deliberate intention and rational direction, man could shape the world of social relations to humane ends. There was no alternative except cynicism or despair, attitudes that Becker had often expressed in private after World War I. Becker deplored the fact that some men had abandoned rational persuasion for irresponsible force. Such recourse was disguised despair or cynicism, and thus not for those who cherished the value of truth and the increase of knowledge.[6]

In fact, Becker's ambivalence appeared in his correspondence with Max Lerner at the very time that his article on constitutions appeared. He said that Lerner dismissed too easily the threat of dictatorship and suppression of civil liberties posed by unrestrained majority rule. Under proper conditions, he said, the people were a great beast. Individual representatives of the people were ordinarily good fellows, humane and sensible with respect to things they understood, but collectively they could easily become something else. Lerner, he continued, had a romantic faith in the humanity and good sense of the people that Becker did not share. Again, the problem was to regulate the minority who controlled economic welfare without sacrificing the intellectual minority represented by Lerner and Becker. Freedom did not mean

[5] *Ibid.*
[6] *Ibid.*

much unless it meant freedom to discuss the ends and means of social organization, and the people would sacrifice this freedom if they believed that this would get them what they wanted.[7]

In answering Becker, Lerner appeared more extreme in his collectivism than Becker was, even though he had the same estimate of the masses. He said that Becker's point about the deep divergence between the scientific and powerful few and the moronic many was terribly true, but it only strengthened his conviction that the way to progress was not through an elite but to socialize the knowledge and the power of the elite. For the next generation, liberalism and democracy must carry on the task, Lerner contended, but eventually it would and must be taken over by a Communist society.[8] Lerner, who had just been offered the position of editor of the liberal news magazine, *The Nation,* later wrote that since he was aiming at socialism, he would not quarrel with Becker's statement that Lerner's program was something approaching Communism.[9]

Although Becker was becoming more aware of the threat to the good society posed by dictatorship in Europe, for a professor of modern European history he was still singularly unaware in 1938 of the trend of world affairs. A freshman student at Boise Junior College had read his article in *The Nation,* "How to Keep Out of War," where he made the statement: "I do not think there will be, in the near future, a European war involving Great Britain." The girl was interested not in Becker's erroneous prognostication about war, but in what she considered his faulty grammar.[10]

By 1938 also, world events had not yet advanced sufficiently to cause Becker to doubt the validity of subjective relativism. In a review article of Harry Elmer Barnes' *History of Historical Writing,* Becker insisted that written history tells us more about the writer's own times than it does about the

[7] Becker to Lerner, March 25, 1938, Becker Papers.
[8] Lerner to Becker, November 6 [1938], Becker Papers.
[9] Lerner to Becker, January 4, 1939, Becker Papers.
[10] Eleanor Burns to Becker, April 6, 1938, Becker Papers.

times of which he writes. Barnes, therefore, should have forgotten "entirely about the contributions of historians to present knowledge" and should have concentrated "wholly upon their role in the cultural pattern of their own time." Historiography should be a history of history subjectively understood (the fable agreed upon, the pack of tricks played on the dead), rather than a history of the gradual emergence of historical truth objectively considered.[11]

Becker's review of Barnes, though not in fact favorable, was done with such skill that even Barnes praised it along with many others. Barnes read the review with pleasure and felt that his book was justified if for no other reason than that it stimulated Becker to produce one of his best essays.[12] Merle Curti said that he came home too tired even to read the *Times,* picked up the *Review,* read the Becker review, and was so exhilarated that he read it aloud to his wife. When had any historian combined such wit, wisdom, and profundity in dealing with the history of historical writing, he asked.[13] James Westfall Thompson of California said that Becker's thought was so subtle, his criticism so keen, that the sense of it would elude Barnes. Doubtless Barnes would feel complimented by having his book made a peg to hang a whole article on. Said Thompson: "The article is a masterly example of the gentle art of literary assassination, so adroitly done that the victim probably feels no pain." [14] And Becker himself wrote that everyone seemed to like his article, "even Barnes." [15]

By the end of 1938, however, Becker appeared to be a little less friendly toward Communism and a little more friendly toward democratic capitalism. He said that the hopes and expectations of leaders of revolutions are betrayed by that tough old nut, history. In the Russian Revolution, history betrayed the Marxist utopian dream; in the French Revolu-

[11] "What is Historiography?" in *American Historical Review,* October, 1938, pp. 20-28.
[12] Barnes to Becker, October 19, 1938, Becker Papers.
[13] Curti to Becker, October 28, 1938, Becker Papers.
[14] Thompson to Becker, November 28, 1938, Becker Papers.
[15] Becker to Henry ?, December 29, 1938, Becker Papers.

tion, history betrayed the liberal democratic dream of equality and fraternity. On the basis of their own theory, he continued, Marxists should take it for granted that the bourgeois classes will fight for their interests. Christian or liberal philosophy would justify Becker in sacrificing his interests for the welfare of mankind, but on the basis of Marxian philosophy, he would be a fool to work for Communism. As a professor — a tool of the capitalism which supported him — why should he not fight for his own class and interests? [16]

Becker's mention of Christian philosophy as a justification for humanitarianism introduces a new note in Becker's philosophy of life. Earlier, one of the editors of Becker's high school textbook, *The Story of Civilization,* suggested that Becker change the section of the book which denied by inference the divinity of Christ. This had caused the company to lose an adoption of the book in the San Francisco schools.[17] Becker's hostility to religion is no great mystery, given his regard for Voltaire and the French philosophes, but all of a sudden God seems to have gotten into his life. In a letter to Beard, Becker closed with the supplication "God keep and preserve you," and to another correspondent, he said, "may God have you in his Most Holy keeping." [18]

If Becker seemed a little less friendly to Communism, he had not yet abandoned the subjective relativism on which Communism was grounded. He wrote to Charles Beard about a book by Maurice Mandelbaum, *The Problem of Historical Knowledge,* which was a refutation of relativism and included the relativism of Becker, Beard, and others. The crucial refutation of relativism was achieved by denying that there was, as the relativists claimed, any distinction between facts and interpretation of facts. According to Mandelbaum, the historical account was a tissue of facts, nothing else, and the tissue of facts, set forth in their natural context, provided their own meaning.[19] What Mandelbaum was saying, and

[16] Becker to Louis Gottschalk, November 26, 1938, Becker Papers.
[17] Robert D. Williamson to Becker, June 21, 1938, Becker Papers.
[18] Letters of December 27 and 29, 1938, Becker Papers.
[19] Becker to Beard, December 27, 1938, Becker Papers.

what Becker and Beard denied, was that the *what* of history was fact, but so also was the *why* or interpretation. Thus the *why*, or interpretation, is to be found in the sources and is not to be imposed by the historian. Beard dubbed Mandelbaum's rejection of relativism as patently absurd.[20]

By 1939, when it was becoming clear that democracy was threatened both from the left and from the right, a very significant change begins to appear in Becker's attitude toward democracy. Germany had not yet invaded Poland, but the German-Russian pact made it obvious that democracy was fighting with its back to the wall. As a result, democracy began to appear to Becker as something more worth keeping than he previously believed. The vehicle for expressing this change of heart was an article in the *Yale Review*, "When Democratic Virtues Disintegrate," and because the article is so important as a reflection of Becker's new attitude, it is deserving of some analysis in depth.[21]

In the article, Becker said that an intensification of ideological warfare found him besieged on all sides by people of widely differing views because he seemed not to be supporting their particular cause. On the one hand, he was branded as a Communist, but on the other, he was damned by Communists who said that his social sympathies should have made him a Communist "if he had only had the guts." One Communist accused him of giving aid and comfort to the enemy because the aim of Communism, the classless society, was of such transcendent importance that his criticism of Stalin for using chicane and brutality to attain this end looked like treason to the cause. At the opposite extreme, one woman labeled him a social Fascist because he had said in public that "reason, we suspect, is a function of the animal organism, and truth no more than the perception of discordant experience pragmatically adjusted for a particular purpose and for the time being." [22]

---

[20] Beard to Becker, December 31, 1938, Becker Papers.
[21] *Yale Review*, June, 1939, pp. 649-66. This article was later published in the book, *New Liberties For Old*.
[22] *Ibid.*

Becker then went on to show that democracy functioned best when the issues were minor ones, but stood in danger of violating its own principles when the going got rough. Good Marxian doctrine declared that "ideas are merely a function of the practical activities, without validity except as instruments in the effective solution of social conflicts." But this doctrine, suitable for Communist and Fascist purposes, had no place in liberal democratic ideology. Yet there was the danger that under stress, democracy would destroy its very foundation, particularly freedom of speech, and thus raise the question of whether it was inevitable that the virtues of democratic government should disintegrate when most needed.[23]

Despite its many failures, Becker continued, democracy had many virtues — "substantial virtues behind glittering generalities." Democracy was based on the assumption that mankind in general were rational creatures motivated by good will toward their fellow men. Hence democratic government fostered tolerance, humane dealing, fraternity. It encouraged men to be good neighbors, to cultivate their minds, to clarify their ideas by inquiry and discussion, and by reasonable concessions, to accommodate individual interests to the common good. Democracy assumes the worth, the dignity, and the creative capacity of the individual; its chief aim is maximum individual self-direction with a minimum of compulsion. Ideally, means and ends are conjoined in the concept of freedom: freedom of thought that truth may prevail; freedom of occupation that careers may be open to talent; freedom of self-government that no one may be compelled against his will.[24]

But in Becker's eyes, the substantial virtues of democracy could be realized only under the proper conditions of general equality. Democratic government was a pact for mutual advantage, but to realize these advantages, the people must be informed, inequalities of status and possession must not be too great, and citizens must be sufficiently easy in their circumstances and in their security in the future to harbor good will,

[23] *Ibid.*
[24] *Ibid.*

tolerance, consideration for others, and the belief that differences can be settled peacefully by compromise. With industrialization and growing economic class differences, the greatest problem of all and the most serious threat to democracy was the flagrant inequality of possessions and opportunities. People began to accept the notion that there was a higher law than the law of private property, and they questioned whether social welfare could be achieved best through a modified system of private enterprise or through the complete socialization of the means of production and distribution. Said Becker: "The essential problem of liberal democracy, therefore, is to preserve that measure of freedom of thought and political action without which democratic government cannot exist, and at the same time to bring about, by social regulation of economic enterprise, that measure of equality of possessions and of opportunity without which it is no more than an empty form." [25]

In spite of the disintegration of democratic virtues, Becker saw hope for American democracy in the long tradition of workable representative government. Orderly society must be held together either by force or by accepted tradition, and American democracy would endure as long as this essential American tradition remained reasonably intact. The core of this tradition was neither habitual practice of wide tolerance nor profound faith in reason but a settled habit of managing political affairs by means of representative government. Since the habit of representative government had amply justified itself by more than three centuries of uninterrupted success, he said, no amount of free criticism would convince us that the theory of representative government is a superstition as long as the institution itself continued to function reasonably well. [26]

Becker believed that history would give this country time to make the proper adjustments in democracy to stop the disintegration of democratic virtues. "This settled habit of man-

[25] *Ibid.*
[26] *Ibid.*

aging our affairs by representative government is the strongest guarantee we have for the persistence of democratic institutions in the crisis which confronts us," he declared. Inertia of habit was a powerful influence that would carry the country beyond the point where conviction faltered and would enable democratic institutions to outlast for a long time the disintegration of democratic virtues. But the country should remember that even the most confirmed and excellent habit cannot forever survive the loss of those qualities which alone in the long run can give it any value.[27]

While this article was no Fourth-of-July eulogy of democracy, it was the most favorable thing that Becker had said about democracy in many a year.

As Hitler's successes in Europe mounted, Becker's attitude toward democracy became increasingly sympathetic. In a series of lectures delivered at the University of Virginia in 1940, he declared that mankind had four choices of social organization — liberal or collective democracy, Socialism, Communism, and Fascism in descending order of attractiveness. Of these, Becker now clearly preferred liberal democracy because both its ends and its means were conducive to progress and the good society. He still believed that the ideal of democracy, developed to permit men to govern themselves in a heavenly city on earth, had been betrayed by concentration of wealth and class division which prevented the achievement of equality promised by democracy. The result was that democracy was being abandoned in the world as unworkable. But if democracy could curtail excesses of economic enterprise without sacrificing other aspects of freedom, it would still be the world's best hope for the future.[28]

If Becker's notions about the values of democracy were altered by the policies of Stalin and Hitler, so also was his attitude toward war. Instead of denouncing war as an instrument for settling human differences and insisting that

[27] *Ibid.*
[28] These Page-Barbour Lectures were later published as *Modern Democracy* (New Haven, 1941).

there was no such thing as a just war, as he had previously done, Becker now conceded that war might be justified to save those countries where democracy existed, for submission to aggressors, he said, would merely lead to more aggression. Becker's change of heart toward democracy, it should be noted, resulted in his change of mind about the justification for war.[29]

Although the assault on modern democracy caused Becker to look with more favor on democracy as a social system, it did not appreciably alter his interpretation of earlier American society and the American Revolution. His thesis in 1940 was still based on the assumption of a dual revolution, one part of which was to democratize an aristocratic society. Yet at the end of the thesis, as we have noted, and contrary to the interpretation of most of Becker's disciples, the internal social revolution for democracy never really came off. Now Becker said that there emerged from the Revolution three classes — one of conservative aristocrats, one of liberal middle classes, and one of disfranchised lower-class republicans, progressives, liberals, and radicals. This latter group not only failed to achieve democracy at the time of the Revolution, but it also failed at the time of Andrew Jackson. Later extension of the suffrage to eliminate oppression meant little, Becker declared, for political control still remained in upper-class hands.[30] If Becker was saying to his followers that the American Revolution did not really achieve a social revolution, he was also denying the Turner thesis as an explanation of Jacksonian Democracy.

As the democracies of Europe disappeared one by one under the impact of Hitler's tanks and Stuka bombers, Becker seems to have gained a corresponding appreciation for the virtues of democracy. Having long made cynical references to these virtues as "glittering generalities," he now saw them as "Some Generalities That Still Glitter." In an article with this title, he also began to doubt the very relativism on which he had

[29] *Ibid.*, p. 96.
[30] *Ibid.*, pp. 43-48.

constructed his philosophy of history. And with this article, Becker took a long stride away from forty years as a publicist for collectivism and back toward the scholarly discipline of the historian.[31]

In what appears as a thinly-veiled confession of his own past attitude toward democracy, Becker showed how Hitler had changed men's minds, including his own. Said he: "Long familiarity with democracy as a going concern, by disclosing its glaring defects and discords, has bred in many quarters a half-cynical skepticism which is alternately directed against the democratic reality as something scarcely worth preserving, and against the ideal as something impossible to achieve." Some men only half believed in democracy and accepted it somewhat perfunctorily, but "less so now that Hitler has brought into strong relief its essential virtues." [32]

Becker blamed this cynical attitude on changes in men's concept of democracy. Democracy assumed that a tolerably just and rational society could be established only through the freest exercise of human reason, but a critical examination of these assumptions left doubts about the capacity of the average human mind to perceive that which is true and cleave to that which is good. This doubt, he said, arose from a conception of human reason different from that of the early supporters of democracy. Early proponents said that democracy was government by laws, not men, the result being impersonal and rational rather than personal and arbitrary government.[33]

Early exponents of democracy constructed their system on a basis of absolute rather than relative values. In the eighteenth century, said Becker, reason was believed to be a bit of the universal intelligence placed within man to make manifest to him the universal reason implicit in things and events, and thus reason was looked upon as an entirely reliable guide to

[31] "Some Generalities That Still Glitter," first published in the *Yale Review*, 1940, was republished in *New Liberties For Old* (Yale University Press, New Haven, 1941). Quotations by permission of Yale University Press. Page references are to the book edition.

[32] *Ibid.*, pp. 124-26.

[33] *Ibid.*, pp. 126-27.

correct thinking and right conduct. Natural law was viewed as absolute, as the regular order of facts by which God ruled the universe. Inseparable from reason and law was the idea of intellectual detachment, the notion of the objective or right-thinking man. Ordinary men might be swayed by passion and interest, but scholars would achieve complete detachment, determine the facts, and then let the facts speak for themselves.[34]

But the doctrines of evolution and relativism changed this earlier view of reason. Now, rational right-thinking man had ceased to be considered the center of our intellectual system, and the world must be thought of not as a creation but as a self-conditioned becoming. Man is part of that becoming, part of the evolutionary process, an animal organism that is what he successively becomes. His mind, like the rest of him, is at any moment what his biological and cultural inheritance and conditions of time and place have made it.[35]

Thus did intelligence and reason lose their sovereign rights and commanding position to evolution and relativism, according to Becker. Darwin and Freud made intelligence a purely material process to explain biological and psychological phenomena. Mind was part of the process, useful to organisms because, by facilitating adjustment to environment, it enabled them to attain desired ends. Reason was merely a function of the organism's total activity, and truth was a coherent integration of activities that proved successful in attaining these desired ends. Reason was simply the docile agent and front for the subconscious, serving the individual by providing him with "good reasons" for doing what his submerged and un-plumbed desires impelled him to do. With the universe divested of rational purpose and the mind of man reduced to a biological character, ideas could no longer be understood apart from the conditions of time and place in which they appeared. Ideas in law and government were regarded as weapons in the mundane conflict for attaining practical ends.

[34] *Ibid.*, pp. 128-31.
[35] *Ibid.*, pp. 131-32.

"To determine the truth of an idea in the world of logical concepts," Becker said, "was less important than to estimate its function in a world of social relations." [36] In plainer words, the end justified the means, regardless of "truth."

Under these circumstances, said Becker, democracy naturally fell victim to evolution and relativism. The cardinal doctrines of the democratic faith could be most conveniently understood as an ideology in relation to the conflicts of a bygone revolutionary age. These doctrines were neither true nor false, but were either "glittering generalities" incapable of realization or bourgeois ideas emerging from a capitalist economy because they were suited to the interests of a ruling class. No longer was it self-evident that man was created with certain inalienable rights: man had only such rights as he could win for himself. Democracy was not an ideal projection of immutable truths but an imperfect and mutable going concern which would change with new social conditions. Natural law and constitutions were imperfect and temporary products of time and place; judges and legislators were influenced by social consequences, by the class to which they belonged; government in democratic countries was cynically defined as government of the people, by lawyers, for special pressure groups. [37]

The new assumptions of evolution and relativism about the nature of man and mind caused the traditional foundations of law and morality to crumble away, Becker maintained. If reason was merely an instrument biologically developed to serve the interests of the organism, its pronouncements could never be disinterested. If truth was relative, nothing could be really true; if morals varied with the customs of time and place, any custom that got itself established was moral, and one system of morality was as good as another. If ideas were inspired by individual or class interest, the success of an idea in promoting individual or class interest was the only test of its validity. Ideas became weapons to rationalize the social conflicts within nations and the imperial conflicts between

[36] *Ibid.*, pp. 132-33.
[37] *Ibid.*, pp. 134-36.

them. Ideas were the servants of power while justice was the interest of the strongest.[38]

Naturally, Becker continued, Marxism flourished in this new milieu created by the doctrines of evolution and relativism. The cardinal doctrines of Marx were that the social structure is conditioned by the economic factors of production and distribution, and that social change or progress results not from a conflict of ideas but from a conflict of interests between ruling and dispossessed classes. Marxian doctrines provided a persuasive ideology for oppressed workers whose hopes were thwarted by democracy. Marxian analysis of capitalism justified their grievances while its philosophy of history assured them that their collective efforts to destroy the existing system were supported by the forces that shape human destiny. Bourgeois or proletarian social ideas were social products, weapons to be employed in class conflict, and if the proletarians were successful, the superior truth of proletarian ideas would thereby be demonstrated.[39]

Eventually, Becker continued, the implications of those philosophies became implicit in the attitude of common men who were innocent of philosophy and unaware of implications. Their attitude was shaped in part by the machine age and the need to adjust to the machine. Machines released on demand a measurable mechanical force without having any concern for the use to which this force was put. They remain impassive to righteous indignation, wishful thinking, or moral imperative. In using machines, man must dispense with wishful thinking and the moral imperative. In all walks of life, the test was not the right-thinking man but the man who could deliver. The disposition was to say "that's that" to whatever was, and if someone protested that what was ought not to be, that it contravened some established principle of law or justice or morality, the answer was a cynical "so what?" [40]

[38] *Ibid.,* pp. 136-39.
[39] *Ibid.,* pp. 139-40.
[40] *Ibid.,* pp. 140-42.

One of the chief victims of the "that's that and so what" philosophy has been democracy, according to Becker. Reflecting the insensitiveness to moral implications of conduct and the anti-intellectual trend of thought deriving from critical analysis and harsh experience in a ruthlessly competitive economy, these cynical words are the symbol and measure of the disintegration of democratic virtues, of conventional lip service and half-cynical devotion which we give to the democratic ideal. Admitting that democratic method calls for compromise by rational discussion and mutual concession, we take for granted that the reasons advanced will not be honest ones but merely "good reasons" to camouflage selfish interests. The recent Supreme Court fight was a good example, Becker said, for Roosevelt's enemies believed that his reform proposals disguised a desire for power while his friends believed that opponents defended the Court, not as a bulwark of democratic liberties, but as a bulwark of class privilege.[41]

For more than half a century, Becker contended, the anti-intellectual, relativist, or activist philosophy that "might makes right, justice is the interest of the stronger" had insidiously worked its way into the fabric of democratic thought and practice. Now, under threat of economic collapse and social frustration, it had been exalted to the level of a complete philosophy in countries which had frankly abandoned democracy. Both Communism and Fascism paid tribute to certain ideal values, such as the welfare and happiness of the community or the progress of mankind, but both assumed that the abstract entity is realized in an inspired leader to whom the truth has been revealed and the direction of affairs committed. Both represented a direct attack upon intelligence, an unqualified denial of any obligation to be guided by rational thinking or humane dealing. Both subordinated the individual man to the common good as the leader saw it; both subordinated reason to will, identified law and morality with naked force as an instrument of will, and accorded value to the disinterested search for truth only if the leader judged it to be

[41] *Ibid.*, pp. 142-43.

useful in reaching practical ends. Thus the relativist, anti-intellectual trend reached a final fantastic form that truth and morality are relative to the purposes of any egocentric somnambulist who can impose his unrestrained will on the world.[42]

In spite of his own contributions to the relativism that he now denounced and his own cynical attitude toward democracy over many years, Becker now saw that democracy was the one bright hope for the good society. "Hitler and Stalin represent an exorbitant price for a little wisdom," he declared. "But they have at least done something to strengthen the cause of democracy." Their brutal activities had revealed the advantages of democratic institutions with the rational and humane values traditionally associated with them, so that men could now refer to the Declaration of Independence without apology. Hitler and Stalin had achieved this revival of faith in democracy by "reducing to an absurdity the principle that law and morality are nothing more than the right of the stronger." [43]

Seeing now how relativism had contributed to the rise of Stalin and Hitler, Becker came to the realization that complete relativism was not the answer that he had once considered it to be. To insist that justice is the right of the stronger eliminates right and justice, leaving nothing but what is, that which is "existential." There is no place for law or morality or even reason. If reason is a functional instrument to serve the biological organism, he declared, its main function is "to discriminate the relatively true from the relatively false, the dependable fact from the deceptive illusion," so that the organism can pursue its best interests. Becker could not discard relativism completely, but, said he: "The fallacy is to suppose that because truth is in some sense relative it cannot be distinguished from error, or that the margin of error cannot be progressively reduced." The civilizing of man was due to his reasoning capacity to distinguish fact from illusion

[42] *Ibid.,* pp. 144-45.
[43] *Ibid.,* pp. 145-46.

and to prefer values that exalt humane and rational qualities of human personality.[44]

Becker now came to understand that the good society he so much desired could not be based upon relativism but must be grounded in something called "truth" which he had so long derided. As he said, one of the values affirmed by the traditional democratic ideology was "to believe that in the long run all values are inseparable from the love of truth and the disinterested search for it." But since truth has some relation to "facts," this was a far cry from Becker's earlier view that facts did not speak for themselves and with a little judicious manipulation they could be made to say almost anything we want them to say. Whatever the limitations of reason, he now said, it was folly to renounce it since it is the only guide we have in our quest for the good society. The chief virtue of democracy (whose values were inseparable from the love of truth and the disinterested search for it) was that it accepted rational and humane values as ends and provided the most favorable conditions for achieving these ends.[45]

Although Becker had obviously come a long way from his earlier ideas about objective truth, he still could not reject relativism entirely. This appears in an exchange of letters in 1940 with Carl Horwich, a student at Wayne University, who was writing a thesis on Becker. Horwich asked for a copy of "What are Historical Facts?," the paper in which Becker had virtually eliminated objective facts in history. Becker's reply was that the paper had never been published: it was intended to be provocative and to elicit discussion, he said, but was not in shape to be made use of "as expressing my considered opinion on the subject," and for this reason he did not care to have it used in Horwich's paper.[46] Becker had made no such protest, however, when Barnes had earlier praised the paper as philosophically on a level with the new physics. Also in his letter, Horwich took the view that relativism entered history,

---

[44] *Ibid.*, pp. 146-49.
[45] *Ibid.*, pp. 149-51.
[46] Becker to Horwich, May 8, 1940, Becker Papers.

not in the facts themselves, which existed independent of the mind of the historian, but in the organization and synthesis of the facts.[47] In his reply, Becker distinguished between an event and the "facts," or what we know about the event. An alleged event becomes a fact for us when the evidence and the inferences we draw are sufficient to convince us, and this capacity to accept evidence and draw inferences is always changing. Thus the "facts" are relative, since they are not something objective and material in the outer world but only something that the mind is convinced is true.[48] Habit is a powerful force in human affairs, and Becker's long immersion in relativism obviously made any complete break with the past extremely difficult.

This exchange of ideas with Horwich over the nature of history posed some of the real problems that face every historian. Are facts something that can be established as absolute and true, or are facts themselves relative to time, place, and circumstance as Becker implied? How close can the historian get to the truth if the love of truth and the disinterested search for it form his basic philosophy? Is it possible for the historian to be objective in collecting the facts themselves, and if so, does that objectivity still prevail when he arranges and narrates these facts? Or is it at this point that subjective relativism takes over?

Some of the answers were provided in 1940 by Louis Gottschalk, who often expressed the notion that Becker was his model, but who appeared to disagree somewhat with the master on the nature of history. The difference came with Gottschalk's distinction between historical method (the collection and testing of evidence) and historiography (the selection, arrangement, description, and narration of the facts).

Unlike Becker, or at least the Becker before 1940, Gottschalk believed that historical method was scientific. Considering truthfulness as the highest norm of historical selection, he believed that millions of historical facts can be established as

---

[47] Horwich to Becker, June 2, 1940, Becker Papers.
[48] Becker to Horwich, June 11, 1940, Becker Papers.

true. This, of course, assumes that there is some absolute called truth which does not depend upon the historian for its validity.[49] Certainly this was not Becker's view of facts at an earlier date, even though by 1940, he, too, was talking in terms of the disinterested search for truth.

Subjectivity or relativism entered in Gottschalk's scheme of things when historical method ended and historiography began. Facts are the unfinished materials of history which must be selected and arranged by the historian, then described and narrated. Whereas historical method was scientific, historiography, said Gottschalk, was art, polemic, propaganda, or special pleading. Every historian has biases, overt or subconscious, and he is dangerous in proportion to his failure to recognize these biases. Historians can prove single facts or sequences of facts, but they cannot maintain, unless they insist that their own interpretations are the only ones, that there can be objectivity in the evaluation, selection, emphasis, and arrangement of these facts.[50]

Like Becker, Gottschalk believed that the historian should be openly committed to some philosophy or code of ethics. He should know whether he is materialist or idealist, liberal or conservative, religious skeptic or religious devotee, or a believer in progress or the imperfectibility of man. Historical writing which has no philosophical or ethical basis, which does not show development, rise, fall, growth, decay, futility, or sterility, cannot be good narrative, and narrative is the essence of history. In order to determine whether things grow or decay, one must have a philosophy of ends and a standard of good or bad. Apparently Gottschalk did not see that he differed in any way with Becker, for he praised *The Heavenly City* as "the most beautiful piece of historical writing that any contemporary in America has produced."[51]

[49] Louis Gottschalk, "The Evaluation of Historical Writing," in *The Practice of Book Selection*, Chicago University Studies in Library Science, (Chicago, 1940), pp. 101-15.
[50] *Ibid.*
[51] *Ibid.*

All of which only raises further questions about the differences between historical method and historiography, between fact and interpretation. If the historian is committed to a cause, as Gottschalk and Becker approved, is there any possibility that he will use scientific method or attempt to arrive at the truth even in the collection of his facts? How can anyone be sure that the committed historian's "facts" themselves are really "facts" that have some correspondence with the event itself? In short, are differences among historians due to interpretation of facts which can be established as "true," or are their differences the result of disagreement over the facts themselves? And finally, is the meaning or interpretation of the facts something that is imposed by the subjective historian, or is the meaning of a fact also a fact?

Gottschalk was not the only admirer of Becker's work at this late stage of Becker's career. Charles Beard praised Gottschalk's work on historiography (and thus Becker's) by saying that there was more sound sense about historical writing in Gottschalk's few pages than in mighty volumes under that head. As for *The Heavenly City,* Beard agreed with Gottschalk that it was among the best — better, in fact, than anything done since 1776 and as near perfect as mortal man could expect.[52] Gottschalk sent Beard's letter to Becker who presumed that Beard meant *The Heavenly City.*[53] One of the editors of Silver, Burdett and Company wrote, "As I told you a number of years ago, you are much more than a Professor of History: you are one of our leading philosophers."[54] And Robert Palmer declared that a great many people at Princeton followed everything that Becker said or wrote with great interest. Could Becker come to Princeton where the circle of Becker's admirers was large? Palmer confessed that he had known Becker "mostly as a sage," but after reading Becker's 1922 article on the Danton letter in the *American Historical Re-*

---

[52] Beard to Gottschalk, April 28, 1940, Becker Papers.
[53] Becker to Gottschalk, June 2, 1940, Becker Papers.
[54] Robert D. Williamson to Becker, July 3, 1940, Becker Papers.

view, Palmer was impressed by Becker's "enormous technical erudition." [55]

Becker's change of heart in reference to war and isolationism is also increasingly evident in 1940. A committee of historians, of which Becker's liberal friend and great admirer, Henry Steele Commager, was a member, requested Becker's support. Calling themselves "The Committee to Defend America by Aiding the Allies," this group proposed to make a frank and open declaration of American sympathy, to extend all material assistance short of war, and to work for repeal of the isolationist Johnson Act.[56] That the appeal was successful is attested by a correspondent who later said that he was interested and pleased, but not surprised, to see Becker's name on a petition for all-out aid to Britain, Russia, and China. Becker, he said, had cured him of "Oxforditis." [57]

Just before the United States became involved in World War II, Becker's distinguished academic career began its decline. He retired officially at Cornell in 1941, although he was to continue as University Historian at a reduced salary. Smith College offered him a year appointment as research professor at $8,000, but Becker would accept for a half year only. Smith, he mused, paid him "a good bit, apparently for residing in the community and giving them the benefit of my distinguished presence. I can't afford to turn down money, especially money obtained under false pretenses." [58]

Retirement from active teaching at Cornell did not mean retirement from writing, however, particularly about Hitler's threat to democracy. In an article, "The Old Disorder in Europe," Becker insisted that Hitler's "new order in Europe" was neither new nor an order. It was simply the "old disorder" with new names: political absolutism (totalitarian state), orthodoxy (regimentation), and military imperialism (struggle for living space). The leader replaced the absolute

---

[55] Palmer to Becker, September 23, 1940, Becker Papers.
[56] Committee to Becker, June 5, 1940, Becker Papers.
[57] Charles Lightbody to Becker, July 29, 1941, Becker Papers.
[58] Becker Papers, May, 1941, especially Becker to Max Lerner, May 9, 1941.

monarch, regimentation of conduct and opinion took the place of religious and political orthodoxy, and the struggle for living space meant the conquest of neighbors who also needed living space. Hitler's plan of a Pan-German state embracing the heart of Europe had now succeeded, but it was only a fulfillment of an earlier Pan-German dream.[59]

But Becker insisted that political and international order in Europe, to have value for the present and future welfare of mankind, must be founded on freedom, not slavery. There must be established and observed rules of public and private law, and an effective concensus that the rules are, or can be made to be, practically expedient and morally defensible. Under the old effort to create political and international order, the "most fundamental concept was that political authority derives from law, and law from the consent of the people." These ideas were especially true of the liberal democratic revolution from the seventeenth to the nineteenth centuries, a revolution which imposed representative assemblies on monarchs who would be absolute and drew up constitutions to limit governments and guarantee the rights of subjects.[60]

With the world in a frightening state of international disorder, Becker now paid high tribute to Hugo Grotius as the founder of modern international law. Instead of condemning Grotius for giving aggressors "good" reasons for waging predatory wars, as he had done earlier, Becker now praised Grotius for refuting the claim that "equity is where the strength is" and for discovering laws which states would be morally bound to observe. More than anyone else, Grotius discredited the doctrine that "might was right" and gave reality to the concept that states must follow established rules in their relations with each other. Even when the rules of international law broke down

---

[59] "The Old Disorder in Europe," *Yale Review,* 1941, republished in *New Liberties for Old,* pp. 152-81. Quotations used by permission of Yale University Press.
[60] *Ibid.*

and war resulted, nations had been forced to recognize certain rules in order to maintain the favorable opinion of neutrals.[61]

Becker insisted that Hitler, Stalin, and Mussolini were not entirely responsible for the breakdown of law and order which occurred after 1914. Defects and discords of the modern economic system leading to political corruption and bitter class conflict, ruthless political competition for economic advantage leading to war, and new conceptions of the nature of man which undermined traditional ideas of reason, morality, and law, had all contributed to the belief that justice was the right of the strongest. The question now was whether the admitted defects of the old order could be remedied by renouncing its virtues and destroying all that had been gained over the centuries in the form of ethical values and legal procedures.[62]

What Hitler, Stalin, and Mussolini did was to renounce the assumptions and procedures by which any new and better order had ever been created, said Becker. They frankly accepted and ruthlessly applied the doctrine that justice was the right of the stronger. They subordinated reason to will, identified force and chicane as instruments of will, and accorded value to the individual and the disinterested search for truth only if these served their purposes. For them, law had no origin but the decree of the leader, and no sanction but force. There were no rights, but only favors conferred for blind obedience. Diplomacy was an integral part of political and military strategy, and treaties were instruments of deception to be broken deliberately whenever convenient. War was not a last resort but an integral part of total policy, for the leader was not bound by rules and could begin war without warning and wage it without restraint. The ultimate justification was that the leader was either realizing the dialectic of history or fulfilling the mission of the superior race, and to such men the end justified the means.[63]

[61] *Ibid.*
[62] *Ibid.*
[63] *Ibid.*

To Becker, however, the Western world never had a state or empire of any notable culture or civilization where power was not restrained by law or custom and not supported by tacit or explicit approval of its subjects. Even Napoleon, who came closest, failed because his claims to unrestrained power brought both disillusionment on the part of the French people and repeated coalitions on the part of other nations. Hitler might succeed where Napoleon failed, but if he did, Europe, and especially the German people, would fail. As Becker said: "It does not profit a nation, any more than a man, to gain the whole world and lose its own soul." In the end, he predicted that the "new order" would be defeated by mounting opposition from without and within — opposition generated by the disorder which the "new order" created.[64]

Becker frankly acknowledged his change of heart on the issues of war and democracy when the articles that he had published after 1936, mainly in the *Yale Review,* were republished as a collection in 1941 under the title of the first article, *New Liberties For Old.* In the introduction, Becker said that his first article had been intended to show how the idea of liberty, formerly conceived in terms of emancipation of the individual from social restraints, had come to be identified in the twentieth century with social regulation, especially economic regulation, of individual freedoms which were largely won in the nineteenth century. The earlier concept of liberty was derived from the liberal-democratic social philosophy of the eighteenth century; the later concept came from Karl Marx and his disciples. As Becker said, the common theme throughout all of the articles was democracy and the way in which democracy was to be defended, particularly from the encroachments of totalitarianism.[65] As we have seen earlier, however, a reader of the original article, "New Liberties for Old," might well have had the impression that the Becker of 1936 was really not so sure that capitalistic democracy was superior to Communism.

[64] *Ibid.*
[65] *Ibid.,* introduction.

Then came Becker's acknowledgment that Hitler and Stalin had changed his mind about the justification for war. Becker said that he had added one paragraph to the original article, "Loving Peace and Waging War," as a reflection of his new outlook. Still believing that the total result of war was futility, Becker conceded now that nations could not always avoid war. In the world as it was, any nation must regard national independence as the primary condition for promoting the interests of its people, and it could not promote these interests by tamely submitting to military conquest and thus committing suicide. In a community of demented men, no one can afford to act always in a rational manner; and in the presence of nations that regard war as a valid means of promoting national interests, other nations sometimes had to fight.[66]

But even more important was Becker's confession that he had changed his mind about the virtues of democracy. He warned his readers that there would be found in these essays "some inconsistencies in statement or difference in emphasis or implication," an indication that he had altered his views over the previous six years. In particular, the discerning critic would note in the last two essays "a certain tone or temper not present in the others — an attitude toward democracy a little less detached and critical, a little more cordial and defensive." The reason, a simple one, was that Hitler had compelled men [Becker] to reappraise democracy in comparison with Hitler's "new order." And, continued Becker, "with every passing year it has become more obvious than it was before that the defects of our democratic way of life, in comparison with the defects of the new order, are negligible, and that its liberties are of all our possessions the ones we cherish most and least wish to surrender." Becker said he did not think that he had ever doubted or denied this, a statement difficult to accept in the light of his long-expressed criticism of democracy, but that now, like many other Americans and "thanks to Stalin and

[66] *Ibid.*, pp. xv, 72-73.

235

Hitler," he was more sure of it than ever. Said he: "If Stalin and Hitler have taught me something, so much the better." [67]

Coming from a man who was once far enough on the left to be identified with Communism, who had convinced his students that he considered the Communist Party the only intelligent party in the country, and who had once said that the defects of democracy made democracy hardly worth preserving, this confession as to the virtues of democracy must loom much larger in Becker's career than Becker would acknowledge. "These superficial inconsistencies," he said, "do not trouble me," but the inconsistencies were much more than superficial, and the fact that Becker noted them suggests that he, too, may have considered them more than superficial. A man of less courage and honesty would have said nothing, and his "guilt" would have gone largely undetected. Since it takes great courage for a scholar to admit to error, Becker must be highly commended for this acknowledgment of previous aberrations in judgment.

Again, as Becker noted, there was good enough reason for his now favorable evaluation of democracy. He believed that "the primary values of life, upon which in the long run all other values depend, are intelligence, integrity, and good will." The three went together as a unit, for any one, without the restraining influence of the other two, could as readily lead to evil as to good. "If I criticize democracy," he continued, "it is only to defend it the better; if I defend it, I do so only because it aims in theory, and only in so far as it attempts as well as may be in practice, to achieve the good life by giving free scope to intelligence, rewarding integrity, and promoting good will among men and nations." [68]

The "new" Becker appears also in a 1941 introduction to a reissue of *The Declaration of Independence*. The original book, published in 1922 at a time when Becker was extremely disillusioned about both war and progressive democracy, was in effect a debunking book. More than anyone else, Becker

[67] *Ibid.*, pp. xv-xvi.
[68] *Ibid.*, pp. xvi-xvii.

taught students of American history that the philosophy of the Declaration did not, in fact, represent the reality of 1776, that the Declaration was filled with "glittering generalities" mainly honored in the breach throughout American history, and that, in fact, the Declaration was better apologized for than praised by Americans.

As already noted, by 1940 Hitler had convinced Becker that Americans need no longer apologize for the Declaration, and in this introduction in 1941 the salubrious influence of Hitler is again made manifest. Events throughout the world had directed attention "to the immemorial problem of human liberty," Becker declared, and none more so than "the incredible cynicism and brutality" of Hitler. Now men everywhere were forced to reappraise the validity of half-forgotten ideas and to entertain convictions as to the substance of things not evident to the senses. One conviction was that "liberty, equality, fraternity" and "the inalienable rights of men" were phrases, "glittering or not," that denoted the fundamental realities that men will always fight for. Now, far from being a propaganda document full of "glittering generalities," Becker called the Declaration "the famous American charter of political freedom." [69]

During the war, Becker had the opportunity to put into practice his new-found philosophy that in the end all values rested on the disinterested search for truth. Becker acted as spokesman for a group of historians who reported to General Arnold late in 1943 on two questions: (1) how seriously had Germany's war potential been eliminated by American bombing, and (2) what would be the probable German reaction to a landing in Europe? Arnold believed that the bombing had seriously damaged Germany's war potential and that Germany would capitulate quickly after an Allied landing. The committee, basing its judgment on history, believed that the Nazi war machine still had great potential and that the Germans

[69] Carl L. Becker, *The Declaration of Independence* (Alfred A. Knopf New York, 1942), introduction. Quotations used by permission of Alfred A. Knopf, Inc.

would fight until Germany was invaded. Arnold apparently took a somewhat high-handed position with the committee, but when Becker told him that unless he wanted an honest report, there was no need to report at all, he "cooled off" quickly and thanked the committee for its "dispassionate and objective report." [70]

As the war progressed and the prospects for an Allied victory grew brighter in 1943-44, Becker thought of the shape of things to come after the war, but this time his thinking was more mature and realistic than it had been after World War I. Having learned that countries sometimes had to fight to preserve the values that foster civilization, Becker was prepared to look at the postwar period with less of the disillusionment and cynicism that characterized his thinking after 1918. Involved, also, was his long-held subjective relativism as a philosophy of history.

In a book, *How New Will the Better World Be,* Becker designated war and unemployment as the two most pressing problems in the world. Knowledge that could be used beneficially was often wasted on destructive wars, wars which were made more devastating by the very technological revolution that should have benefited mankind. Technology, in turn, created unemployment, for at the same time that production increased, failure of distribution and consumption reduced employment and curtailed the market. War ended unemployment temporarily, but while countries sometimes had to fight for principles, the total effect of war was harmful for all. The "better world" after the war would have to solve these two major problems, and the solutions would not be as easy as some thought.[71]

Taking a leaf from the history which he had witnessed, Becker urged Americans not to "return to normalcy" as they had done after World War I. They would need to adjust

[70] J. Duane Squires to Phil Snyder, November 29, 1955, Becker Papers.

[71] Carl L. Becker, *How New Will the Better World Be?* (Alfred A. Knopf, New York, 1944), pp. 4-21. Quotations used by permission of Alfred A. Knopf, Inc.

habit, thought, and conduct to rapid change, a difficult thing to do especially if sacrifice of interests was involved. Due to cultural lag, there would be futile attempts to solve new problems with old formulas, and especially Americans would have to fight the temptation to return to isolation.[72]

In urging Americans not to return to the 1920's, Becker revealed much of the climate of opinion that had shaped his own thinking, teaching, and writing. Of the period he said: "It was a time of skepticism and disillusionment. So far from having made the world safe for democracy, the war had only intensified social and international conflicts. Young people, having been promised a new and better world, found only a worse one, and were therefore in a mood to believe in nothing. Many of their elders, writers and college professors, equally disillusioned, taught them to place a low value on 'ideals.' The real motives of men and nations, it was said, were always selfish, the professed motives never sincere. Democratic government, like any other, so it was said, was designed to benefit the few at the expense of the many. To imagine that men could become good or the world made better was a vain thing; to get yours while the going was good was the only wisdom." [73]

Now Becker could see that isolationism, including his own, had been disastrous. Now it was easy to see how mistaken the democracies were, he declared, for by prompt and decisive action they could have stopped Hitler. Again Becker blamed the historians. Much of isolationism stemmed from the cynical approach of American historians who depicted the war as just another imperialist conflict of European powers over interests rather than principles. Historians had helped to create the impression in the 1920's that this country had been dragged into a war for the interests of European countries, and thus Americans decided to let Europe stew in its own juice. Instead of embracing isolationism, the United States should have joined the League of Nations and worked in

[72] *Ibid.,* pp. 22-33.
[73] *Ibid.,* pp. 34-35.

close alliance with the other democracies to preserve peace. Wilson's policies were thus not an "idealistic crusade to reform the world" but a realistic, hard-headed way of serving American interests.[74]

Becker's experiences had now brought him back from the extreme left and flirtations with Communism to a position considerably closer to the middle of the road. He declared that we cannot change the past, though his own writings had preached the doctrine that every man can create almost any past that he desires. But we can help to shape the future. Liberals, in contrast with conservatives and reactionaries, are concerned with the better world of tomorrow, he continued, but the chief weakness of liberals was that in living too much in the ideal world of tomorrow, they are prone to forget or ignore how inert and toughly resistent the world of today really is. If conservatives look back to a Golden Age that never existed, liberals look forward to a Golden Age that in fact cannot be created. Idealists expect too much too soon; they should expect much, he said, but not the impossible.[75]

Becker also realized that, unlike the New Historians who stressed the evils of the past and present in order to direct men's attention to the better future, other men often saw good in America's past and present. He quoted Goethe, "America, you have it better," a view prevalent in such eighteenth-century observers as Crèvecoeur, Franklin, Lafayette and many others. As for the present, he related the story of the Greek proprietor of an ice cream and candy store who had been here only five years: "I like it fine. I am a Greek Jew. So what? No ones asks me am I a Greek Jew. I pay the rent on time? Yes. So I am okay. My candy and ice cream is good, high class. So the boys and girls should worry I am a Greek Jew. I am here as good as the next one. The children, they go to school. There is nothing to pay. They read and speak American better than me. Already I am not understanding the words they use. Already they are not Greeks any

[74] *Ibid.*, pp. 36-43.
[75] *Ibid.*, pp. 44-48.

more, but Americans. In America is better chance for all poor people like me." [76] The implication was that the United States was built on the profound belief that this was a country where everything was better. This was certainly not the philosophy and history that Becker had embraced for forty years.

In considering the postwar world, Becker realized that nationalism was stronger than any notion of a fellowship of mankind in general, and that the "better world" of tomorrow would have to live with nationalism. Democratic revolutions had replaced monarchs with "the will of the people" — the loyalty of the people to themselves, the country they loved, the liberties they had won. Nationalism had replaced all other allegiances, causing men to fight and die for nationalism. Nationalism had defeated the notion of international democracy; and even Communism, which theoretically was based on international socialism of the proletariat, had been modified by nationalism. The great danger, that the strong national states would use power unjustly, had also to be the only hope, for the national state would be dominant, and the hope was that the power of the great national states would be used to promote general principles rather than selfish interests. [77]

Becker believed that democracy was really the key in both national and international affairs. The ideal of democracy is that people will forget personal and private interests and support measures designed for the common good. If interests between and within nations cannot be reconciled by agreement, the result is civil strife or war. In both instances, power is inevitable, but power can be used for good as well as for evil. All would depend on how power was used after the war, but if each country considered only its own interests, without regard to the interests of others, Becker said, the chances of peace were not good. [78]

[76] *Ibid.,* p. 52.
[77] *Ibid.,* pp. 71-74.
[78] *Ibid.,* pp. 79-86.

Once again Becker refuted much of the basis for his philosophy of many years. He downgraded Freudian thinking by speaking of the subconscious, which enables men to conceal "real reasons" by offering "good reasons." We have overdone this concept, Becker said, and now there was the danger of becoming "wise guys" who believe that man's real motives are always sordid and his professed motives never sincere. In addition, Becker again stressed the need to weigh the good and the bad of the past, not simply to emphasize the bad. He praised the British Empire for having prevented a victory by Hitler, and said that the British Empire should be judged, not by its isolated failures, but by its general achievements.[79]

Hitler had indeed taught Becker that not all was bad about American society and that there was much that was worth fighting for. Far from a war to get Britain out of a mess for a second time, Becker went on, this country was fighting for independence and the cause of human freedom. In fact, "freedom-loving people" should have stopped Hitler before he got started. And as for the status quo, Becker rejected the notion that saving the status quo was not a desirable objective. Europeans fled Europe to seek the status quo of America which gave them life, liberty, and a livelihood, he said, and in spite of its shortcomings, this country was still the hope of the world. There were some things about the status quo that no one wanted to preserve, but, he urged, we must put these undesirable aspects in their proper relation to the fundamental aspects of the status quo which we most certainly want to retain. In thinking about the new and better world, we must not lose sight of the status quo as a whole, "its fundamental virtues as well as its superficial defects." [80]

Becker then went on to point out the fundamental virtues of the status quo which were so well worth keeping. The primary purpose of the war was to preserve the status quo in its fundamentals, he declared, even if this involved retention of its defects. These fundamentals were what they had been

[79] *Ibid.*, pp. 91-96.
[80] *Ibid.*, pp. 108-13, 126-28.

since 1789 (and, we might add, many of them before that): sovereign political independence, a free economic system tempered by essential social regulation, constitutional guarantees against freedom from arbitrary arrest and imprisonment, freedom to choose one's occupation and to pursue this occupation freely, and freedom of religion, speech, press, learning, and teaching. All of these fundamentals could be improved, but they were the fundamentals of the status quo, what we were fighting for, and what the Axis powers would destroy. If we would get something better, we must first save this status quo, for the new and better world would be firmly grounded on the old world.[81]

Having long advocated social democracy as a solution for the country's economic problem of underconsumption, Becker naturally believed that collectivism was the wave of the future; but now, he said, it should be modified. Since this trend was irreversible in his view of things, the only question was which brand of collectivism the American people would choose: Fascism, Communism, Socialism, or Social Democracy. Fascism and Communism demanded that we give up all three democratic liberties — private economic enterprise, freedom of speech and press, and self-government. Socialism eliminated only one, private economic enterprise. By contrast, Social Democracy required only regulation of private economic enterprise, not elimination, but left the other democratic freedoms intact. Thus the good society demanded that we choose Social Democracy.[82]

In advocating increased collective democracy for the future, Becker now saw that the American democracy of the past, which he had long criticized so freely, had more virtues than he had previously acknowledged. Modern democracy was the result of opposition to European absolutism of the seventeenth and eighteenth centuries, he said, when the mass of the people, oppressed and exploited, had few rights. Except in England, Holland, and the American colonies, people had no safe-

[81] *Ibid.*, pp. 128-33.
[82] *Ibid.*, pp. 134-57.

guards against arbitrary search, arrest, and imprisonment, and no right to trial by jury. The English, American, and French revolutions "were directed against this form of dictatorship, class privilege, and social regimentation." Instead of a propaganda document designed to camouflage the defects of an aristocratic society, the Declaration of Independence in Becker's eyes now appeared as the classic expression of the philosophy of liberal democracy.[83]

In the realm of international affairs, Becker believed that the old nationalism must be discarded, that complete internationalism was as yet impossible, and that a combination middle ground of nationalism for local problems and internationalism for world problems must be established. This international order must be based on a realism, not present in the League of Nations, that war was not always the worst of all evils and that it was impossible to transfer power of unequal states to a league of equal states. Most important of all, wars could not be eliminated unless economic problems were solved, and this called for elimination of trade barriers and control of international exchange. Becker believed that the solution for Europe was a United States of Europe where economic conflicts, if not others, could be eliminated.[84]

When he proposed a United States of Europe, Becker again demonstrated that the past few years had greatly changed his concepts about the historical development of his own country. He said that conditions for a United States of Europe were not as favorable as those had been for a United States of America. Americans were mostly of English origin, and thus had similar political institutions, economic practices, customs, morality, and religion. During the Revolution they came to think of themselves as forming one nation. When they adopted their Constitution, they did so not only to prevent war but also for positive political ends, such as promoting the general welfare. Said he: "The Constitution of 1787 did not make the people of the thirteen colonies one nation. On the con-

[83] *Ibid.*, p. 137.
[84] *Ibid.*, chs. VII and VIII.

trary, it was but the formal expression of a union already existing and easily cemented because the people included in it had all much the same needs and interests, and much the same ideas about how they could best be safeguarded and promoted. In short, the conditions for creating a United States of America were about as favorable as they well could be." [85]

This account of early American history, emphasizing concensus rather than conflict, was a far cry from Becker's earlier accounts of the period, and, one might add, much more realistic. Had he used the sources correctly in writing his dissertation, he would have found that concensus rather than conflict *was* the key to middle-class colonial society, and that this concensus continued when Americans were faced with British imperialism as a threat to their democratic, middle-class society. Becker's account of the Constitution, again emphasizing concensus rather than conflict, has little in it of the Beard interpretation of the Constitution; and certainly it explains much better than does Beard why the Constitution received a landslide endorsement by some sixty-five per cent of the voters in 1787-88.

In other ways, too, Becker had become more realistic in his approach to international affairs. "Those of us (and unfortunately there are many) who think that we are a nation of starry-eyed idealists who have been twice tricked by the British into a European war in order to 'pull their chestnuts out of the fire' have read the history of their country to little purpose," he said. "The truth is rather that the existence and friendliness of the British Empire, and the power of the British fleet, have for more than a century enabled us to roast our own chestnuts at leisure and eat them in security." [86] Again Becker was repudiating Charles Beard's as well as his own interpretation of World War I. And judging by his approval of the past accomplishments of the British Empire and its role in the postwar world, Becker might well have

[85] *Ibid.,* p. 182.
[86] *Ibid.,* pp. 188-89.

sympathized with Winston Churchill who said that he did not become prime minister to preside over the dissolution of the British Empire.

These second thoughts about the validity of subjective relativism, the concensus origins of American democracy, and the fallacies of American isolationism left Becker groping for a viable philosophy of history, and by 1944 he still had not found a satisfactory answer. He well understood that history could not be a science, for unlike the subject matter of science, the subject matter of history, man, could learn about himself and thus change his habits. Marxism, he said, was a prime example, for millions of men accepted Marxism as true, whether or not it was, and thus acted differently from what they would have done had they never learned about Marx. Hence there could be no laws of history as there were laws of science.[87]

Becker did believe that the historian, unlike the scientist, must deal with the question of causation in history. The scientist could dispense with the concept of cause and merely describe sequences and relations, reducing them to mathematics whenever possible. But the historian cannot dispense with causes unless he is a mere antiquarian or statistician. The reason is that he is concerned not only with the actions of men but with their purposes, desires, and aspirations. Men's actions have value and purpose, and the historian writes history in such a way as to give these actions meaning and significance. Historians must take into account men's values and purposes in order to explain why men behave as they do, what they aim to accomplish, and whether or not they succeed. For the historian, causes are on the everyday practical level of human activity, not on the scientific or philosophical level.[88] What Becker should also have said was that these causes, as well as the events themselves, could be found in the sources and thus did not depend on the subjective interpretation of the historian.

[87] Becker to Gottschalk, September 3, 1944, Becker Papers.
[88] *Ibid.*

When he dealt with causation in history, however, Becker's thinking left something to be desired. He could see that if historical causation is placed on a practical human level, most historical events have multiple causes because many people with various reasons for acting are involved. But then Becker reverted to subjective relativism by saying that the causes of the French Revolution must be multiple, not because different participants had different reasons for involvement, but because of the subjective historian and the age in which he lives. Having stressed multiple causation in the French Revolution, however, he declared flatly that the American Civil War had only one cause, slavery, and that American historians had been too clever by half in finding other causes for that momentous event.[89] Becker could have added that American historians, including himself, had also been too clever by half in finding class-conflict causes for the American Revolution.

As the end of Becker's career drew near, the elderly historian seemed to be attempting to atone for the mistakes that he had made and to warn others not to commit the same errors. His last effort as an academic was a series of lectures, delivered at the University of Michigan in 1944 and published after his death in 1945 under the title *Freedom and Responsibility in the American Way of Life.* To some of his disciples Becker appeared to be repeating himself endlessly but a more plausible explanation might be that he was desperately anxious to convey to the current generation the wisdom that had come to him in the last few years of his life and to correct the erroneous conceptions of American history that he had been so instrumental in implanting.

In his first lecture, "The American Political Tradition," Becker again emphasized the good rather than the evil of American political development. He said that his lectures "might properly be devoted to those broad general rights or freedoms upon which our system of government rests, and which, according to the Declaration of Independence, all just governments exist to secure." Then speaking of American

[89] *Ibid.*

constitutions, he emphasized what many today seem prone to forget: "For every right or freedom that they confer they impose, implicitly if not explicitly, a corresponding obligation or responsibility." Rights entail responsibilities, he declared, for freedom unrestrained by responsibility becomes mere license, while responsibility unchecked by freedom becomes mere arbitrary power.[90]

Becker could now see that throughout its history America had always been a haven for the poor, a place where the good had greatly outweighed the bad. Quoting Goethe again, "America, you have it better," and repeating the story of the Greek Jew candy maker that "In America everything is better for poor people like me," Becker made this significant statement: "This is the essential fact: in America everything has always been better for poor people." Because immigrants found here the best opportunity to do what they liked and get what they wanted, America had always been, and had been thought of by Europeans, as the land of the free because it was the land of opportunity.[91]

Nearly forty years too late, Becker returned to the Turner thesis of the frontier as an explanation for the climate of opinion in pre-Revolutionary America. He pointed out that free or cheap land provided great freedom and opportunity — freedom from social and religious conventions and restraints, freedom to establish a due form of government. Then he cited Franklin on the idea that European society with its hopelessly impoverished working classes crowded together "could never develop in America so long as any man with a little gumption could go elsewhere and become the independent owner of a farm. It was this situation that defeated every attempt to transplant and perpetuate in the New World the aristocratic social structure and upper-class political domination that prevailed in the old." [92] Yet Becker had depicted

[90] Carl L. Becker, *Freedom and Responsibility in the American Way of Life* (Alfred A. Knopf, New York, 1945), pp. 1-3. Quotations used by permission of Alfred A. Knopf, Inc.

[91] *Ibid.*, pp. 6-9.

[92] *Ibid.*, pp. 8-10.

precisely this aristocratic social order in New York as the foundation for his dual-revolution thesis.

While stating that conditions in America were not conducive to aristocracy, however, Becker performed the almost incomprehensible feat of clinging to the Becker thesis. Having just said that there was no aristocratic social structure or upper class political domination in the colonies, he returned to the contradiction that political control and social prestige were the prerogatives of a few interrelated landowning and merchant families. Then came the contradiction again that poverty and servility in the European sense were virtually unknown, and any young man of character and ability could acquire an education and property. But this was followed by the statement that the American Revolution "was as much an uprising of the populace against the better sort as it was an uprising of the better sort against British control." And finally his statement that distinctions virtually disappeared as a political force in 1828 with the election of Jackson differs considerably from his earlier view that the widening of the franchise by 1828 made no difference as aristocrats still controlled the country.[93]

After indulging in all of these contradictions, Becker delivered what should have been the *coup de grace* to the Becker thesis. Said he: "It may now be said that during the eighteenth and nineteenth centuries the people of the United States enjoyed *a greater degree of political liberty, social equality, and widely based material prosperity* than has ever fallen to the lot of any other people." This happy state was won, not by desperate struggles against the oppressions of men, but by the unremitting effort to appropriate available rich resources. Warning Americans that they had taken their freedoms too much for granted, he concluded: "Our political freedom and social equality were the casual and lavish gift of nature rather than anything won by war or revolution." [94]

[93] *Ibid.*, pp. 10-11.
[94] *Ibid.*, p. 17. Italics added

If the American people at the time of the Revolution "enjoyed a greater degree of political liberty, social equality, and widely based material prosperity than has ever fallen to the lot of any other people," where is the climate of opinion that would produce Becker's "dual revolution"? The unfortunate truth is that "what may now be said" in 1944 about the great advantages for the common American at the time of the Revolution could just as easily have been said in 1907 when Becker wrote his thesis, for this was what the logic of his evidence said. But if he had followed the logic of his evidence in 1907, there would never have been a "Becker thesis."

Thus by 1944 did the prodigal return, if not completely, at least much of the way back to the fold of the scholarly historian, although he was unable to abandon entirely the faulty logic that had characterized his work for more than forty years. With his statements that "all values are inseparable from the love of truth and the disinterested search for it" and that while truth was in some sense relative, it was folly to believe that the relatively true could not be distinguished from the relatively false, Becker abandoned much of the subjective relativism on which his philosophy of history rested. And with his conclusion that Americans of the eighteenth and nineteenth centuries enjoyed more economic, political, and social equality than any other people at any time, he virtually destroyed his thesis that colonial society was class ridden and that the American Revolution was primarily a social revolution to democratize that society. What had once been "glittering generalities" to the cynical Becker had now become sterling generalities that indeed still glittered brightly.

At the very time that Becker was undermining his own thesis, however, other historians were in the process of perpetuating the interpretation of American history that the master was abandoning. A case in point was the work of Merrill M. Jensen, *The Articles of Confederation*, which appeared in 1940. Starting with a class-ridden society of rich

250

against poor, privileged against under-privileged, and enfranchised against disfranchised, Jensen pictured the Articles of Confederation as a victory of lower-class radicals over upperclass conservatives in the struggle to democratize American politics and society. The extent of social revolution in Jensen's account rested, however, on the degree to which the revolutionary state constitutions represented a victory for the forces of democracy, and as we have seen, progressive historians differed fundamentally on this question.[95]

Two other prominent historians of early America, Carl Bridenbaugh and John C. Miller, were also perpetuating the Becker thesis, even to the contradictions that haunted Becker for so long. Using contemporary sources, both men built up a concept of colonial society as middle-class, democratic, and abounding in opportunity for the common man. Yet after demonstrating why there was so much concensus among Americans about the desirability of their social order, and why they had perfectly logical reasons for opposing British imperial encroachments, both men imposed a class structure and a class conflict that their own evidence refuted.[96]

The great pity was that Becker did not live to undo completely the damage that his philosophy of history and his interpretation of eary American history had wreaked on history as a scholarly discipline. He died unexpectedly in 1945, leaving the process of retraction barely begun, and whether he would have pushed it to its logical conclusion must always remain a moot question. It must have taken a tremendous amount of courage to repudiate, to the extent that he did, nearly forty years of work. What is clear, however, is that the full implications of Becker's reconversion from propagandist to historian have not yet been fully appreciated even though a quarter of a century has passed since his death.

[95] Merrill M. Jensen, *The Articles of Confederation: An Interpretation of the Social-Constitutional History of the American Revolution* (Madison, 1940).

[96] Carl and Jessica Bridenbaugh, *Rebels and Gentlemen: Philadelphia in the Age of Franklin* (New York, 1942), ch. I; John C. Miller, *Origins of the American Revolution* (Boston, 1943), chs. I-III, XXI.

It is something of a tragedy that this man, who could engender such loyalty and devotion in students and colleagues, whose thoughts on history had both breadth and depth, and who wrote with a style that will live long as a model for others to emulate, is now honored for what he was before 1940 rather than what he became after that date. Unfortunately, he is still remembered as the historian who believed that "history is only a pack of tricks we play on the dead" and that the facts of history, with a little judicious manipulation, "can be made to say, within reason, whatever we want them to say." Would, instead, that we could say of him, as he himself came to believe, that in the long run, "all values are inseparable from the love of truth and the disinterested search for it."

IX. EPILOGUE

> "Becker was widely recognized as a masterly craftsman and held in the highest esteem for his magnificant command of a research technique that he affected to make little of. There is nothing in the known record challenging his devotion to truth, though he had made it clear from a very early date that he was happily indifferent to pursuing truth for the sake of vindicating the hallowed rules governing the quest."
>
> — Leo Gershoy, 1949

WERE it not for the fact that the Becker thesis long outlived its creator, this story of Carl Becker might well end in 1945. Becker had come nearly full circle from scholarly historian, through subjective relativist and class interpreter of early American history, and almost back to scholarly historian. Had he lived a few more years, the circle might have been complete. But the thesis which bears his name still lives with us, and in fact has become an integral part of a conflict involving not only revolution in the past but revolution in the present and future. For this reason it is essential that we trace briefly what has happened to the Becker thesis from 1945 to the present.

Among the many expressions of admiration following Becker's death, that of his colleague at Cornell, George H. Sabine, indicated how deeply ingrained the Becker philosophy had become. In a long biographical introduction to Becker's last book, *Freedom and Responsibility in the American Way of Life* (the University of Michigan lectures of 1944), Sabine praised Becker for the very detachment that Becker had so long denied. Sabine considered Becker to be a great artist, and accepting at full face value Becker's statement in *The Eve of*

253

the Revolution that his sources could not be verified, Sabine declared that "verifying a work of art is nonsense." Recognizing that Becker "pursued the sources only as far as suited his purpose," Sabine apparently did not know how Becker pursued sources or for what purpose, and thus he believed that Becker used his sources "meticulously and with a fine historical understanding." Although Sabine asserted that Becker would not engage in dishonest selection or distortion of evidence, he still sanctioned Becker's philosophy of "prompting the fact according to his own judgment of what it ought to say." Each reader must decide whether, as Sabine claimed, Becker fulfilled "his own ideal of the high calling of the historian." And if, as Sabine said, Becker achieved "an idealism without illusions and a realism without cynicism," we must remember that he achieved this philosophy almost too late in life to be of any value.[1]

Robert R. Palmer, while still very much a Becker admirer, was somewhat more critical of his former major professor than was Sabine. Palmer agreed with most of what Sabine had to say about Becker, but he confessed that he had become dissatisfied with the pragmatist and subjectivist element in Becker's thinking, as well as the fact that Becker's pronounced judgments were not always his real beliefs. Palmer declared that Becker viewed economics mainly through the Socialist critique, that he was perhaps more concerned with literary style than with content, and that "freedom" loomed much larger in Becker's thinking than did "responsibility." Palmer well understood that part of Becker's difficulty lay in a plethora of admiring students and a paucity of critics. But he did not point out the obvious reason for this: Becker trained graduate students in European history while he wrote mainly in American history, so he never had to face really critical graduate students. Posterity will also have to judge the correctness of Palmer's statement that Becker's responsibility

---

[1] Becker, *Freedom and Responsibility*, pp. vii-ix, xii-xiii, xvi, xx-xxviii, xxxvi, xxxviii, xli, xlii. Quotations used by permission of Alfred A. Knopf, Inc.

was mainly to mankind in general, and, despite his philosophy, to the truth.[2]

In all probability, Leo Gershoy came close to capturing the general favorable attitude th.... prevailed toward Becker both before and after his death. Gershoy, who had written to Becker that he had once been invited to a dinner because another guest wanted to touch the man who had sat at Becker's feet,[3] wrote as follows: "A few voices may occasionally have been lifted from the side of the specialists to regret what they considered his unprofessional predilection for philosophy, but none ever contested his superb professional competence. Becker was widely recognized as a masterly craftsman and held in the highest esteem for his magnificant command of a research technique that he affected to make little of. There is nothing in the known record challenging his devotion to truth, though he had made it clear from a very early date that he was happily indifferent to pursuing truth for the sake of vindicating the hallowed rules governing the quest. Outside of his brilliant doctoral dissertation on political parties in New York on the eve of the Revolution and his *Declaration of Independence* he did not make what is formally called an 'original contribution to learning.' " Gershoy went on to say that Becker was no savant interested in swelling the body of factual information, and thus the widespread recognition of his extraordinary talents, which made him a dominant force in American historiography in his late years, was a tribute to the discrimination of his colleagues in the field.[4]

Other former students also reflected the adulation which Becker had engendered in students during his lifetime and which remained after his death. One reported that students soon discovered "one of the truly rare minds of our times" behind Becker's monotone, and that by the end of Becker's first term at Cornell the "Becker cult" was in full boom,

[2] Palmer to Sabine, November 17, 1945, Becker Papers.
[3] Gershoy to Becker, November 22, 1944, Becker Papers.
[4] Carl L. Becker, *Progress and Power* (Alfred A. Knopf, New York, 1949), introduction by Leo Gershoy, pp. xxix-xxx. Quotations by permission of Alfred A. Knopf, Inc.

"although without the hero worship and awe that later came to characterize it." Becker's criticisms of student papers were, however, "far more pointed in their critical attitude towards the language employed than toward the scholarly apparatus." This student believed that Becker's subjectivity precluded any possibility of an original philosophy or doctrine in historiography which Becker's disciples could follow, so "instead, what they worshipped was the man and the mind."[5] Frank Klingberg asserted that the article, "Kansas," did as much for Becker's reputation as Turner's frontier article had done for him,[6] while Richard R. Smith, an editor and publisher, reported that Becker had come to be considered probably the top man in his field.[7] And one former student declared that while Becker never bothered to return student papers, "what any university needs, is not more marble halls, but more teachers of the stature of Carl Becker."[8]

On the professional side, the Becker thesis continued with undiminished popularity even though it had virtually been emasculated by the master himself. For example, John D. Hicks, who had consolidated his two-volume text into one volume for use in military and civilian classes during the war, abandoned any previous reservations about the dual revolution and accepted it completely.[9] Richard B. Morris and John R. Alden also discovered class conflict in a society where cheap land provided great economic opportunity and high wages, and where political rights were widely held.[10] And in 1954, Lawrence Henry Gipson wrote as follows: "With

[5] Barnet Nover to David Hawke, February 10, 1950, Becker Papers.
[6] Frank Klingberg to Phil Snyder, November 10, 1955, Becker Papers.
[7] Richard R. Smith to Phil Snyder, November 14, 1955, Becker Papers.
[8] Margaret Dorrah Battaile to Phil Snyder, December 8, 1955, Becker Papers.
[9] John D. Hicks, *A Short History of American Democracy* (Boston, 1943, 1946). For the Becker-Beard thesis, see pp. 48, 49, 53, 85, 103, 119. But on the conservatism of the Revolutionary state constitutions, see pp. 100-101.
[10] Richard B. Morris, *Government and Labor in Early America* (New York, 1946). For evidence of an open society, see pp. 26, 32-34, 44-48, 52, 149. For class confict, see pp. vii, 51-56, 188. John R. Alden, *The American Revolution, 1775–1783* (New York, 1954), pp. 150-57, 171, 225, 265, 268.

respect to the electorate that selected the lawmakers, everywhere, as was true in England, there existed what might be called a political aristocracy made up of qualified males who enjoyed the right of franchise and a monopoly of public office — as against the great mass of the disfranchised, whose persons and property were subject to regulation and taxation without true representation." [11]

When Becker was criticized, which was seldom, the charges were directed more at his philosophy of history than at the history which he actually wrote. Acknowledging that Becker had exerted "great influence on his generation," Homer C. Hockett believed that Becker's reputation would rest more "on his scholarly, thoughtful, and well-written books on political ideas and social tendencies, such as *The Declaration of Independence* and *How New Will the Better World Be*, than on his purely political works." Hockett considered Becker as "a political philosopher and an essayist" whose interest in literary form sometimes exceeded his concern for subject matter; but he also believed, as did others, that Becker had done good orthodox research in his *History of Political Parties* and *Declaration of Independence*. In fact, Becker's belief that one "cannot recover the past" was a denial of the very foundation on which Becker's own historical work rested, Hockett concluded, for indubitably Becker had recovered enough of the past to make possible a truthful version of an important aspect of it. [12]

On the whole, however, the attitude toward Becker was far more one of adulation that of criticism, and thus it is not surprising that the first full-length biography of Becker by Charlotte Watkins Smith contained little that was critical either of his subjective relativism or of the kind of history that he wrote. Smith's biography began as a doctoral dissertation,

[11] Lawrence Henry Gipson, *The Coming of the Revolution, 1763–1775* (Harper and Brothers, New York, 1954), pp. 2-4. As did Alden, Gipson in reality proved that there was a "War for Independence" rather than an "American Revolution." Quotations used by permission of Harper & Row, Publishers, Incorporated.

[12] Homer C. Hockett to Phil Snyder, January 6, 1956, Becker Papers.

and given the general acceptance of Becker's philosophy of history and of his thesis on the Revolution, it would have taken a brave graduate student, even if she had been so inclined, to have stormed the formidable barricades of the "Becker cult." [13]

One can easily agree with many of Smith's judgments about Becker. There is no doubt that his "commanding position among twentieth-century American historians is unquestioned," that his name was prominent in any study of historiography, that he wrote with superb skill and is still one of few historians who is accounted a writer, a man of letters, someone worth reading for pleasure, and that he was accepted among philosophers as a colleague. There is also no doubt that he influenced the political ideas of public men who read his books, and "helped to shape the political beliefs of great numbers of American citizens who learned most of what they know of modern history from his high-school textbook." [14]

While one must agree with all of these statements, there is one serious fault with the Smith biography: the author did not know enough about the sources in early American history and thus was not in a position to judge the kind of history that Becker wrote. She assumed that his dissertation was really a scholarly work based on wide and extensive research, but only by checking Becker's sources would she have known how far Becker's subjective relativism and his progressive philosophy influenced his use of these sources. She did not realize that Becker used evidence to promote his own view of what the world should be in the future by showing how bad the past had been. Curti was much closer than Smith to the real Becker when he said earlier that Becker's skepticism was instrumental in achieving the goals which social radicals desired. Had she known this Becker, Smith would then have realized why Becker would say in his review of Well's *Outline*

---

[13] Quotations reprinted from Charlotte Watkins Smith: *Carl Becker: On History & the Climate of Opinion.* © 1956 by Cornell University. Used by permission of Cornell University Press.

[14] *Ibid.,* pp. vi-vii.

of History that the facts do not speak for themselves, and with a little judicious prompting, they can be made to say, within reason, whatever we want them to say — an idea which she omitted in her discussion of this writing, but which is absolutely fundamental to any real understanding of Becker.[15]

Although she recognized changes in Becker after 1940, Smith did not fully grasp the significance of these changes. She insisted, for example, that Becker's attitude toward relativism after that date did not indicate a change of mind on Becker's part but merely reflected a change of situation. But this is not what Becker himself believed. Furthermore, when Becker stated that in the long run all values depended on the disinterested search for truth, he was showing a different Becker from the one who would use history to play tricks on the dead. And of course, not being versed in early American history, Smith did not realize that Becker had repudiated the Becker thesis by undermining the kind of society on which that thesis rested. The Becker after 1940 could not have written *The Eve of the Revolution,* for like Samuel Adams, he had come to realize that there are values in the world that men fight for.[16]

Inadvertently, perhaps, Smith caught the old Becker but not the new in her last paragraph. Becker had presented a copy of *The Heavenly City* to her father-in-law, the philosopher T. V. Smith, with this witty autograph: "This certainly isn't history. I hope it's philosophy, because if it's not, it's probably moonshine: — or would you say the distinction is over subtle?" As Smith concluded, what did it matter whether it was moonshine or philosophy, history or myth, if it helped men to find enduring values amid perishing occasions?[17] But after 1940 one does not find the levity and skepticism that marked the earlier Becker. Life had indeed become real and earnest with the advent of Stalin and Hitler upon the scene. For suddenly Becker had discovered that real history, the disinterested

[15] *Ibid.,* pp. 49, 68, 114-15.
[16] *Ibid.,* p. 87.
[17] *Ibid.,* p. 212.

search for truth, was the only enduring foundation for the good society. Moonshine and myth were no longer good enough.

In addition to Charlotte Smith, two other writers, Cushing Strout and Burleigh Taylor Wilkins, have attempted to evaluate Becker's work since 1956. Both men, and especially Wilkins, condemn pragmatic, skeptical, or subjective relativism as a sound philosophy of scholarship, and both realized that Becker at the end of his career virtually abandoned the relativism that he had embraced so long. Like Smith, neither Strout nor Wilkins were specialists in early American history, and therefore could not judge the validity of Becker's historical writing, although Wilkins was somewhat critical of the scholarship in Becker's doctoral dissertation but did not carry his criticisms to their logical conclusions. As a result, both men believed that Becker, in practice, violated his professed philosophy and actually produced detached, objective history.[18]

As Becker had predicted, however, the winds of relativity were apt eventually to sweep away his own "moonshine," or subjective-relativist interpretation of American history, and dump it unceremoniously into the junkyard of myth. As early as 1938,[19] but more particularly after World War II, scholars began to subject the progressive interpretation of the Revolution and Constitution to the cold logic of evidence, and what

[18] Cushing Strout, *The Pragmatic Revolt in American History: Carl Becker and Charles Beard* (New Haven, 1958); Burleigh Taylor Wilkins, *Carl Becker: A Biographical Study in American Intellectual History* (Cambridge, 1961).

[19] My own contribution to the controversy was a Ph.D. Thesis, "The Road to Revolution in Massachusetts," started in 1938 and completed in 1945; "Democracy in Colonial Massachusetts," *New England Quarterly* (September, 1952); "Restriction of Representation in Colonial Massachusetts," *Mississippi Valley Historical Review* (December, 1953); "Economic Democracy Before the Constitution," *American Quarterly* (Fall, 1955); "Liberalism, Conservatism, and History," *Centennial Review, VII* (Summer, 1963); "Reinterpretation of the Revolution and Constitution," *Social Education, XXI* (March, 1957); *Middle-Class Democracy and the Revolution in Massachusetts, 1691–1780* (Ithaca, 1955); *Charles Beard and the Constitution* (Princeton, 1956); *Reinterpretation of the Formation of the American Constitution* (Boston, 1963); and with my wife, B. Katherine Brown, *Virginia, 1705–1786: Democracy or Aristocracy* (East Lansing, 1964).

started as a trickle became a flowing stream by the mid-1950's.

For nearly fifteen years, an animated controversy, especially involving Becker and Beard, has continued over how Americans are to interpret their Revolution and Constitution. A detailed account of this controversy is not possible here, but readers who are interested can follow its outlines in the footnote references. Suffice to say that it has found its way into articles in professional journals,[20] monographs on particular

[20] For example, see Frederick B. Tolles, "The American Revolution Considered as a Social Movement: A Re-Evaluation," *American Historical Review*, October, 1954; Cecelia M. Kenyon, "Men of Little Faith: The Anti-Federalists on the Nature of Representative Government," *William and Mary Quarterly*, January, 1955; "Republicanism and Radicalism in the American Revolution: an Old-Fashioned Interpretation," *William and Mary Quarterly*, April, 1962; " 'An Economic Interpretation of the Constitution' After Fifty Years," *Centennial Review*, Summer, 1963; Edmund S. Morgan, "The American Revolution: Revisions in Need of Revising," *William and Mary Quarterly*, January, 1957; Merrill M. Jensen, "Democracy and the American Revolution," *Huntington Library Quarterly*, August, 1957; Sung Bok Kim, "Introduction to the Origin of the Constitution of the United States," *Kyung Pook University Liberal Arts and Sciences College Review* (Taegu, Korea), vol. I, 1958; Milton M. Klein, "The Rise of the New York Bar: The Legal Career of William Livingston," *William and Mary Quarterly*, July, 1958; "Democracy and Politics in Colonial New York," *New York History*, July, 1959; "Prelude to Revolution in New York: Jury Trials and Judicial Tenure," *William and Mary Quarterly*, October, 1960; Roy N. Lokken, "The Concept of Democracy in Colonial Political Thought," *ibid.*, October, 1959; David F. Trask, "Historians, the Constitution, and Objectivity: A Case Study," *Antioch Review*, Spring, 1960; Bernard Bailyn, "Political Experience and Enlightenment Ideas in Eighteenth-Century America," *American Historical Review*, January, 1962; Richard B. Morris, "Class Struggle and the American Revolution," *William and Mary Quarterly*, January, 1962; John Higham, "Beyond Concensus: The Historian as Moral Critic," *American Historical Review*, April, 1962; Jack R. Pole, "Historians and the Problem of Early American Democracy," *ibid.*; Jack P. Greene, "The Flight from Determinism: A Review of Recent Literature on the Coming of the American Revolution," *South Atlantic Quarterly*, Spring, 1962; John Cary, "Statistical Method and the Brown Thesis on Colonial Democracy" with a rebuttal by Robert E. Brown, *William and Mary Quarterly*, April, 1963; David Syrett, "Town-Meeting Politics," *ibid.*, July, 1964; Michael Zuckerman, "The Social Context of Democracy in Massachusetts," *ibid.*, October, 1968.

problems,[21] anthologies containing conflicting interpretations

[21] Examples are Clinton L. Rossiter, *Seedtime of the Republic: The Origin of the American Tradition of Political Liberty* (New York, 1953); Edmund S. Morgan, *The Birth of the Republic, 1763–1789* (Chicago, 1956) and *The American Revolution: A Review of Changing Interpretations* (Washington, 1958); David S. Lovejoy, *Rhode Island Politics and the American Revolution* (Providence, 1958); Forrest McDonald, *We The People* (Chicago, 1958); Benjamin Fletcher Wright, *Concensus and Continuity, 1776–1787* (Boston, 1958); Robert R. Palmer, *The Age of the Democratic Revolution* (Princeton, 1959); Marcus Cunliffe, *The Nation Takes Shape* (Chicago, 1959); Lee Benson, *Turner and Beard: American Historical Writing Reconsidered* (Glencoe, 1960); Chilton Williamson, *American Suffrage from Property to Democracy: 1760–1860* (Princeton, 1960); Charles R. Grant, *Democracy in the Connecticut Frontier Town of Kent* (New York, 1961); Esmond Wright, *Fabric of Freedom, 1763–1780* (New York, 1961); Stanley Elkins and Eric McKitrick, *The Founding Fathers: Young Men of the Revolution* (Washington, 1962); Hannah Arendt, *On Revolution* (New York, 1963); Paul Goodman, *The Democratic-Republicans of Massachusetts: Politics in a Young Republic* (Cambridge, Mass., 1964); John Higham, *History: The Development of Historical Studies in the United States* (Englewood Cliffs, N.J., 1965); Nicola Matteucci, *Charles Howard McIlwain E La Storiographia Sulla Rivoluzione Americana* (Bologna, 1965); Forrest McDonald, *E Pluribus Unum: The Formation of the American Republic, 1776–1790* (Boston, 1965); Morton Borden, *Parties and Politics in the Early Republic, 1789–1815* (New York, 1967); Carl Ubbelohde, *The American Colonies and the British Empire, 1607–1763* (New York, 1968).

Several more recent books attest to the continuing vigor of the controversy. On the concensus side, Jackson Turner Main, *The Social Structure of Revolutionary America* (Princeton, 1965), pictures early American society as predominantly middle class, and Bernard Bailyn, *The Ideological Origins of the American Revolution* (Cambridge, 1967), contends that the American Revolution was not a social revolution.

In opposition, however, are other books which indicate that the Becker-Beard thesis dies hard. J. R. Pole, for example, in his *Political Representation in England and the Origins of the American Republic* (New York, 1966), interprets American society as elitist and Whig rather than middle class and democratic. Richard B. Morris, who appeared at various times to veer away from Becker and Beard, seems to have returned to an emphasis on the social revolution in *The American Revolution Reconsidered* (New York, 1967). And finally, Merrill M. Jensen, who in various introductions to his *Articles of Confederation* and in a recent collection of sources left the impression of a retreat from his 1940 position, has returned to the progressive interpretation with renewed vigor in his latest book, *The Founding of a Nation: A History of the American Revolution, 1763–1776* (New York, 1968).

by various authors,[22] introductions to collections of documents,[23] introductions to reprints of older books,[24] book reviews,[25] college textbooks,[26] and even books for American

[22] Sidney Fine and Gerald S. Brown, *The American Past: Conflicting Interpretations of the Great Issues*, 2 vols. (New York, 1961); John C. Wahlke, *Causes of the American Revolution* (Boston, 1962); John Higham, *The Reconstruction of American History* (New York, 1962); Grady McWhiney and Robert Wiebe, *Historical Vistas: Readings in United States History* (Boston, 1963); Donald Sheehan, *The Making of American History*, 3rd ed., 2 vols. (New York, 1963); George Athan Billias, *The American Revolution: How Revolutionary Was It?* (New York, 1965); Ross M. Robertson and James L. Pate, *Readings in United States Economic and Business History* (New York, 1966); Allen F. Davis and Harold D. Woodman, *Conflict or Concensus in American History* (New York, 1966); Esmond Wright, *Causes and Consequences of the American Revolution* (Chicago, 1966); Gerald N. Grob and George Athan Billias, *Interpretations of American History* (New York, 1967); Michael G. Kammen, *Politics and Society in Colonial America: Democracy or Deference?* (New York, 1967); Paul Goodman, *Essays in American Colonial History* (New York, 1967); Jack R. Pole, *The Advance of Democracy* (New York, 1967); Barton J. Bernstein, *Towards a New Past: Dissenting Essays in American History* (New York, 1967); Jack P. Greene, *The Reinterpretation of the American Revolution* (New York, 1968), and *The Ambiguity of the American Revolution* (New York, 1968); Richard J. Hooker, *The American Revolution: The Search for a Meaning* (New York, 1970).

[23] Winton U. Solberg, ed., *The Federal Convention and the Foundation of the Union of the American States* (New York, 1958); Gottfried Dietze, ed., *The Federalist . . .* (Baltimore, 1960); John Braeman, ed., *The Road to Independence: A Documentary History of the Causes of the American Revolution: 1763–1776* (New York, 1963); Frank Freidel and Norman Pollock, eds., *Builders of American Institutions* (Chicago, 1967).

[24] John C. Miller, *Origins of the American Revolution* (Boston, 1959); Merrill M. Jensen, *The Articles of Confederation* (Madison, 1963).

[25] Such reviews are legion and too numerous to list. See for example the Bookshelf, *Wall Street Journal*, November 24, 1958; Jackson T. Main's review of McDonald, *We the People*, in *The Nation*, June 13 and August 15, 1959; Oscar Handlin's review of Lee Benson, *Turner and Beard*, in the *American Historical Review*, October, 1961; John M. Murrin, "The Myths of Colonial Democracy . . . ," and rebuttal by Robert E. and B. Katherine Brown, *Cithara* (November, 1965 and May, 1966).

[26] Examples are T. Harry Williams, Richard N. Current, and Frank Freidel, *A History of the United States*, 2 vols. (New York, 1959); Jennings B. Sanders, *A College History of the United States*, vol. I (Evanston, Ill., 1962); John R. Alden, *The Rise of the American Republic* (New York, 1963); John A. Garraty, *The American Nation: A History of the United States* (New York, 1966); Oscar Theodore Barck, Jr., and Hugh Talmadge Lefler, *Colonial America* (New York, 1968).

and foreign high school students.[27] There have also been numerous sessions at scholarly meetings devoted to the theme of social revolution and counterrevolution in the Revolution-Constitution period.

In essence, the new interpretation of the Revolution and Constitution that has emerged has tended to emphasize consensus rather than conflict and continuity rather than change. Contrary to the earlier views of Becker, and those of Beard, Schlesinger, Parrington, Jameson, Jensen, and others that colonial society was undemocratic, that the American Revolution was a class war to democratize that society, and that the Constitution represented a conservative counterrevolution designed to check the gains of democracy, historians have in recent years attempted to explain the Revolution and Constitution as products of an already-functioning democratic society. Widespread economic opportunity due to the frontier and an insatiable demand for labor, an extensive electorate that included most free adult white men, equitable representation that gave farmers control of politics, extensive religious toleration, the best educational system in the world at that time for the common man, and a predominantly middle class rather than upper-lower-class society did not provide the class-conflict milieu which was basic for the progressive interpretation.

In broad contours, the change over the years in Becker's interpretation of the Revolution and Constitution delineates this current controversy among historians. Once the early advocate of the class-conflict, undemocratic view of colonial society, by 1944 Becker had come around to the realization that eighteenth-century Americans "enjoyed a greater degree of political liberty, social equality, and widely based material prosperity than has ever fallen to the lot of any other people."

In spite of Becker's own change of heart about the nature of American colonial society, and regardless of a mounting volume of literature supporting Becker's final considered

[27] Bernard Feder and Jack Allen, *Viewpoints: USA* (New York, 1967); *La Rivoluzione Americana,* a cura di Nicola Matteucci (Bologna, 1968).

judgment, the "Becker cult" lives on among some segments of the profession with almost undiminished vigor. If it is as difficult to free an enslaved man as it is to enslave a free man, it is also as Herculean a task to eradicate a myth as it is to instill a truth.

In modified form, the views of Arthur M. Schlesinger confirm the above truism. Schlesinger, who had been a major contributor to the progressive interpretation of the American Revolution, remained a firm believer in the integrity of Becker's scholarship for several years after abundant evidence had appeared that the Becker thesis rested on quicksand. In a foreword to the 1960 printing of Becker's *History of Political Parties,* Schlesinger characterized the book as a "minor classic in historical literature" and "still a seminal work for students of the American Revolution." Then Schlesinger ended his foreword with this eulogy: "In research method as well as in content, objectivity and interpretation it is a model of what a work of historical scholarship should always strive to be." [28] Yet within five years, Schlesinger wrote a manuscript on colonial America which annihilated Becker's thesis along with his own earlier interpretation.[29] When the manuscript was published in 1968, three years after Schlesinger's death, he was severely criticized as an apostate who had sold out progressive history.[30]

If the reputation of Becker as a scholar remained unimpaired long after his death, a recent correspondent confirms the fact that the Becker philosophy of pre-1940 is still very much with us. This historian expressed great admiration

[28] From Carl L. Becker, *The History of Political Parties in the Province of New York,* 2nd printing (Madison, The University of Wisconsin Press, © 1960 by the Regents of the University of Wisconsin), forward. Used by permission of the University of Wisconsin Press.

[29] Arthur M. Schlesinger, Sr., *The Birth of a Nation: A Portrait of the American People on the Eve of Independence* (New York, 1968).

[30] Review by Gordon S. Wood, *William and Mary Quarterly* (July, 1969). Wood himself, in his recent book, *The Creation of the American Republic, 1776–1787* (Chapel Hill, 1969), perpetuates the old progressive contradiction of a class-ridden society and a social revolution on one hand, and a democratic society and a war to preserve democracy on the other.

for Becker even though he had suspected a fatal flaw in Becker as a man living up to an image of himself as farm boy turned philosopher. His admiration for Becker did not rest on such a "silly" basis as whether Becker was right or wrong in the history he wrote. Who cared? Right or wrong, Becker and Parrington had what every great historian must have — they were endlessly provocative and they knew how to write. Both had, and still have, the ability to excite. As for "truth" in history, he asked, who wanted historians who reached a final truth? What counted was the original provocation, for no great historian, especially an intellectual historian, ever had the truth. His virtue was not that he arrived at the truth himself but that he stimulated others to seek their own truths. Thus for this admirer the early Becker still lives on as the model of the great historian.

Whatever the final outcome of the present controversy over Becker and the American Revolution as a social movement, there can be no doubt that Becker raised some fundamental issues about philosophy of history which every historian must confront. What are historical facts, and are there facts and interpretations or merely facts telling us "what" and other facts telling us "why"? What is the function of the historian, that of propagandist for a cause or scholar with a legitimate discipline? Is written history only a pack of tricks that we play on the dead, or should it be a body of information, as accurate as human frailty can assemble, which tells humanity how it arrived at its present state of development? Is it possible for the historian to be both "committed" and a "scholar," or by definition, does the one function preclude the other?

The historian is not the only one, however, who can profit from the career of Carl Becker. In a world rife with social revolution, Americans are facing the fundamental task of deciding what kind of social order they desire for the future. In making the choice, they should be aware of the fact that those advocates of change who use Becker's subjective relativism and class interpretation of the Revolution to promote social revolution beyond the bounds of democracy are following the "old" Becker of 1900 to 1940, not the "new" Becker of 1940 to 1945. Americans might well remember, as Becker said, that Stalin and Hitler represented an exorbitant price to pay for a little knowledge, and that in the end all values are inseparable from the love of truth and the disinterested search for it.

BIBLIOGRAPHY

Adams, James Truslow. *New England in the Republic, 1776–1850.* Boston, 1926.

—— *Revolutionary New England, 1691–1776.* Boston, 1923.

Adams, John. *The Works of John Adams.* Charles Francis Adams, ed., 10 vols. Boston, 1850-56.,

Alden, John Richard. *The American Revolution, 1775–1783.* New York, 1954.

—— *A History of the American Revolution.* New York, 1969.

Arendt, Hannah. *On Revolution.* New York, 1963.

Bailyn, Bernard. *The Ideological Origins of the American Revolution.* Cambridge, Mass., 1967.

—— "Political Experience and Enlightenment Ideas in Eighteenth Century America," *American Historical Review* (Jan., 1962).

Beard, Charles A. *An Economic Interpretation of the Constitution of the United States.* New York, 1913, 1935.

—— and Mary R. Beard. *The Rise of American Civilization.* New York, 1927.

—— "That Noble Dream," *American Historical Review* (Oct., 1935).

—— "The World as I Want It," *Forum and Century* (June, 1934).

—— "Written History as an Act of Faith," *American Historical Review* (Jan., 1934).

Becker, Carl Lotus. Becker Papers. John M. Olin Research Library, Cornell University, Ithaca, N.Y.

—— *Beginnings of the American People.* Boston, 1915.

—— *The Cornell Tradition: Freedom and Responsibility.* Ithaca, N.Y., 1940.

—— *The Declaration of Independence: A Study in the History of Political Ideas.* New York, 1922, 1942.

—— "Detachment and the Writing of History," *Atlantic Monthly* (Oct., 1910).

—— *Detachment and the Writing of History: Essays and Letters of Carl L. Becker.* Phil L. Snyder, ed. Ithaca, N.Y., 1958.

—— *The Eve of the Revolution: A Chronicle of the Breach with England.* New Haven, Conn., 1918.

—— "Everyman His Own Historian," *American Historical Review.* (Jan., 1932).

—— *Everyman His Own Historian: Essays on History and Politics.* New York, 1935.

—— *Freedom and Responsibility in the American Way of Life.* New York, 1945.

268

—— *The Heavenly City of the Eighteenth-Century Philosophers.* New Haven, Conn., 1932. Eleventh Printing, 1957.

—— *The History of Political Parties in the Province of New York, 1760–1776.* Madison, Wis., 1909, 1960.

—— *How New Will The Better World Be.* New York, 1944.

—— *Modern Democracy.* New Haven, Conn., 1941.

—— *Modern History: The Rise of a Democratic, Scientific, and Industrial Civilization.* New York, 1931.

—— "Mr. Wells and the New History," *American Historical Review* (July, 1921). Also in *Everyman His Own Historian,* pp. 169-90.

—— *New Liberties for Old.* New Haven, Conn., 1941.

—— *Progress and Power.* Palo Alto, Calif., 1936 and New York, 1949.

—— "Some Aspects of the Influence of Social Problems and Ideas upon the Study and Writing of History," *Publications of the American Sociological Society,* VII (1912). Also in *American Journal of Sociology* (March, 1913).

—— *The United States: An Experiment in Democracy.* New York, 1920.

Beer, George Louis. *The English-Speaking People: Their Future Relations and Joint International Obligations.* New York, 1917.

Benson, Lee. *Turner and Beard: American Historical Writing Reconsidered.* Glencoe, Ill., 1960.

Bernstein, Barton J., ed. *Towards a New Past: Dissenting Essays in American History.* New York, 1967.

Billias, George Athan, ed. *The American Revolution: How Revolutionary Was It?* New York, 1965.

Billington, Ray Allen, ed. *The Reinterpretation of Early American History: Essays in Honor of John Edwin Pomfret.* San Marino, Calif., 1966.

Borden, Morton. *Parties and Politics in the Early Republic, 1789–1815.* New York, 1967.

Braeman, John, ed. *The Road to Independence: A Documentary History of the Causes of the American Revolution, 1763–1776.* New York, 1963.

Bridenbaugh, Carl and Jessica. *Rebels and Gentlemen: Philadelphia in the Age of Franklin.* New York, 1942.

Brown, Robert E. *Charles Beard and the Constitution.* Princeton, N.J., 1956.

—— "Democracy in Colonial Massachusetts," *New England Quarterly* (Sept., 1952).

—— "Economic Democracy Before the Constitution," *American Quarterly* (Fall, 1955).

—— "Liberalism, Conservatism, and History," *The Centennial Review* (Summer, 1963).

—— *Middle-Class Democracy and the Revolution in Massachusetts, 1691–1780.* Ithaca, N.Y., 1955.

—— *Reinterpretation of the Formation of the American Constitution.* Boston, 1963.

———— "Reinterpretation of the Revolution and Constitution," *Social Education* (March, 1957).

———— "Restriction of Representation in Colonial Massachusetts," *Mississippi Valley Historical Review* (Dec., 1953).

———— with B. Katherine Brown. *Virginia, 1705–1786: Democracy or Aristocracy?* East Lansing, Mich., 1964.

Burnette, O. Lawrence, Jr. See Frederick Jackson Turner.

Burr Papers. Papers of George Lincoln Burr. Cornell University Library, Ithaca, N.Y.

Cary, John. "Statistical Method and the Brown Thesis on Colonial Democracy" with a rebuttal by Robert E. Brown, *William and Mary Quarterly* (April, 1963).

Chitwood, Oliver Perry. *A History of Colonial America.* New York, 1931.

Cunliffe, Marcus. *The Nation Takes Shape, 1789–1837.* Chicago, 1959.

Davis, Allen F. and Harold D. Woodman, eds. *Conflict or Concensus in American History.* Boston, 1966.

Dietze, Gottfried. *The Federalist: A Classic on Federalism and Free Government.* Baltimore, Md., 1960.

Elkins, Stanley and Eric McKitrick. *The Founding Fathers: Young Men of the Revolution.* Washington, D.C., 1962.

Feder, Bernard and Jack Allen, eds. *Viewpoints: USA.* New York, 1967.

Fine, Sidney and Gerald S. Brown, eds. *The American Past: Conflicting Interpretations of the Great Issues.* 2 vols. New York, 1961.

Gipson, Lawrence. *The Coming of the Revolution, 1763–1775.* New York, 1954.

Goodman, Paul. *The Democratic-Republicans of Massachusetts: Politics in a Young Republic.* Cambridge, Mass., 1964.

———— ed. *Essays in American Colonial History.* New York, 1967.

Gottschalk, Louis. "The Evaluation of Historical Writing," *The Practice of Book Selection.* Chicago University Studies in Library Science. Chicago, 1940.

Grant, Charles R. *Democracy in the Connecticut Frontier Town of Kent.* New York, 1961.

Greene, Jack P., ed. *The Ambiguity of the American Revolution.* New York, 1968.

———— "The Flight from Determinism: A Review of Recent Literature on the Coming of the American Revolution," *South Atlantic Quarterly* (Spring, 1962).

———— ed. *The Reinterpretation of the American Revolution, 1763–1789.* New York, 1968.

Grob, Gerald N. and George Athan Billias, eds. *Interpretations of American History: Patterns and Perspectives.* 2 vols. New York, 1967.

Hicks, John D. *The Federal Union: A History of the United States to 1865.* Boston, 1937.

———— *A Short History of American Democracy.* Boston, 1943, 1946.

Higham, John. "Beyond Concensus: The Historian as Moral Critic," *American Historical Review* (April, 1962).

—— *History: The Development of Historical Studies in the United States.* Englewood Cliffs, N.J., 1965.

—— ed. *The Reconstruction of American History.* New York, 1962.

Hooker, Richard J., ed. *The American Revolution: The Search for a Meaning.* New York, 1970.

Jameson, J. Franklin. *The American Revolution Considered as a Social Movement.* Princeton, N.J., 1926, 1957.

Jensen, Merrill. *The Articles of Confederation: An Interpretation of the Social-Constitutional History of the American Revolution, 1774–1781.* Madison, Wis., 1940, 1959, 1963.

—— "Democracy and the American Revolution" in *The Huntington Library Quarterly* (Aug., 1957).

—— *The Founding of a Nation: A History of the American Revolution.* New York, 1968.

—— ed. *Tracts of the American Revolution, 1763–1776.* Indianapolis, 1967.

Kammen, Michael G., ed. *Politics and Society in Colonial America: Democracy or Deference?* New York, 1967.

Kenyon, Cecelia M. "'An Economic Interpretation of the Constitution' After Fifty Years," *The Centennial Review* (Summer, 1963).

—— "Men of Little Faith: The Anti-Federalists on the Nature of Representative Government," *William and Mary Quarterly* (Jan., 1955).

—— "Republicanism and Radicalism in the American Revolution: An Old-Fashioned Interpretation," *William and Mary Quarterly* (April, 1962).

Kim, Sung Bok. "Introduction to the Origin of the Constitution of the United States" in *Kyung Pook Univ. Liberal Arts and Sciences College Review,* Vol. I. (Taegu, Korea, 1958).

—— "The Manor of Cortlandt." Unpublished Ph.D. dissertation, Michigan State University, 1966.

Klein, Milton M. "Democracy and Politics in Colonial New York," *New York History* (July, 1959).

—— "Prelude to Revolution in New York: Jury Trials and Judicial Tenure," *William and Mary Quarterly* (Oct., 1960).

—— "The Rise of the New York Bar: The Legal Career of William Livingston," *New York History* (July, 1959).

Lokken, Roy N. "The Concept of Democracy in Colonial Political Thought," *William and Mary Quarterly* (Oct., 1959).

Lovejoy, David S. *Rhode Island Politics and the American Revolution.* Providence, 1958.

Main, Jackson Turner. *The Social Structure of Revolutionary America.* Princeton, N.J., 1965.

Matteucci, Nicola. *Charles Howard McIlwain E La Storiographia Sulla Rivoluzione Americana.* Bologna, 1965.

—— *La Rivoluzione Americana.* Bologna, 1968.

McDonald, Forrest. *E. Pluribus Unum: The Formation of the American Republic, 1776–1790.* Boston, 1965.

———— *We The People: The Economic Origins of the Constitution.* Chicago, 1958.

McWhiney, Grady and Robert Wiebe, eds. *Historical Vistas: Readings in United States History.* Boston, 1963.

Miller, John C. *Origins of the American Revolution.* Boston, 1943, 1959.

———— "Religion, Finance and Democracy in Massachusetts," *New ·England Quarterly* (March, 1933).

———— *Sam Adams, Pioneer in Propaganda.* Boston, 1936.

Morgan, Edmund S. *The American Revolution: A Review of Changing Interpretations.* Washington, D.C., 1958.

———— "The American Revolution: Revisions in Need of Revising," *William and Mary Quarterly* (Jan., 1957).

———— *The Birth of the Republic, 1763–1789.* Chicago, 1956.

Morris, Richard B. *Government and Labor in Early America.* New York, 1946.

———— *The American Revolution Reconsidered.* New York, 1967.

———— "Class Struggle and the American Revolution," *William and Mary Quarterly* (Jan., 1962).

———— ed. *The Era of the American Revolution: Studies inscribed to Evarts Boutell Greene.* New York, 1939.

Murrin, John M. "The Myths of Colonial Democracy and Royal Decline in Eighteenth-Century America," *Cithara* (Nov., 1965, and May, 1966).

Nevins, Allan. *The American States During and After the Revolution.* New York, 1924.

New York Historical Society *Collections* (1885).

Odum, Howard W., ed. *American Masters of Social Science: An Approach to the Study of the Social Sciences Through a Neglected Field of Biography.* New York, 1927.

Ogg, Frederic A. and P. Orman Ray. *Introduction to American Government: The National Government.* 5th ed. New York, 1935.

Palmer, Robert R. *The Age of the Democratic Revolution: A Political History of Europe and America, 1760–1800.* Princeton, N.J., 1959.

Parrington, Vernon Louis. *The Colonial Mind, 1620–1800.* Vol. I of *Main Currents in American Thought: An Interpretation of American Literature from the Beginning to 1920.* 3 vols. New York, 1927-1930.

Pole, Jack R., ed. *The Advance of Democracy.* New York, 1967.

———— "Historians and the Problem of Early American Democracy," *American Historical Review* (April, 1962).

———— *Political Representation in England and the Origins of the American Republic.* New York, 1966.

Robertson, Ross M. and James L. Pate., eds. *Readings in United States Economic and Business History.* Boston, 1966.

Robinson, James Harvey. *The Humanizing of Knowledge.* New York, 1923.

———— *The Mind in the Making: The Relation of Intelligence to Social Reform.* New York, 1921.

———— *The New History: Essays Illustrating the Modern Historical Outlook.* New York, 1912, 1965.

Rossiter, Clinton L. *Seedtime of the Republic: The Origin of the American Tradition of Liberty.* New York, 1953.

Sanders, Jennings B. *A College History of the United States.* 2 vols. Evanston, Ill., 1962.

Schlesinger, Arthur M., Sr. *The Birth of the Nation: A Portrait of the American People on the Eve of Independence.* New York, 1968.

—— *The Colonial Merchants and the American Revolution, 1763–1776.* New York, 1918, 1957.

—— *New Viewpoints in American History.* New York, 1922.

Sheehan, Donald, ed. *The Making of American History.* 2 vols. New York, 1950, 1963.

Smith, Charlotte Watkins. *Carl Becker: On History & the Climate of Opinion.* Ithaca, N.Y., 1956.

Smith, David G. *The Convention and the Constitution: The Political Ideas of the Founding Fathers.* New York, 1965.

Smith, Theodore Clarke. "The Writing of American History in America from 1884 to 1934," *American Historical Review* (April, 1935).

Solberg, Winton U. *The Federal Convention and the Foundation of the Union of the American States.* New York, 1958.

Strout, Cushing. *The Pragmatic Revolt in American History: Carl Becker and Charles Beard.* New Haven, Conn., 1958.

Syrett, David. "Town-Meeting Politics," *William and Mary Quarterly,* (July, 1964).

Thayer, Theodore. *Pennsylvania Politics and the Growth of Democracy, 1740–1776.* Harrisburg, Pa., 1953.

Thorpe, Francis Newton, ed. *The Federal and State Constitutions, Colonial Charters, and Other Organic Laws . . . .* Washington, D.C., 1909.

Tolles, Frederick B. "The American Revolution Considered as a Social Movement: A Re-Evaluation," *American Historical Review* (Oct., 1954).

Trask, David F. "Historians, the Constitution, and Objectivity: A Case Study," *Antioch Review* (Spring, 1960).

Turner, Frederick Jackson. Turner Collection. The Henry E. Huntington Library. San Marino, California.

—— *The Early Writings of Frederick Jackson Turner: With a List of All His Works.* Comp. by Everett E. Edwards. Madison, Wis., 1938.

—— *Essays in American History: Dedicated to Frederick Jackson Turner.* New York, 1951.

—— *Frederick Jackson Turner's Legacy: Unpublished Writings in American History.* Ed. by Wilbur R. Jacobs. San Marino, Calif., 1965.

—— *The Frontier in American History.* New York, 1920, 1947, 1962.

—— *Wisconsin Witness to Frederick Jackson Turner: A Collection of Essays on the Historian and the Thesis.* Compiled by O. Lawrence Burnette, Jr. Madison, Wis., 1961.

Ubbelohde, Carl. *The American Colonies and the British Empire, 1607–1763.* New York, 1968.

Van Tyne, Claude H. *The Causes of the War of Independence: Being the First Volume of a History of the Founding of the American Republic.* New York, 1922.

—— *The Loyalists in the American Revolution.* New York, 1902, 1929.

Wahlke, John C., ed. *Causes of the American Revolution.* Boston, 1962.

Wilkins, Burleigh Taylor. *Carl Becker: A Biographical Study in American Intellectual History.* Cambridge, Mass., 1961.

Williamson, Chilton. *American Suffrage from Property to Democracy, 1760–1860.* Princeton, N.J., 1960.

Wright, Benjamin Fletcher. *Concensus and Continuity, 1776–1787.* Boston, 1958.

Wright, Esmond. *Fabric of Freedom, 1763–1800.* New York, 1961.

Zuckerman, Michael. "The Social Context of Democracy in Massachusetts" *William and Mary Quarterly* (Oct., 1968).

INDEX

absolutism, 72, 196
Adamic, Louis, 202
Adams, Henry, 76n., 109-11
Adams, James Truslow, 131-32, 161-63, 206-07
Adams, John, on New York, 49-50; as a "radical," 53; evidence of opportunity, 88; and American Revolution, 88-90; and Declaration of Independence, 120, 143
Adams, Samuel, 99-100, 111, 208, 259
"Afterthoughts on Constitutions," 209-12
Albany, 16, 26, 73
Alden, John, 256, 263n.
Allen, Jack, 264n.
American Historical Association, 11, 21, 137, 144, 150-61, 182-83, 197, 199
American Historical Review, 12, 15, 20, 109n., 113n., 150n., 183n., 188, 197n., 214, 230, 261n.
American Journal of Sociology, 79n.
American Legion Monthly, 191
American Leviathan, The, 182
American Masters of Social Science, see Odum
American Revolution, and the Becker thesis, vii, 5, 11, 12, 14-57, 61-62, 85-92, 94, 99-102, 134, 167-68; and Turner, 5, 11, 12, 61-62; and Schlesinger, 19, 93-94, 132-34; and Van Tyne, 134-36; and Jameson, 163-66; and Channing, 84-85; and Declaration of Independence, 116-32; and conservatism, 6, 9-10, 12, 53; and liberalism, 45, 121-22, 187, 260-65; recent interpretation of, 260-65. See Jensen, Bridenbaugh, Miller, Morris, Pole, Main
American Revolution Considered as a Social Movement, The, 163-66
American States During and After the Revolution, The, 163
anarchy, 127-30
Andrews, Charles McLean, 99n., 140

Andrews, G. G., 159n., 188
An Economic Interpretation of the Constitution of the United States, 93, 208. See Beard
Anglophiles, 135
anticapitalism, 58-59, 97, 111, 124. See capitalism, collective democracy
Appleton-Century-Crofts, vi., 150n.
apprentices, 34, 122
Arendt, Hannah, 262n.
aristocracy, 4, 12, 14-57, 84-91, 97-103, 133, 134, 248-49
Arnold, General, 237
Aronson, Moses, 191
art, and history, 144, 152, 253-54
Articles of Confederation, 167, 250-51. See Jensen
artisans, and mechanics, 18, 20, 28, 30, 102. See Sons of Liberty
assembly, 28, 30, 31, 40
Atlantic Monthly, 72n.

Bacon, Lord, 67
Bacon's Rebellion, 62
Bailyn, Bernard, 261n., 262n.
ballot, 29, 51, 56. See franchise, voters
Baltimore Sun, 192
Bancroft, George, 80, 141-42
Barck, Oscar Theodore, Jr., 263n.
Barnes, Harry Elmer, 63-64, 143n., 197-98, 213-14
Bassett, John Spencer, 112, 141n.
Battaile, Margaret Dorrah, 256n.
Beard, Charles A., and relativism, 61; and the Constitution, 62, 85, 91, 93, 132, 136, 161, 167-68, 202, 207, 208, 245, 261, 262n., 264; and Robinson, 64, 143; philosophy of history, 81-82, 142-43, 158, 182, 183, 197, 200-201; social philosophy, 137-38, 200-201; and Becker, 93-95, 137-38, 166-67, 183, 191, 215, 230; President of A.H.A., 183, 197; and *The Rise of American Civilization*, 166-67, 205
Beard, Mary, 166-68

275

social democracy. See collective democracy

"Social Forces in American History," 59-60

Social Foundations of Education, 199

Social Frontier, 184

Social Ideas of American Educators, The, 184, 199-200

Socialism, 68, 76, 104-06, 111, 112, 129-30, 182-84, 193, 195-97, 199-200, 219, 241, 242

social reform, 58, 64-66, 129

social revolution, and American Revolution, 23-57, 163-66. See Becker thesis

Solberg, Winton U., 263n.

"Some Aspects of the Influence of Social Problems and Ideas Upon the Study and Writing of History," 79-82, 158-59

"Some Generalities That Still Glitter," 220

Sons of Liberty, 18, 19, 45-48, 50, 187

Spanish Civil War, 202-03

specious present, 153-54, 175

"Spirit of '76," 142-43

Spirit of the Laws, 175

Spitzer, Norman, 181n.

Squires, J. Duane, 238n.

Stalin, Joseph, 216, 219, 226, 233, 235, 236, 259

Stamp Act, 17, 18, 42-45, 89

Stanford University, 184-85, 189

St. Augustine, 172-73

Story of Civilization, The, 215

Strout, Cushing, 260

subjective relativism, and Becker, 13, 72-75, 79-82, 95, 97, 112, 116, 137-70, 182, 193-95, 198, 209, 213, 215, 223-28, 246-47, 250, 258-60; and Communism, 183, 195-96; and Fascism, 183; and progressivism, 58-97; and Robinson, 114-16; and Turner, 8, 12, 13, 59-61. See truth, philosophy of history

Suffolk Resolves, 50

suffrage. See franchise

Supreme Court, 202, 225

Syrett, David, 261n.

Tawney, Richard Henry, 64

Tea Act, 47

tenants, 16, 27, 28n., 32, 41, 52

testimony, 198, 210

"That Noble Dream," 197

Thayer, William Roscoe, 79n.

Thomas, Norman, 182, 202

Thompson, James Westfall, 214

Todd, A. J., 83

Tolles, Frederick B., 261n.

Tories, 19. See Becker thesis

town meetings, 88

Townsend, W. B., 191n.

Townshend Acts, 47

Trask, David F., 261n.

Trotsky, Leon, 202

truth, and Becker, 20, 22, 72-75, 79, 96, 98, 102, 112-13, 197-98, 209, 212, 222, 223, 226, 227, 237, 250, 259, 260, 267; and Gottschalk, 228-29; and relativity, 72, 78, 79, 96, 101, 112-13, 194-95, 226; and Robinson, 140; and Turner, 1, 7-9, 12

Turner, Frederick Jackson, and Becker, 2-13, 15, 19, 23-24, 39-40, 58-62, 75, 85-86, 108, 143-44, 147-50, 159, 199, 248; and frontier thesis, 6, 9, 105-06, 256; and the "New History," 61, 143; philosophy of history, 1, 3, 5-12, 59-60, 82, 143, 147-50; and the Revolution, 6, 9-12, 17, 19, 24, 25; social philosophy, 4-7, 58-59; and Simons, 59

Ubbelohde, Carl, 262n.

unfranchised classes, 18, 19, 26-57, 89, 187

United States: An Experiment in Democracy, The, 102-08, 110

United States of Europe, 244

United States Publishers Assn., Inc., vi, 98n.

upper classes, 18, 20-57, 90-91

Van Doren, Carl, 187-88, 191

Van Shaack, Peter, 186-87

Van Tyne, Claude H., 77, 134-36, 162, 207